WOMEN TEACHERS ON THE FRONTIER

A frontier schoolmistress as remembered by Edward Eggleston from his boyhood in the 1840s in Vevay, Switzerland County, Indiana, and portrayed in his book The Circuit Rider.

WOMEN TEACHERS ON THE FRONTIER

Polly Welts Kaufman

YALE UNIVERSITY PRESS
New Haven and London

Designed by Nancy Ovedovitz and set in Garamond No. 3 type by Brevis
Press. Printed in the United States of America by The Murray Printing
Company, Westford, Massachusetts.

Library of Congress Cataloging in Publication Data
Kaufman, Polly Welts, 1929–
    Women teachers on the frontier.
    Bibliography: p.
    Includes index.
    1. Women teachers—United States—History—19th century. 2. Edu-
cation—United States—History—19th century. 3. Women pioneers—
United States—History—19th century. I. Title.
LB2837.K35 1984   371.1'0088042   83–14699
ISBN 0–300–03043–6

1   3   5   7   9   10   8   6   4   2

CONTENTS

Appendixes

Maps

The manuscripts were followed closely, with only a few exceptions. Unusually long sentences and paragraphs were broken up and punctuation for quotations standardized. The notation *sic* was not used. If a word is misspelled, it indicates that the writer misspelled it. Words spelled correctly in one place, however, were corrected if misspelled in another. Because the McLench reminiscence is an oral history, proper names were corrected as necessary and punctuation standardized.

The diary of Arozina Perkins was divided into seven chapters with explanatory titles added. The style of the entries was regularized in keeping with the style of the original diary. There is evidence that the diarist revised her journal at a later time. In pencil she completed proper names and added a few parenthetical statements. She also appears to have removed certain pages. The completed names are printed without notation, but added parenthetical statements are enclosed in parentheses and printed in italics to indicate hindsight. When a page is missing from the diary, a notation is made within the text. Brackets have been reserved for editorial clarification.

With the exception of a long introductory lyric poem and three pages of religious reflections, nothing was omitted from the Perkins diary. In order to clarify the essential experiences of Cynthia Bishop and Martha Rogers, repetitions and extra detail were eliminated from their letters. Four of Martha Rogers's letters are summarized. The letters from the other teachers are presented in their entirety. The McLench reminiscence omits only a section called "Miscellaneous Notes," added a few weeks after the original interview.

The women were highly literate and they were teachers. If a few obvious slips were corrected by the editor, it was done because we can assume that they did not intend to have their errors, often made in haste, go down in history.

Sources for quotations from the teachers and information about their origins and their later lives are provided in Appendix D, "Lives of the Pioneer Women Teachers." Except in cases where the source is more extensive than the format of this appendix allows, they are not repeated in

the footnotes. For convenient reference, page numbers for the Arozina
Perkins Diary refer to the pages of this book.

~~~~~~~~~~ ACKNOWLEDGMENTS ~~~~~~~~~~

Such a work as this study of antebellum pioneer teachers, involving the search for the future lives and origins of a group of women unconnected by kin or place and joined only by common goals and shared actions, depends heavily upon the good services of others. Virtually without exception, archivists and county clerks, historians and volunteer officers of historical societies responded to my queries. Often they did not have the answers, but they always looked.

Some persons answered not only one query but a second and more. Each answer seemed to lead to another question. Ruth M. Blair, manuscripts librarian at the Connecticut Historical Society, and the society's staff aided me from the beginning of the study to the end, making the Arozina Perkins Diary and the NPEB Papers readily accessible and helping me find answers raised by the manuscripts themselves. Steven Hallberg, manuscripts librarian at the Oregon Historical Society, worked with me at long distance to supply the materials necessary for the annotation of the McLench reminiscence. Without Janet E. Peterson of the Marshfield Historical Society, the story of Arozina Perkins would never have been complete. Anna Dermody, reference librarian at Johnson State College, used her free time to help me find the details of Perkins's early years, and Sarah Cartwright of the Iowa State Historical Department found information about Fort Des Moines and Fairfield that helped me understand Perkins's life in Iowa. Elaine D. Trehub, college history librarian at Mount Holyoke College, got me off to a good start in my search by leading me to the facts about the future lives of the twenty-four Holyoke alumnae in the study. In Indiana, Dorothy Lower and Delia Bourne of the staff of the Allen County Public Library and Carolyn Autry of the Indiana Historical Society found several pioneer teachers who settled in their state. Ms. Autry also made the Calvin Fletcher manuscripts accessible. Near the end of the study, Ronald E. Butchard ran the names of the pioneer teachers through his computer listing of five thousand teachers of the freedmen. We were both excited when he came up with some matches. He led me to Frank J. J. Miele, archivist at the Amistad Research Center in New Orleans, who willingly sent me letters by three of the pioneer teachers written fifteen years after I had lost track of them.

The search for authentic historical pictures unexpectedly led me to some descendants of the pioneer teachers. Sharing photographs and stories were Gertrude Hobbs, of Salem, Oregon, Mary Gray McLench's great-grand-daughter; Elizabeth Wilson Buehler, of Portland, Oregon, and Janet Wilson James, of Cambridge, Massachusetts, direct descendants of Elizabeth Millar Wilson. In Concord, Massachusetts, librarian Marcia Moss introduced me to Gladys Clark, grandniece of Rebecca Clark, who, instead of a photograph, had a wonderful story. Other persons who went out of the way to find pictures were Robert M. Cochran, Edie Blender, and Versa Smith of Hancock County, Illinois; Winifred Huffman of the Greenville, Illinois, public library; Alex Toth of the Pacific University library; Charles J. Frey, Cullom-Davis Library of Bradley University in Peoria, Illinois; James Leonardo of the Cowles Library, Drake University, Des Moines, Iowa; Myrna Williamson, State Historical Society of Wisconsin; Mary K. Dains, State Historical Society of Missouri; Jean Elkington, Oregon Historical Society; Nadia A. Halpern, University of Vermont; Doris M. Perry, Allen County–Fort Wayne, Indiana Historical Society; Ann Bauer, Vermilion County, Illinois Museum Society; Mary Bennett and Christie Dailey, Iowa State Historical Department; and Lucinda Burkepile, New Haven Colony Historical Society. Special thanks to my nephew, Jeremy G. Welts, who did not question my sudden request to locate a particular picture in the Mariners' Museum in Newport News, Virginia.

Without the encouragement and advice of several scholars in the field of women's history, this book would not have reached the dimensions that it did. Mary Ann Ferguson read the diary as it was first transcribed and urged me to go ahead with it. Anne Firor Scott encouraged me to prepare the letters for publication. Kathryn Sklar and Julie Roy Jeffrey read the final manuscript and made helpful recommendations. Glenda Riley generously criticized the study in an early stage and offered the opportunity for its first publication. At meetings where I presented my findings useful formal comments were offered by Barbara Finkelstein, Andrea Hinding, Alanna Brown, and Nancy Hoffman. Special thanks for support and suggestions from Geraldine Clifford, Margaret K. Nelson, Sue Armitage, Tom Dublin, Laurie Crumpacker, Louise Stevenson, Eileen McDonagh, Claudia Bushman, and Eugenia Kaledin. And I shall always be particularly grateful to Edmund S. Morgan, who first introduced me to the excitement of working with historical manuscripts and documents.

In addition to the librarians at the Boston Public Library, Schlesinger Library, Maine State Library, Vermont Historical Society, New Hampshire Bureau of Vital Statistics, New England Historic Genealogical Society, and the federal archives in Waltham, Massachusetts, I would like to acknowledge those researchers who dug into their files and helped me find what happened to just one more teacher. From the Midwest, South, and West they include, in Illinois: Betty Albsmeyer, Quincy Public Library; Cynthia Peters, Newberry Library; Idabel Evans, Historical Society of Montgomery County; Marjorie Taylor, Cass County Historical Society; and county clerks Roscoe McDaniel, Hancock County; Shirley Eldredge, Edgar County; George J. Petefish, Cass County; and Eunice May Russell, Montgomery County; in Iowa: Grace W. Holihan, Maquoketa, and Anne Kintner, Grinnell College; in Indiana: Sarah E. Cooke, Tippecanoe County Historical Association, and Phyllis Walker, Morgan County Public Library; in Michigan: Frederick Honhart, Michigan State University; in Wisconsin: John O. Holzhueter, Historical Society of Wisconsin; in Ohio: James B. Casey, Western Reserve Historical Society; W. E. Bigglestone, Oberlin College; in Minnesota: Louise Johnson, Washington County Museum; Richard Hofstad, Minneapolis Atheneum; Steven Nielsen, Ruth Bauer, and Dallas Lindgren, Minneapolis Historical Society; in Missouri: Helen Mitzel, Bunceton; in Alabama, Annwhite Fuller, Huntsville–Madison County Public Library; in Oregon: Bruce Berney, Astoria Public Library, and Addie Dyal, Marion County Historical Society; in Nevada: Eric N. Moody, Nevada Historical Society; and in California: Maude K. Swingle, California Historical Society; Carol Jarvis, Mills College Library; Teresa Bodine, California State Library; and Judith Strong Albert for research at the Bancroft Library.

Especially helpful in New York state, where vital records before 1880 do not exist, were David Brumberg, Cornell University; Field Horne, Saratoga County Museum; Barbara Aldrich, Saratoga town historian; Frances P. Hale, Essex County Historical Society; Sharon Pocock, Bergen town historian; Doug Welch, St. Lawrence County Historical Association; Virginia Wolfe, Franklin County Historical Society; Marjorie Allen Perez, Wayne County historian; Lorna Spencer, Cattaraugus County Historical Museum; Mrs. John Cannon, Delaware County Historical Society; Edward Oetting, State University of New York, Albany; and Kathleen Facer, Batavia Public Library. Finally, from New England, particular thanks to Vermont town clerks Anna K. Buxton, Orwell; Priscilla Wilson, Waitsfield; Therese Magnant, Worcester; and to Polly Darnell, Sheldon Museum, Middlebury, and Linda Dotson, Green Mountain Junior College; in Maine: town clerks Barbara Kane, Otisfield, and M. Munsey, Topsham; and Brother Theodore Johnson, United Society of Shakers, Poland Spring; in New Hampshire: Harold and Esther Wyatt, Meredith, and Virginia Berry, Brewster Academy; in Massachusetts: Harold F. Worthley, Congregational Library, Boston; Sarah Phillips, Framingham State College, and Eleanor O'Donnell, American Antiquarian Society; and in Connecticut: Thomas Manning, Franklin; Karl Stofko, East Haddam Historical Society; and Henrietta Larson for research in the Connecticut State Library.

My special thanks to Judy Kelly, who transcribed the Arozina Perkins Diary and graciously responded to my typing requests, to Barbara Elam for sharing insights and keeping other things going, to Charles Grench for his continued encouragement, and to Charlotte Dihoff for shepherding the book through production. Finally, and most especially, to my family, to whom this book is dedicated: Rog, for his critical judgment and willingness to listen; Kathy for her bright example; and Roger for maps, photography, critiques, copyreading, and his essential partnership.

≈≈≈≈≈≈≈≈≈≈≈≈ INTRODUCTION ≈≈≈≈≈≈≈≈≈≈≈≈

The schoolmarm from the East is a stock character in stories about the Old West. Her genteel poverty, unbending morality, education, and independent ways make her character a useful foil for the two other female stock characters in Western literature: the prostitute with the heart of gold and the long-suffering farmer's wife. The feminine schoolteacher is also helpful in providing the masculine hero with the opportunity to display chivalry and prove his natural nobility.

Miss Mary, Bret Harte's schoolmistress of Red Gulch, who is an orphan from Boston, is a symbol of purity in contrast to the town's good-hearted prostitute with "money plenty." She agrees to take responsibility for the prostitute's boy who, in an ironic twist, is revealed to be also the son of the drunkard Miss Mary hoped to reform. Hamlin Garland's teacher, Lily Graham, is town bred, and, although younger, her manners and education qualify her to interfere directly in the life of a downtrodden farmer's wife. The best-known fictional Western teacher of all, Owen Wister's Molly Wood, left Vermont to teach in Wyoming because she was too pure to marry an unacceptable man chosen for her by her family and too proud to depend on their declining resources. She allows the Virginian to prove his true nobility but is forced to confront her own self-righteousness before she wins his hand.[1]

The character of the eastern schoolmistress in the West is an intriguing one and her very occurrence in the literature of the West demonstrates her existence on the frontier. Her portrait is, of course, a stereotype based on the prescriptive literature of the time. The schoolmistress is the ideal woman about whom myths were made: moral, self-sacrificing, discreet, dedicated to the welfare of children, and capable of bringing out the best in men. She is unconcerned with personal goals or needs.

Fortunately, the letters, reminiscences, and a diary of members of a group

1. Bret Harte, "The Idyl of Red Gulch," *Luck of Roaring Camp and Other Sketches* (Boston: Houghton Mifflin, 1869), pp. 72–88; Hamlin Garland, "Lucretia Burns," *Other Main-Travelled Roads* (New York: Harper & Bros., 1892), pp. 81–115; Owen Wister, *The Virginian: A Horseman of the Plains* (New York: Macmillan, 1902).

of single women teachers who did travel from the East to teach on western frontiers before the Civil War allows them to tell their own remarkable stories. Of the nearly six hundred women who were sent West to teach by the National Board of Popular Education and its Boston affiliate in the decade following 1846, the names of nearly two hundred and fifty are known. By reading their words and learning why they accepted the National Board's challenge and what happened to them after they arrived in the West, the reader can go beyond the stereotype of the ideal woman and see actual women, distinct individuals, trying to live up to their ideals while supporting themselves and working alone to survive in their new communities. Information has been uncovered about the subsequent lives of nearly 40 percent of the women who have been identified by name. And although their original commitment was to teach only two years in the West, two-thirds of the women chose the West for their future homes.

The number of single women teachers who journeyed from the East to teach in the West and South before the Civil War would probably approach a thousand if all the threads could be followed "back East" from the new western schools or "out West" from the many eastern seminaries or academies. The movement continued throughout the nineteenth century and into the present day. It attracted such women as Olive Pickering, who in 1878 journeyed by rail and stage from New Hampshire to Montana, where she married and became the mother of Jeannette Rankin, the first woman to be elected to the United States House of Representatives.[2]

Yet several recent studies of western women pass by this movement westward of single women. Reluctant wives of overland pioneers and prostitutes are among the women migrants to the West currently studied. One recent work simply discounts the single eastern women who taught in the West under the National Board, undoubedly lacking the information that a large proportion of them remained as early settlers and were responsible for training young women teachers from the families who preceded them. A major history of education dismisses the National Board's efforts, stating that it failed.[3]

There is room, however, for a variety of pictures of the nineteenth-century West. The edge of settlement was not fixed in place or time but moved in every direction. It was both rural and urban. Schools were established early

---

2. *Notable American Women: The Modern Period,* Barbara Sicherman and Carol Hurd Green, eds. (Cambridge: Harvard University Press, 1980), pp. 566–68.

3. John Mack Faragher, *Women and Men on the Overland Trail* (New Haven: Yale University Press, 1979); Lillian Schlissel, *Women's Diaries of the Westward Journey* (New York: Schocken Books, 1982); Marion S. Goldman, *Gold Diggers and Silver Miners: Prostitution and Social Life on the Comstock Lode* (Ann Arbor: University of Michigan Press, 1981); Sandra L. Myres, *Westering Women and the Frontier Experience, 1800–1915* (Albuquerque: University of New Mexico Press, 1982), p. 248; Lawrence A. Cremin, *American Education: The National Experience, 1783–1876* (New York: Harper & Row, 1980), p. 146.

in the process not only because children needed to learn their three Rs but because community leaders knew that a school brought respectability to a town or area and made it attractive to new settlers. At the same instant, individual pioneer teachers met a variety of frontier conditions. When diarist Arozina Perkins reached the frontier town of Fort Des Moines late in 1850, its population of five hundred was barely able to support a school. Before the decade ended, Des Moines was the state capital and its population more than ten times larger. Two hundred miles to the east, Mary Hitchcock chose the small center of Princeton in Cass County, Illinois, for her school. Bypassed by the railroad, it was vacated within two decades. While Mary Hitchcock was teaching in Cass County, another letter writer, Sarah Ballard, married in the Wisconsin Dells region and taught in the first successful school of a new settlement. In a frontier town in the Missouri Ozarks, Sarah Ballard's classmate Martha Rogers recorded a classic gunfight and knifing between two men on horseback.

Any study of women who chose to go West must acknowledge the tremendous diversity among them and the differences in their perceptions and conditions. Several authors have emphasized the immediate oppression of the four-to-five-month overland journey for married women of a childbearing age but have underplayed the settlement years. They neglected the significance of the antebellum journeys of such women as Mary Jane Megquier, who more than once traveled by ship to San Francisco, hoping to escape the social restrictions of a small Maine town.[4] Groups of antebellum women choosing the West who scarcely have been studied include Catholic sisters who located mother houses in the West and founded schools and hospitals on the frontier and teachers in missions to Indian nations, who reflected a complex combination of respect for the culture of the native people and the desire to change their ways.[5]

4. After divorcing her husband, Mary Jane Megquier eventually returned to Winthrop, Maine, saying before she left San Francisco: "We dine at seven in the evening and then comes the frolic and dancing. Shant I miss them at home." See U.S. Manuscript Census, Kennebec County, Maine, 1860, p. 136; 1870, p. 265; Robert Glass Cleland, ed., *Apron Full of Gold; The Letters of Mary Jane Megquier from San Francisco, 1849–1856* (San Marino, CA: Huntington Library, 1949), p. 99.

See also the stories of such "California widows" as Lucinda Mann who traveled West to find their absent husbands in J. S. Holliday, *The World Rushed In: The California Gold Rush Experience* (New York: Simon & Schuster, 1981), pp. 453–54.

5. Examples of remarkable stories not fully told include that of Mother Joseph of the Sisters of Charity of Providence, who superintended the building of Providence Academy in Vancouver, Washington, in 1857 and of Mother Angela Gillespie of the Sisters of the Holy Cross, founder of Saint Mary's College in South Bend, Indiana, in 1855. A useful list of western schools established by Catholic sisters before the Civil War is the very list used by Catharine Beecher in calling attention to the need for Protestant evangelical women teachers in the West. See Catharine Beecher, "An Address to the Protestant Clergy of the United States," in *The Evils Suffered by American Women and American Children: The Causes and the Remedy* (New York: Harper & Bros., 1946), pp. 18–19. For Mother Joseph, see Lucile McDonald, "Mother Joseph," in Western Writers of America, *The Women Who Made the West* (New York:

As the frontier period is extended in time beyond the Civil War, the diversity of pioneer women increases. Enterprising women, both single and married, set up boardinghouses and millinery shops or proved homestead claims. Concerned women nurses and doctors traveled to the West. Desperate women became camp followers or washerwomen or prostitutes. Adventurous women included explorers like Isabella Bird and the uncounted Mountain Charleys.[6] While this book presents only the group of single antebellum women who used teaching as their opportunity for a new life in the West, it acknowledges all the women now known to have joined the westward migration and others yet to be discovered. Unifying them all was the hope for opportunity and self-development and the belief that it was their right, even duty, as Americans to settle and improve the new land, regardless of the existence of a native population. The West, however, did not always meet its promise, and some, like one-third of the pioneer teachers, did return East. One of the goals of this study is to examine the differences between the teachers who settled in the West and those who, in the end, chose the East.

Who were the pioneer women teachers? Did they share characteristics that made them different from more conventional women of their times, making them receptive to the call from the West? "The West is my enthusiasm," said Amy Chapman of Palmyra, New York, as she left the East in 1853. She would teach in the West and South for her entire life. "I previously determined to devote the remainder of my life to teaching," wrote Flora Davis Winslow, a widow with a small son from Portland, Maine, as she left

---

Doubleday & Co., 1980), pp. 120–29. For Mother Angela Gillespie, see *Notable American Women, 1607–1950; a Biographical Dictionary,* Edward T. and Janet W. James, eds. (Cambridge: Harvard University Press, 1971), hereafter cited as *NAW,* vol. 2, pp. 34–35. For a recent corrective to the omission of the work of Catholic sisters see Susan Peterson, "Religious Communities of Women in the West: The Presentation Sister's Adaptation to the Northern Plains Frontier," *Journal of the West* 21 (April 1982): 65–70.

See Ethel McMillan, "Women Teachers in Oklahoma," *Chronicles of Oklahoma* 27 (Spring 1949): 2–32 and Kay Graber, ed. *Sister to the Sioux: Memoirs of Elaine Goodale Eastman, 1885–91* (Lincoln: University of Nebraska Press, 1978).

6. For example, see Christie Daily, "A Woman's Concern: Millinery in Central Iowa, 1870–80," *Journal of the West* 21 (April 1982): 26–32; Joseph W. Snell, ed. "Roughing It on Her Kansas Claim: The Diary of Abbie Bright, 1870–71," *Kansas Historical Quarterly* 37 (Autumn 1971): 233–63 and 37 (Winter 1971): 394–428; Sheryll Patterson-Black, "Women Homesteaders on the Great Plains Frontier," in Sheryll and Gene Patterson-Black, *Western Women in History and Literature* (Crawford, NB: Cottonwood Press, 1978), pp. 15–31; Isabella Bird, *A Lady's Life in the Rocky Mountains* (Norman: University of Oklahoma Press, 1960); *Mountain Charley or the Adventures of Mrs. E. J. Guerin, Who Was Thirteen Years in Male Attire* (Norman: University of Oklahoma Press, 1968); Mari Sandoz, *Miss Morissa, Doctor of the Gold Trail* (New York: Hastings House, 1955); Christiane Fischer, ed. *Let Them Speak for Themselves: Women in the American West, 1849–1900* (New York: Dutton, 1978).

for Michigan in 1852. "I felt there was a wider sphere of usefulness there than here."

Daughters on the declining hill farms or of the waning group of independent rural craftsmen of the Northeast, the pioneer teachers were also the daughters of the first generally literate women. Their mothers had been raised in the revolutionary period with the expectation that women should prepare an educated citizenry for the new republic. Out of Republican ideals had come the impetus for the burgeoning of private academies and seminaries all over the Northeast in advance of public secondary education. During the first decades of the nineteenth century many academies opened their doors to girls, and new seminaries were founded for the purpose of educating young women.[7] As more women seized the opportunity to increase their life choices by acquiring secondary education, school districts began to realize the advantages of employing women rather than men as teachers. At mid-century, town officials in Concord, Massachusetts, found that pupils under women teachers had improved more than those taught by men. "And surely, this being the fact," the town report stated, "it is not good economy to employ a man to teach those Schools, when the services of a woman, of the best qualifications, can be obtained for two-thirds or three-fourths the expense."[8]

Another new option for self-support outside their homes or neighbors' homes included factory work; and, indeed, at least three of the pioneer teachers worked in the Lowell Mills first to raise money for their education.[9] Although they did offer the possibility of a different life from that of their mothers, both options were extremely limited. As for schools, by mid-century, competition for district school positions kept salaries low and available jobs few in number.

Scarcity of eastern district school positions alone would not be reason enough for a single woman to leave her family and friends for an uncertain future in the West. If it had been, the numbers of antebellum women who went West to teach would have been even larger. The critical impetus for the pioneer women teachers was the empowerment each woman accepted from Protestant evangelical religion. Each one was a young girl during the end of the Second Great Awakening which swept in successive waves over western New York and rural New England. In fact, only women who could prove

7. Linda K. Kerber, *Women of the Republic: Intellect and Ideology in Revolutionary America* (Chapel Hill: University of North Carolina Press, 1980); Mary Beth Norton, *Liberty's Daughters: The Revolutionary Experience of American Women, 1750–1800* (Boston: Little, Brown, 1980); Nancy F. Cott, *The Bonds of Womanhood: "Woman's Sphere" in New England, 1780–1835* (New Haven: Yale University Press, 1977).

8. *Annual Report of the School Committee of the Town of Concord, Year Ending April 1, 1855* (Concord, Massachusetts, 1855), p. 15.

9. See Thomas Dublin, *Women at Work: The Transformation of Work and Community in Lowell, Massachusetts, 1826–1860* (New York: Columbia University Press, 1979).

membership in an evangelical church and describe their conversion experiences were accepted by the National Board of Popular Education. If God willed that they were to serve Him by teaching in the West, the women believed it was their duty to go. By transferring authority to God, each woman began the process of separating herself from dependence on her family to reliance upon her own conscience and her own self.[10]

When the personal empowerment each woman acquired through her faith in God was combined with a romantic view of the West and the need simply to support herself, each woman's choice to take the risk of migrating West was a logical one. Because the pioneer women teachers were highly intelligent and articulate, undoubtedly among the brightest persons in their home communities, teaching was the route they chose to achieve independence. Expanding on her reasons for choosing to teach in the West, Michigan-bound Flora Davis Winslow stated: "I teach school because I wish to be independent and not beholden to my friends for a livelihood. I go West to do the Will of my Heavenly Father."

Women poured into teaching in the West as they had previously in the East. Indigenous women followed the example of the pioneer teachers, often directly trained by them. While in 1848 only twenty-three of 124 teachers in Iowa were women, by 1865, women constituted nearly 65 percent of the state's teachers. By 1870, in the combined ten North Central states, 56 percent of the teachers were women. Teaching, despite its low pay, was considered such a desirable, not to mention respectable, position on the Comstock Lode that when twenty public school posts were advertised in Virginia City in 1877, 120 unmarried women applied for them.[11]

Like their brothers, the pioneer teachers possessed restless spirits as they searched for more useful lives and the chance to influence their own destinies. Unlike their brothers, their choices were limited to positions that met society's expectations for women as defined in the fictional characters of Miss Mary of Red Gulch and Molly Wood of Bear Creek. A significant number of the women dedicated themselves to teaching for their entire lives. But for the teachers who desired upward social mobility and the possibility of a settled life, marriage to a successful man remained the most certain route.

10. Nancy F. Cott, "Young Women in the Second Great Awakening in New England," *Feminist Studies* 3 (1975): 15–29.

11. Thomas Morain, "Departure of Males from the Teaching Profession in Nineteenth-Century Iowa," *Civil War History* 26 (June 1980): 161–70; Julie Roy Jeffrey, *Frontier Women: The Trans-Mississippi West, 1840–1880* (New York: Hill & Wang, 1977), p. 90; Wayne E. Fuller, *The Old Country School: The Story of Rural Education in the Middle West* (Chicago: University of Chicago Press, 1982), pp. 159–60; Goldman, *Gold Diggers*, p. 29.

For the story of country schools in the Rocky Mountain and Plains states, see *Country School Legacy: Humanities on the Frontier* (Silt, CO: Country School Legacy, 1981). Andrew Gulliford was the project director. See also ERIC ED 211 243–254 and ED 211 266–280.

Had such professional opportunities as the ministry, the law, or medicine been open to them, surely it was women like those who went West to teach who would have been the pioneers.

PART I

THE SHARED EXPERIENCE

1848 to 1854 and Beyond

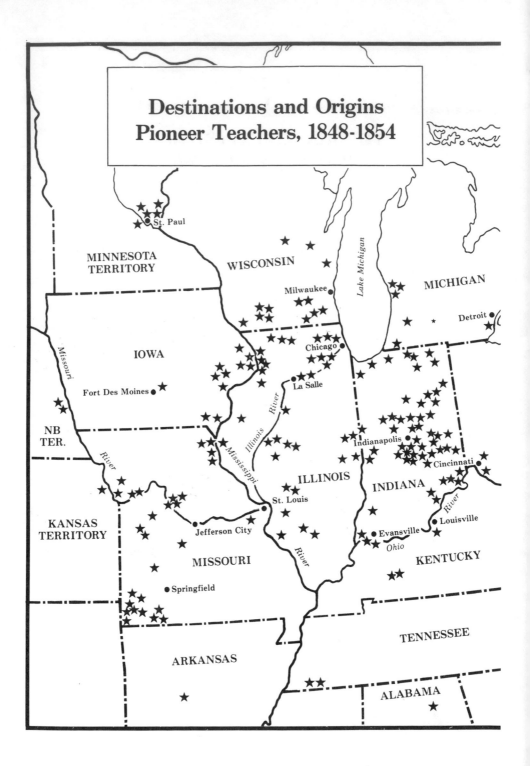

**Destinations and Origins
Pioneer Teachers, 1848-1854**

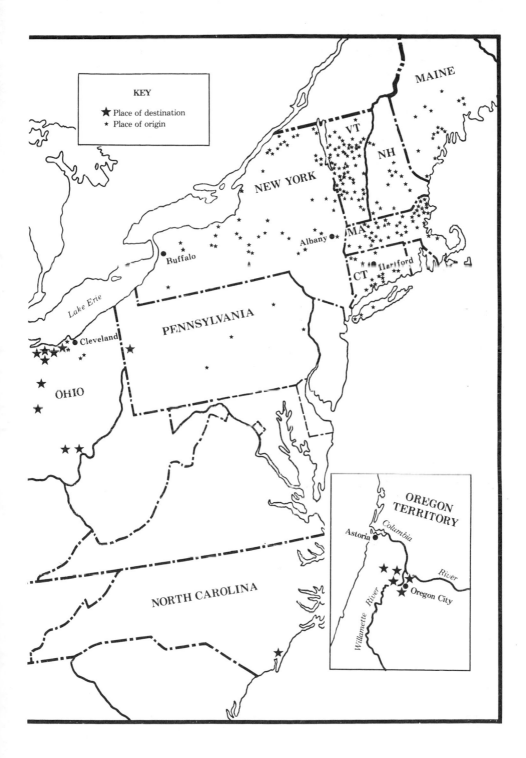

KEY

★ Place of destination
★ Place of origin

MAINE

VT

NH

NEW YORK

Albany

MA

Buffalo

CT   Hartford

Lake Erie

PENNSYLVANIA

Cleveland

OHIO

OREGON
TERRITORY

Astoria

Columbia

River

Willamette River

Oregon City

NORTH CAROLINA

The urge to go West, which swelled to a fever pitch after 1848, was shared by a virtually unnoticed group of nearly six hundred single women from northern New England and upper New York state. Because they participated in the westward migration within the acceptable and familiar vocation of teaching, the extraordinary quality of their decisions as single women willing to uproot and relocate themselves far away from their families has been little recognized.

"The fact is, " wrote Arozina Perkins, a twenty-three-year-old New Haven teacher, in September 1849, "I have been in a perfect fever for several months about it, but of late my excitement has been alarming. Probably it will reach a crisis soon. I hope if it should turn, to be calmer. But it shall *not* turn. I *must* go out in the Spring class of the National Board and my dear mother *must* give her consent and blessing."[1]

Excerpts from the diary of Arozina Perkins, one reminiscence, and the letters of seven other teachers sent out by the National Popular Education Board in the decade following 1846 allow the teachers to tell their stories in their own words. Some returned home and painfully described their failures; others stayed and shared the excitement of becoming a part of the building of new communities on the frontier.

The women sponsored by the National Board were not even the first single women to become pioneer teachers in the West. During the 1830s, eighty-eight teachers from Zilpah Grant's Female Seminary in Ipswich, Massachusetts, answered the call to start schools in the valleys of the West and in the South. After confirming for herself the need for teachers in the West during a trip to Ohio and Michigan, Grant established an association in 1835 to loan money to teachers wishing to train at Ipswich for western positions. Her plan, combining specific training and financial aid with placement in the West, was clearly a model for the National Board's program a decade later. By 1839, when Grant left Ipswich, fifty-seven women had been sent West, the majority to Ohio, although Missouri, Michigan, Illinois, and Indiana were also represented.[2]

The Connecticut Historical Society has granted permission for the publication of the Arozina Perkins Diary and the selections from the National Popular Education Board Papers contained in its collections.

The *Journal of the West* has granted permission for the reprinting of the parts of this section which originally appeared in the April 1982 issue of the *Journal of the West* (Copyright 1982 by the Journal of the West, Inc.).

The teachers were first discussed by Kathryn Kish Sklar, *Catharine Beecher, a Study in American Domesticity* (New Haven, Yale University Press, 1973), pp. 178–83, and Jeffrey, *Frontier Women*, pp. 34–36, 90–94.

1. Perkins Diary, p. 75.

2. *Catalogue of the Officers and Members of the Seminary for Female Teachers at Ipswich, Mass., for the Year Ending April 1839* (Salem, 1839), hereafter cited as *Ipswich Catalogue*, pp. 27, 35; Linda T. Guilford, *The Use of a Life: Memorials of Mrs. Z. P. Grant* (New York: American Tract Society, 1886), pp. 183–204; *NAW*, vol. 2, pp. 73–75.

Even as early as the 1820s, Emma Willard's network of alumnae and friends of Troy Female Seminary in New York placed increasing numbers of women teachers in the West as well as in the South, beginning with Ohio. Finally, a year before the National Board was organized, the Ladies' Society for the Promotion of Education at the West in Boston sent its first group of women West to teach. After sponsoring 109 teachers, the Society merged with the National Board in 1852. Indeed, the flow of women teachers from the East seeking greater opportunities in the West has continued to the present time. It is not uncommon for an eastern family to recall a great-aunt who became a teacher "out West" or for a western family to mention that their great-grandmother first came West as a teacher.[3]

Although the women sent by the National Board each pledged to teach for only two years in the West, a search revealing the subsequent lives of nearly 40 percent of the teachers whose full names are known has shown that two-thirds of them succeeded in making a permanent transition from East to West. A majority made homes in growing towns from Indiana west to the border of Nebraska Territory, and a few became pioneer settlers of Oregon and California. When their names are first coupled with the towns of their origins, they appear to be ordinary daughters of native-born northeastern craftsmen and hill farm families. An analysis of their personal and social backgrounds, however, reveals a special group of women whose spirit for independence was rising. Highly literate and spurred by the need to support themselves, they were drawn to the West by a strong sense of mission and by a romantic view. The factor of individual personalities, however, cannot be discounted.

Arozina Perkins first tried out the subject of her going West on the daguerreotypes of the surviving members of her scattered family. She pulled

---

Only twenty-five young men from Andover Theological Seminary and a similar number from Princeton went West or South as teachers or ministers between 1830 and 1835. Thomas Woody, *A History of Women's Education in the United States* (New York: Science Press, 1929), vol. 1, pp. 457–58.

3. Mary J. Fairbanks, ed. *Emma Willard and Her Pupils or Fifty Years of the Troy Female Seminary, 1822–1872* (New York, 1898); *First Annual Report of the Ladies Society for the Promotion of Education at the West* (Boston: 1846), hereafter cited as *Boston Society; Eleventh Annual Report of the General Agent of the Board of National Popular Education* (Hartford: 1858), hereafter cited as *NPEB Report*, p. 7.

At least fifteen women who attended Westfield Normal School in Massachusetts and taught in the West before the Civil War do not show up in the National Board records and may have been recruited by the Boston Society. Their names and locations were compiled from an 1889 survey of alumnae contained in the Westfield State College Archives by Robert T. Brown.

The most famous group of pioneer teachers were the "Mercer girls." In 1864, eleven women teachers were recruited for Seattle by Asa S. Mercer in Lowell, Massachusetts. Two years later he brought to Seattle thirty-six single women who were teachers, dressmakers, and milliners. For their stories, see Flora A. P. Engle, "The Story of the Mercer Expeditions," *Washington Historical Quarterly* 6 (October 1915): 225–37, and Angie Burt Bowden, *Early Schools of Washington Territory* (Seattle: Lowman and Hanford Co., 1935), pp. 189–93.

Zilpah Polly Grant, principal of Ipswich Female Seminary from 1828 to 1839, whose project to train and send teachers to the West was a predecessor of the program of the National Popular Education Board.

them from her trunk and grouped them on a table. "Mother, dear mother," she said, "I have a request to prefer, and it may be quite as favorably listened to by your picture as by your dear self. Now be lenient, and kindly permit your daughter to go out and devote her life to the cause of education and truth and religion in the far west." She thought about how she was often called "enthusiastic" or a "visionary" and dreamed she had three eyes. Her third eye "accounted" she said, "for my seeing things differently from some people."[4]

Arozina Perkins's words reflect the spirit of the movement that sent hundreds of single women teachers to bring education and Protestant evangelical religion to the West before the Civil War. Developed and publicized by Catharine Beecher, the plan of the National Board was to transfer the surplus of single eastern women already trained as teachers to the West, where Beecher estimated two million children lacked schools. She saw Protestant women, in fact, as the redeemers of the West. An essential impetus was the competition from schools already opened by Roman Catholic orders.[5]

After raising money on a lecture circuit and organizing the first two classes at Albany and Hartford in 1847, Beecher requested the board to hire William Slade, former governor of Vermont, as general agent. She soon broke with the organization, partly because she believed that funds would be better spent in establishing endowed female seminaries in the West to train indigenous women teachers. Although board members continued to accept only women who had embraced evangelical religion through a conversion experience, they advocated an end to the sectarianism that threatened to fragment the Protestant cause in the West.[6]

Using Cleveland, Ohio, as a base, Governor Slade and members of the board not only identified western communities that wanted teachers but urged others to open schools using National Board teachers. That the towns were often less concerned with religion than with their need for teachers is evident in a request from the directors of two school districts in La Salle County, Illinois. They wrote that they had "great difficulty to get Competent teachers to train our Schools," but "in regard to Religon in this place,

---

4. Perkins Diary, p. 76.

5. Catharine Beecher (1800–1878) surveyed the number of Catholic schools for girls in such states as Kentucky, Indiana, and Ohio and found them to be more numerous than Protestant academies for girls. Like other professors of evangelical religion in her time, she saw the Catholic church as a threat to the republic, in part, because she believed the church demanded blind obedience of its people by not allowing them to interpret the Bible for themselves. Beecher, "An Address to the Protestant Clergy," pp. 18–19.

6. Because the NPEB Papers used in this study begin in 1848, after Beecher left the organization, the only women included from the first classes are the few whose names came from sources outside the collection. Catharine Beecher, *Educational Reminiscences and Suggestions* (New York: J. B. Ford & Co., 1874), pp. 100–13; *First NPEB Report,* 1848, pp. 9–10; *Fourth NPEB Report,* 1851, p. 16. For an interpretation of Beecher's social philosophy concerning the pioneer teachers, see Sklar, *Catharine Beecher,* pp. 176–83.

William Slade (1786–1859), governor of Vermont from 1844 to 1846, had a long career in politics and journalism before becoming the agent for the NPEB in 1847, a position he held until 1858 when illness forced him to resign and effectively ended the NPEB's activities. *National Cyclopedia of American Biography* (Clifton, NJ: James T. White & Co., 1979), hereafter cited as *National Cyclopedia,* vol. 8, p. 319.

Catharine Beecher, founder of the National Popular Education Board, from an 1848 daguerreotype.

we have no particler Choice as their is some of all kinds in the place, mainly Baptist and Methodist we are not at tall particler on that point."[7]

In the East, centered at his home in Middlebury, Vermont, Slade raised

7. *First NPEB Report,* 1848, p. 9; David Olmstead, A. B. Stebbings, Ira Baker, directors, La Salle County, Illinois, to Co. for Selecting Teachers, 31 January 1849, administration folder, National Popular Education Board Papers, hereafter cited as NPEB Papers.

Governor William Slade, general agent of the National Popular Education Board from 1847 to 1858.

money and recruited women through public lectures, newspaper articles, and visits to the seminaries and academies whose offerings often had come to include teacher training. Only women were accepted, because, like Beecher, Slade believed in woman's special mission to perform the task. The Gold Rush attracted young men to the mines, leaving no one to teach in the West, he explained, "unless the young women of the nation come to the rescue." Sarah Josepha Hale, editor of *Godey's Lady's Book,* publicized the National Board's efforts. She believed that the board's plan provided an opportunity to prove that women were qualified to teach. What is more, she said, without woman's moral influence as teachers in the West, "the gold will prove a curse and not a blessing."[8]

It was not always as easy to recruit qualified women teachers for the West as the board had hoped. Even Mary Lyon, who taught with Zilpah Grant in the early years of Ipswich Seminary before founding Mount Holyoke Female Seminary, was cautious. Although her primary goal, as it had been at Ipswich, was to prepare women to teach and she did place some of her graduates in the West, Lyon told Catharine Beecher that the board's plan lacked specific assurances for teachers. She thought it would be difficult to find willing women who could gain the approval of their families unless a position and salary at a specific place were secured ahead of time and a dependable escort to the location provided.[9]

When it came time for final decisions, it was unusual for more than two or three women in one academy or seminary to decide to go West in a single year. Of the five women expected at Hartford in September 1849, from the Burlington Female Seminary in Vermont, the Reverend John K. Converse, Principal, wrote in late August that at least two would not be coming. Friends of one thought she should study another year, and the parents of another were so unwilling to have her go that she finally decided to look for a position near home. Before merging with the National Board, the Boston Society noted that it was much more difficult to locate teachers than to find positions. They blamed families for keeping their interested daughters from going to the West. Because of family opposition, of sixty teachers applying to the Society in 1848, only eleven actually went West. Six women cancelled at the last minute. In the first three years of operation, the Society reported that more than half of the women who consented to teach in the West were orphans.[10]

Yet, during the peak of the National Board's activities, twice a year twenty or twenty-five experienced women teachers did come forward from all over the Northeast as candidates for western positions. They met in a spring or fall institute at Hartford for six weeks, tuition free, directed by superintendent Nancy Swift, a Vermont native who was especially chosen for the position by Governor Slade. Her reputation for training teachers was built first when she served as principal of the Middlebury Female Seminary while his daughter Jane was a student and later as principal of the Huntsville Female Seminary in northern Alabama on the western edge of the Appa-

8. *Third NPEB Report*, 1850, pp. 11, 16; *Godey's Lady's Book* 38 (April 1849): 294–95; 39 (May 1850): 354–55.

9. Beecher, *Educational Reminiscences*, pp. 97–99; *Third NPEB Report*, 1850, pp. 11, 16. See also Elizabeth Alden Green, *Mary Lyon and Mount Holyoke: Opening the Gates* (Hanover, NH: University Press of New England, 1979), pp. 264–67.

10. J. K. Converse, Burlington, Vermont, to William Slade, 25 August 1849, administration folder, NPEB Papers; *Third Boston Society Report*, 1849, pp. 7–9.

lachians. Swift worked with a voluntary group of prominent Hartford women, called the Committee for Selecting Teachers, to organize the program, examine the teachers, and match them with western schools. She was watchful for potential failures and warned Henrietta Weymouth, a Maine teacher who was in her forties, that the committee believed the positions made "such a draft upon the physical energies of those engaged as teachers" that they could only send women who possessed "vigor of body and elasticity of mind."[11]

An escort, often Governor Slade himself, did accompany the teachers for the first part of the way and made arrangements for each woman's journey at the organization's expense. But from the moment each teacher left the larger group at various points beyond the western end of Lake Erie for her specific destination, she was on her own. Directions for travel were often brief. The directors of the La Salle County schools told their two expected teachers to come "by the lakes to Chicago thence By canal to Marseilles," where they were to call on Mr. L. Kimball, who kept a public house. One teacher was to ask for Joseph Grove, six miles northwest, and the other would find her schoolhouse within three miles.[12]

Martha Rogers describes the last leg of her Missouri journey in one of the letters included in this collection. She rode in a stagecoach from before dawn to after dark for three days and completed her trip in a lumber wagon. When she finally arrived, so exhausted she was sick for three days, she found her teaching position already filled for the summer session. Because the board's financial support ended when the teacher arrived at her assignment, Martha Rogers soon had to make her own plans.

Subsequent support from the board was minimal. Except for an annual circular and help with arrangements for a return trip West after a home visit,

---

11. The eldest daughter in a family of nine, Nancy Swift (1801–1884) moved with her family from Connecticut as a young child to Fairfax, Vermont. She taught in St. Albans before becoming principal of the Middlebury Female Seminary from 1835 to 1838. Governor Swift's daughter, Jane Maria, her student for three years, died in 1838. During Nancy's term, three of her younger brothers, Lucius, Samuel, and Eliphalet, graduated from Middlebury College, which did not open to women until 1883. Because these brothers were each at least ten years younger than she was, it is not difficult to imagine the role she played in their college lives. George H. Swift, comp., *William Swyft of Sandwich and Some of his Descendants, 1637–1899* (Milbrook, New York, 1900), pp. 55, 99–100, 147–48; Samuel Swift, *History of the Town of Middlebury in the County of Addison, Vermont* (Middlebury: A. H. Copeland, 1859), pp. 398–99; Duane L. Robinson, *General Catalogue of Middlebury College* (Middlebury: Middlebury College, 1950), pp. 96, 99, 110; *Catalogue of the Trustees, Instructors & Students of Middlebury Female Seminary* (Middlebury, 1836, 1837, 1838), references from Middlebury supplied by Polly Darnell, Sheldon Museum. For Emma Hart Willard's connection with Middlebury Female Seminary, see *NAW*, vol. 3, p. 611.

Members of the Committee for Selecting Teachers included the wives and a daughter of local judges: Mrs. Thomas Williams, Clarissa Brown Parsons (Mrs. Francis), and Sarah Day. *Sixth NPEB Report*, 1853, p. 28; Nancy Swift, Hartford, to Henrietta Weymouth, 16 April 1850, administration folder, NPEB Papers.

12. David Olmstead, 31 January 1849.

the most important connection with Hartford was letters from the popular and experienced Nancy Swift, whom they had come to trust while at Hartford. But her letters, however sympathetic to a problem described by the teacher, generally arrived after the teacher had resolved the problem herself. Cynthia Bishop's second letter, printed here, is a mixture of a request for advice and a plea for approval of the decision already made. When she started teaching in the new public school in Lafayette, Indiana, she was told not to use the Bible for fear of alienating Roman Catholic students. She described her compromise:"I *shall teach the scholars* the golden rule and many *other Bible precepts, whether I tell them* where I found *them or not."*

Clearly, whether or not the pioneer teacher understood all the consequences of her decision to move to a place she perceived as "a distant and stranger land," to quote Caroline Doughty of Orwell, Vermont, she made a choice unusual for a single antebellum woman. Papers from nearly two hundred of the women survive, including applications, biographical sketches written during the institute, and the letters from the West back to Nancy Swift.[13] From these sources and the very names of the women themselves, it is possible to discover the motivation and futures of many of the pioneer teachers, both individually and collectively. Before turning to take a close look at the diary, letters, and reminiscence of the nine women chosen to tell their stories, it is useful to analyze the common experience they shared as members of a group. Some perceptions will come from teachers whose letters cannot be included in this volume because of space limitations. All the voices serve to keep the immediate personal reality of the combined experience in clear view.

Why the Women Went West to Teach

In analyzing the reasons people went West historian John Unruh defined two useful categories: the "push" factors and the "pull" factors.[14] As teachers the women felt a strong pull to bring education and Protestant evangelical religion to the West, and some possessed a sense of adventure as well; as women they were pushed by a strong sense of personal economic need.

When asked to state their reasons for applying to teach in the West, the teachers often expressed themselves in the same terms. Her mother had died when she was three, Mary S. Adams explained. At the age of fourteen she

13. When Nancy Swift resigned early in 1855, she gave the letters and other papers to Clarissa Parsons at the request of the Committee for Selecting Teachers. They were saved and given to the Connecticut Historical Society by a descendant, Colonel Francis Parsons, in 1937. Nancy Swift, Pittsfield, Massachusetts, to Mrs. Parson, [n.d.], administration folder, NPEB Papers.

14. John D. Unruh, Jr., *The Plains Across; the Overland Emigrants and the Trans-Mississippi West, 1840–60* (Urbana: University of Illinois Press, 1979).

left home and, she wrote in words used by so many of the teachers, "since that time I have depended upon my own exertions for my livelihood and education." Mary Adams had taught for seven years and managed to attend Mount Holyoke Seminary for a year and a half. When she was going to school, Lucy Bell had not planned to become a teacher. After the death of her father, she found she needed to support herself. She had been teaching "for some years." Augusta Moore of Bangor, Maine, who took the La Salle County position, wrote: "I am in debt, and I wish to go where I can *earn* money. . . . Life has lost its *fanciful,* and put its *real* look to me."

When describing their difficulties in finding teaching positions in the East, the teachers also chose similar words. "New England seems to be flooded with teachers," observed Agnes Goulding, a young student at Mount Holyoke. "There is not as much probability of being the instrument of doing good here, as at the West." Elisabeth Bachelder, of Plainfield, Vermont, who was about to celebrate her twenty-seventh birthday, was certain that "a wider field of usefulness was opened at the West."

Some older women simply had been teaching too long in their home communities and needed a change—or at least one family thought so. The brother of Ursula Stevens, age forty-six, and Augusta Stevens, age thirty-four, sent a recommendation to the board for his sisters who were teaching with him in the academy at Hardwick, Vermont, so that "*they* be made the instrument of great usefulness in their field of labor."

Knowing and, in fact, agreeing with the board's mission, several teachers apologized for having an economic motive as well. Betsey Brownell, who went from Vermont to Indiana, explained: "Being dependent upon my own exertions I felt it necessary also to look at the subject in another light, which, I think is not inconsistent with the spirit of doing good." Frances R. Farrand, who had been a teacher in the district schools of northern Vermont for five years, maintained that, after all, salary "*may* be a pure motive, for we are commended to be 'Diligent in business' and surely if a person is always so he will acquire *some* wealth and have a better opportunity for doing good."

Arozina Perkins, who was raised in the Green Mountains of Vermont, was worried not only about her own future but also about her family's descent from respectability. Her grandfather had been a Baptist minister. By the time her father died, she was twenty, and the family had dispersed. Her mother had moved back to her native Marshfield, Massachusetts, and Arozina was supporting herself by teaching. Her older sister was mentally ill and one of her brothers was in jail. On her way West, she met a young minister who showed a great deal of interest in her. She longed to tell him about her brother but held back. After starting school in Fort Des Moines, Iowa, she finally gathered up enough courage to write her suitor about her brother. The response came quite promptly and Arozina was dismayed. "It is as I anticipated; ———— has discarded me *because I am so unfortunate as to have a prodigal brother.* Perhaps it is well, for this fact *might* have been a barrier to his usefulness in the ministry." It was early in March and she was feeling particularly depressed about the problem of relating to her new community. "But if *he,* who *professed* to love me so well, has turned from me, what am I to expect from those who feel *no* interest in me!" Within a week, spring arrived in Iowa bringing, she wrote, "a half dozen of the pleasantest, sweetest days I ever saw," and she felt more hopeful again. [15]

The motives of nearly half of the women who chose to go West through the Board of National Popular Education whose names are known can be found in their applications or biographies. The "push" of economic necessity is clear. Of these, more than two-thirds reveal that they were already on their own, self-supporting by necessity. Of that group, half mention the loss of one or both parents and the adverse effect of the deaths on their lives. The rest are older professional teachers, long on their own, seeking change or higher salaries. Fewer than a third of the entire group either mention that their original parents are both living or appear to be young women looking for positions early in their careers. Information from town vital records and the United States manuscript census shows that in both groups the women came from large families and were most likely to be the eldest daughters. In addition, the median age of the teachers while at Hartford is twenty-five, reducing the other option for family support, marriage, for the majority of the women, whether by choice or not, because of age. [16]

---

15. Perkins Diary, p. 142.

16. The excess of women over men in the Northeast was not as great in 1850 as it would become during and after the Civil War. In the twenty- to thirty-year age group, Vermont, New York, Connecticut, and Maine had slightly more men than women. Massachusetts had 106.46 females for every 100 males and New Hampshire had 102.53 females for every 100 males. *Seventh Census of the United States, 1850* (Washington, D.C., 1863), p. lxxxvi.

The average age of marriage for women in New England in this period was between twenty-three and twenty-four. See Dublin, *Women at Work,* p. 52.

Comparisons can be made between the pioneer women teachers and the Lowell mill girls studied by Dublin and the Mount Holyoke students studied by Allmendinger. One of the major differences between the teachers and the Lowell and Mount Holyoke groups appears to be the extent of the economic need. Dublin finds the Lowell women to have come from "typical male-headed households" and to have gone to the mills in kin networks. The Lowell women also lacked the sense of mission that was a "pull" factor for the teachers. Although the pioneer teachers had similar social origins to the overall Holyoke group studied by Allmendinger, such factors as age and family losses appear to be intensified in the pioneer teacher group. See David F. Allmendinger, Jr., "Mount Holyoke Students Encounter the Need for Life-Planning, 1837–1850," *History of Education Quarterly* 19 (Spring 1979): 27–46. Three of the pioneer teachers explained that they had worked in Lowell to help pay for their education: Cynthia M. Bishop from Georgia, Vermont; Martha Boynton from Carlisle, Massachusetts; and Lucretia M. Morrill from Boscowen, New Hampshire.

The average number of children in their families of origin was between six and seven. The oldest daughter was most likely to leave because she was closest in age to her mother or stepmother and became superfluous sooner. This concept for oldest sons in Vermont is explained by Hal S. Barron in "After the

Mount Holyoke Female Seminary, South Hadley, Massachusetts, attended by at least twenty-four of the National Board teachers.

The women were already experienced teachers who had struggled to prepare for their careers. Two-thirds had taught for three years or more. Their literate letters reveal the high level of their education, whether formal or informal. Although free secondary schools were not yet generally available to girls, nearly 90 percent of the women whose educational backgrounds can be found name the academies or seminaries they attended, usually for a few terms only in alternation with teaching or other jobs. Only three of the twenty-four women known to have attended Mount Holyoke Seminary graduated, and only a handful can be shown to be graduates of normal schools. Like many of her sister teachers, Arozina Perkins attended the coeducational academy in her home town. Each of the four terms, defined by the seasons, cost $3.00, with an increase of $.50 for languages or other advanced studies. Some academies offered "teachers' classes" on a weekly basis. For students who had to leave home to attend academies, room and board in private families cost $1.50 a week. Augusta Hubbell, whose letter

Great Transformation: The Social Processes of Settled Rural Life in the Nineteenth-Century North," paper presented at the Social Science History Association, Nashville, TN, October 1981.

Burlington Female Seminary in Vermont sent more than fifteen alumnae to the National Board for western teaching positions.

follows, incurred a $200 debt while she attended the seminary in Le Roy, New York.[17]

All of the women teachers shared one common "pull" factor, their sense of mission, of bringing Protestant evangelical religion and education to the West. During the institute at Hartford, each woman had to write about the meaning of "regeneration" and describe her personal conversion experience. Supporting letters from their ministers were submitted with their applications. Women who could not meet the religious test were advised to wait. In Arozina Perkins's class, Miss Wooster was refused a western position because she had not yet been converted. Arozina tried to influence her, but Miss Wooster replied that she would have to wait. Since the board knew she was anxious to go West with the group, she explained, they would think her motive for accepting religion was to be chosen as a teacher.[18] Julia Bassett

17. *Catalogue of Lamoille County Grammar School* (Johnson, VT: 1837); *Catalogue of Newbury Seminary* (Newbury, VT: 1851–52) in Vermont Historical Society, *One Hundred Year Biographical Directory; Mount Holyoke College, 1837–1937* (South Hadley, MA: Mount Holyoke College, 1937), hereafter cited as *Mount Holyoke Directory*.

18. Perkins Diary, p. 112.

had wanted to go West earlier "but being a non-professor I could not go," she wrote. "Since I became a member of the church, I have felt more anxious to go." Fanny L. Joslyn, a student at the Burlington Female Seminary, had no less a goal than to "exert a happy influence on the church—the country— and the world."

The significance of the conversion experience in helping nineteenth-century women develop a new way of life has been discussed by historian Nancy Cott. Conversion experiences allowed women to lean on God rather than on men, Cott explained, and helped women form new identities and a sense of purpose in a changing world. Catharine Fortner from Tompkins County, New York, was one of the group of pioneer teachers who came from that part of western New York called the "burned-over district," because of the waves of religious enthusiasm that swept over the region in the first half of the century. She was twenty-six when she described a confrontation with her father over her desire to teach in the West. "I told him the only object I had in view (of going West) was to do good to others," she said, "and I felt as though I could be of greater use elsewhere than here—he *thinks not*. And here I am. I would not cause my friends one hour of sadness needlessly nor would I disobey the command of my Father in heaven. No! rather would I obey God than any other." Without the conversion experience and the goals deriving from it, it is unlikely that many of the pioneer women teachers would have found the courage to leave their homes.[19]

Although Governor Slade's annual reports continued to emphasize the special role of woman in civilizing the West, none of the teachers claims to have felt a special calling because they were women. In their view, their mission derived from a desire to serve God. Although they revered Governor Slade as a kind father, some of them were sometimes a bit amused at his statements. When Arozina Perkins's group gathered in Albany for the last time before leaving for the West, Slade had said, "We come, not with the whirlwind or the storm, but with the still, small, gentle voice of woman." Later, Arozina made a pun on his words when the last of her companions took the Missouri River steamer, the *Tempest,* while she continued on the Mississippi for Iowa. She wrote, "I thought of what the Gov. said, that 'they come not in the *whirlwind* or the storm' but I could testify they had gone in the *Tempest.*"[20]

The final "pull" for many of the pioneer women teachers was the same as the "pull" for many pioneer men—a sense of adventure and a desire to see the West for themselves. After Arozina viewed the "Panorama of the Ohio and

19. Cott, "Young Women in the Second Great Awakening"; Whitney R. Cross, *The Burned-Over District: The Social and Intellectual History of Enthusiastic Religion in Western New York, 1800–1850* (Ithaca, NY: Cornell University Press, 1950).

20. *Third NPEB Report,* 1850, pp. 11, 16; Perkins Diary, p. 121.

the Mississippi Rivers" one evening in New Haven, she longed to go West. The wish of Mary E. Adams from Bangor, Maine, "to visit the Western Country to see something of the world we live in" was more than gratified when she married an Indian agent in Neosho, Missouri, during her first year West. As the letters printed in this collection by Mary Hitchcock reveal, it was her hope "to see more of the country" that influenced her to teach in Illinois.

Still, when it came time to make the final decision, last-minute wavering was not uncommon. Nancy Swift noted on the back of an unexpected letter from Caroline Doughty the words, "failed in courage." Doughty's letter told how she stopped packing her trunks because her friends had so discouraged her. Within the month, Doughty did join the class after all, headed for Indiana and a marriage within four years to the proprietor of a successful grain elevator.[21] She admitted in her biography: "I cannot [say] that I possess such a self-denying, self-sacrificing spirit that I have not some respect to my own comfort and convenience. In my estimate this is a right, for self-preservation is an important law of nature."

When the decision was firm, several women revealed a new sense of self. Just twenty, Maria Welch had recently finished her studies at the Cortland, New York, Academy. She wanted to "try myself alone, and find out what I am."[22] Three of the entire group were widows. Abby Willard Stanton, whose husband had died while away in California, wrote, "I am conscious God has something for me to do. That my future life is to be one of action and not repose."

Training to Be Pioneer Teachers

Although glimpses of the teaching methods advocated at the National Board's institute at Hartford appear in many of the letters as the women describe their eforts to put them into practice, the diary of Arozina Perkins provides the only complete description of the training. It was held in donated rooms at the orphan asylum. Each candidate was expected to pay her traveling expenses to Hartford and board of $1.75 a week during the institute; many had to be granted loans.[23]

21. Charles Blanchard, ed., *Counties of Morgan, Monroe & Brown, Indiana* (Chicago: 1884), p. 211; reference supplied by the staff of the Allen County Public Library, Fort Wayne.

22. Maria Welch returned home and taught in Syracuse for ten years before a brief marriage to a doctor that was ended by his death. He was the brother of her sister teacher, Nancy Harris. She later wrote a travelogue describing a trip with two other women. Maria Welch Harris, *United States Girls Across the Atlantic* (Homer, NY: 1876), reference supplied by Ronald Butchart using the collection of the Cortland Historical Society.

23. Perkins Diary, pp. 102–15; William Slade, Middlebury, Vermont, to Abba Mace, 14 August 1852, administration folder, NPEB Papers.

View of Hartford in 1849 from the American Asylum for the Deaf and Dumb. Looking right from the State House (center, with flag) are the Universalist Church, First Congregational Church, Wadsworth Atheneum, St. John's Episcopal Church, and Second Baptist Church. Looking left from the State House are the City Hall, First Baptist Church, African Congregational Church, and Trinity Catholic Church.

The staff of the institute provided the women with strong female role models. Nancy Swift served as superintendent for ten classes. Like many of the candidates, she was raised as the eldest daughter of a large family in northwestern Vermont, where she taught before becoming a female seminary principal. Her experiences also represented ones immediately facing the teachers. In 1838, Nancy and her younger sister Lydia, who had been her assistant at the seminary, journeyed down the Ohio River to northern Alabama to teach in the western South. Lydia stayed and married, and Nancy returned to New England.[24]

Strong connections to either Ipswich Female Seminary or Mount Holyoke or both were evident in the institute's staff. During her six years with the National Board, Nancy Swift lived with the family of her youngest brother, the Reverend Eliphalet Y. Swift, a trustee of Mount Holyoke and minister to its students. His wife, Catharine, was an early graduate. Lucy Tappan Grosvenor, an Ipswich alumna, directed two classes and Hannah White, a former Ipswich teacher, directed the other four classes. White's niece, Amanda Ferry, who was Swift's assistant, was brought up as a missionary daughter in Michigan. An alumna of Mount Holyoke, Ferry was teaching at Ipswich concurrently with her position in Hartford. Finally, the former principal of Ipswich Seminary, Zilpah Grant herself, by then the widow of William Banister, lectured to the last three classes and traveled West with Hannah White to visit schools.[25]

The Ninth Class (Spring 1851) was held in Cleveland under the direction of Linda T. Guilford (1823–1911), a Mount Holyoke graduate who was the long-time principal of the Cleveland Female Seminary and the author of the life of Zilpha Grant Banister. A collection of Linda Guilford's papers is housed at the Western Reserve Historical Society in Cleveland.

24. Nancy and Lydia Swift joined the Presbyterian Church in Huntsville, Alabama, on 25 November 1838, and Nancy is advertised as the continuing principal of the Huntsville Female Seminary in 1839 with Lydia as her assistant. Nancy resigned sometime before 1846 when a new principal was advertised. Although Lydia married Henry Wright of Perryville, Tennessee, in Huntsville on 23 December 1847, she was living in Lexington, Tennessee, by October 1850, when Nancy traveled with Arozina Perkins and members of her class to spend the winter with Lydia. Lydia's son Henry S. was born in 1850. For Catharine Beecher's connection with the Huntsville Female Seminary and possible clues as to why Nancy Swift went there, see Beecher, *Educational Reminiscences*, p. 80, and Woody, *History of Women's Education*, vol. 1, pp. 388–89. "Session Records of the Presbyterian Church, Huntsville, Ala.," *Valley Leaves* 5 (March 1971): 84; *The Democrat*, Huntsville, AL, 17 August 1839, p. 3; 12 August 1846, p 3; *Southern Advocate*, Huntsville, AL, 1 January 1848, p. 3; U.S. Manuscript Census, 1860, Henderson County, TN, p. 250. Huntsville references supplied by Annwhite Fuller, Huntsville-Madison County Public Library.

Nancy Swift never married but assumed the care of her niece, Helen Swift, who at six, was orphaned by the death of Nancy's brother, Lucius, in 1849. Helen knew all the teachers at Hartford and they often sent messages to her in their letters. Nancy Swift died in Portland, Oregon, in 1884, where she was living with Helen and her husband, Buell Lamberson. Swift, *William Swift*, pp. 55, 99–100; Vital Statistics File, Oregon Historical Society.

25. Eliphalet Swift (1815–1892) served as a western agent for the American Tract Society from 1842 to 1844 and was ordained in Ohio before taking a church in Massachusetts in 1845. His wife was the

The goals of the staff at Hartford were twofold. First, they hoped to turn into pioneer teachers women who most of their lives had been teachers or students in the small district schools of rural New England and New York. Second, they expected the women to introduce specific teaching methods into the West. The latter goal was essential, because the staff knew that the majority of teachers were being hired by communities that believed men teachers were more effective disciplinarians than women and students were best controlled with the rod. The idea presented at Hartford was to awaken the pupil's moral sense and govern with the Golden Rule. The use of Bible readings was urged to set the proper tone, as well as active singing programs, another way to inspire students to high ideals. The introduction of the blackboard was recommended.

The favorite speaker was the charismatic Thomas Gallaudet, known for his work in teaching the deaf. Influenced by Pestalozzi, Gallaudet urged the

---

former Catharine Leach of Pittsford, Vermont. U.S. Manuscript Census, 1850, Hampshire County, Massachusetts, p. 84; *General Catalogue of the Theological Seminary, Andover, Massachusetts, 1808–1909* (Boston: 1908), p. 196.

Lucy P. Tappan attended Ipswich from 1831–32 with her first cousins Susan and Juliana, daughters of Lewis Tappan of New York City, the prominent Abolitionist who helped found the American Missionary Association and Oberlin College. Lucy was probably the "Miss Tappan" of the Detroit Female Seminary who Mary Lyon visited in 1833. She became the second wife of the Reverend Mason Grosvenor in 1849, a former agent of the Western College Society. Earlier he established a female seminary in Hudson, Ohio, where they lived after 1855.

Hannah White (1900–1879) was one of the three daughters of Thomas White of Ashfield, a supporter of Mary Lyon from the beginning. Her sister, Amanda, married the Reverend William Montague Ferry, a missionary on Mackinac Island and in Grand Haven, Michigan. There was a great deal of interest in the Mackinac Island mission at Ipswich Seminary and correspondence between students at each place. Hannah White lived in Newburyport near Zilpah Grant Banister (1794–1874) and was her close friend. Their assistant at Hartford was Anna Bronson, of Winchester, Connecticut, a recent graduate of Ipswich Seminary, where the principals were then Grant's cousin the Reverend John P. Cowles and his wife Eunice Caldwell Cowles, Grant's former student. See *Ipswich Catalogues;* David L. Tappan, *Tappan-Toppan Genealogy* (Arlington, Mass.: 1915), pp. 25, 30, 40; *Obituary Record of Graduates of Yale University, 1880–1890* (New Haven: 1890), hereafter cited as *Yale Graduates,* pp. 291–92; Green, *Mary Lyon,* p. 107; Woody, *History of Women's Education,* vol. 1, p. 370; "To the ladies who support Mary Lyon Grant," Mackinaw, 4 September 1829, in Ipswich Female Seminary collection in the Ipswich Public Library; Guilford, *the Use of a Life:* 274–88; *NAW,* vol. 2, pp. 73–75, 443–47; *Ninth NPEB Report,* 1856, p. 13; *Eleventh NPEB Report,* 1858, p. 15. Zilpah Grant Banister's papers are contained in the College History Collection at Mount Holyoke College and the Ferry family papers in the archives at Michigan State Univeristy. The Essex Institute has a complete collection of *Ipswich Catalogues.*

For a description of Zilpah Grant's lectures on teaching at Ipswich, which correspond to the methods presented at the institute at Hartford, see Leonard W. Labaree, "Zilpah Grant and the Art of Teaching: 1829, as Recorded by Eliza Paul Capen," *New England Quarterly* 20 (September 1847): 347–64.

Other than men who served as trustees, the only connection between the National Board's institute at Hartford and the Hartford Female Seminary appears to be Clarissa Brown Parsons, one of the members of the Committee for Selecting Teachers, who taught at the Seminary under Catharine Beecher. Beecher, *Educational Reminiscences,* p. 77.

teachers to lead from interest and to use reason instead of memorization. An advocate of women's education, he published a book designed to show mothers and teachers how to teach beginning reading by substituting words for letters. His *Child's Book on the Soul,* which taught the child in story form that the soul had a separate existence from the body and was immortal, was mentioned by numbers of teachers in the field as being the favorite of their students.[26]

Arozina and her sister candidates were reviewed and tested in English composition, spelling, music, algebra, and physiology. They practiced calisthenics daily to make their bodies stronger and their movements more graceful and to combat critics who believed women were too delicate to pursue a serious education. The teachers heard inspirational lectures; they visited schools, the insane asylum, art gallery, state house, and historical society; they took walks to the Charter Oak. They were given copies of religious tracts, dictionaries, and, in later years, *Uncle Tom's Cabin.* The arrival of Governor Slade to escort them for the first part of their journey West was the signal that the institute was almost over. Each teacher received her teaching assignment and last instructions from the superintendent. She urged them to exercise "cordiality of manner" and to "censure as little as possible."[27]

The Journey West

The teachers promised to write Nancy Swift within a few months. Undoubt-edly because she had learned from earlier classes that each teacher wanted to describe her journey in great detail, Nancy Swift appointed one or two members of each class to be the official reporters for the part of the trip made as a group. The journeys took from two to four weeks. The pioneer teachers traveled by the "cars" to Buffalo and on lake, river, and canal boats along Lake Erie, down the Ohio River, up and down the Mississippi and the Missouri or along the Michigan-Illinois Canal. They remained together as far as Buffalo, where they broke off into smaller groups at various stopping places until each individual teacher found herself alone on that last journey by stagecoach or farm wagon.

The Lake Erie crossing was the transition from East to West for the pioneer teachers. Mary Arnold from Monmouth, Maine, described her

26. The Reverend Thomas Gallaudet (1787–1851) was a cofounder of the American Asylum for the Deaf and Dumb in Hartford. *Dictionary of American Biography* (New York: Scribner's, 1927–1974), hereafter cited as DAB, vol. 4, pp. 111–12. T. H. Gallaudet, *An Address on Female Education* (Hartford: 1828); *Mothers' Primer* (Hartford: 1840); *Child's Book on the Soul* (Hartford: 1831).

27. Lucy Tappan Grosvenor was the superintendent of the fall 1850 class because Nancy Swift was sick. Perkins Diary, p. 103; "Papers Left in Table Drawer by Mrs. Grosvenor," envelope in adminstra-tion folder, NPEB Papers; *Seventh NPEB Report,* 1854, p. 20; *Eighth NPEB Report,* 1855, p. 18.

The steamer May Flower *carried many of the pioneer teachers across Lake Erie. They viewed the crossing as the passage from East to West.*

feelings. "It seemed like being transported into a new clime and I suppose we were just then beginning to cross the *boundary line* which separates East from West." It was suitable, she thought, that their ship was called the *May Flower,* although she was amused by the differences. "Methinks," she said, "its fanciful decorations, its crimsoned lounges and Brussels carpets were little like the Mayflower of the pilgrims of old when they embarked for these wild shores of America." As will be seen in Martha Rogers's description of the crossing, everybody on board with her was seasick.

Two women in Arozina Perkins's class signed up to go to Oregon in the spring. Elizabeth Miller had family on the way to join her in Oregon; Sarah Smith, a teacher at the Genesee Wesleyan Seminary in Lima, New York, made the decision to go on her own. Governor Slade recruited three more women for Oregon, including Mary Almira Gray from Vermont, whose recollections of the journey are included in this collection. The adventure, starting on the *Empire City* out of New York, was such a significant event in her life that fifty years later she could recall every detail. The following spring, a second group of three teachers made a similar journey to San Francisco, in thirty-one days. Susan A. Lord, a young teacher from Massachusetts, returned from her first assignment in Wisconsin to be part of the group, because she wanted to go farther West.[28]

A few teachers found the trip West somewhat frightening. Arozina Perkins was moved by the homesickness of Annie Flint, from a small town in Maine. "I really pitied the poor girl," she told her diary, "as she promenaded

28. *Fifth NPEB Report,* 1852, pp. 6–7; *Sixth NPEB Report,* 1853, p. 7.

the room, looking so very sober, and heaving such very heartbreaking sighs, and was rejoiced when she told me she had decided she would go on." Less than a year later, Arozina recalled the scene as she reported to Nancy Swift the news of Annie Flint's death in Vermilion County, Illinois.

As Arozina neared her destination after six weeks of travel, she stopped to record the feelings she first experienced when she stepped off the coach in Iowa. "I was in the centre of a wide Western Prairie, and one of the many dreams of my early days was being realized. . . . I tho't how often, when a schoolgirl I had traced out on the map the very spot upon which I now stood." Arozina's hopes soon fell. She found that a rival schoolhouse had been opened. The one thing she had not expected was *not* to be needed.[29]

Although Arozina Perkins was welcomed into a family right away, other teachers were faced with the immediate problem of where to stay. As Sarah Ballard's first letter shows, the women often found it necessary to assert themselves immediately over the issue of living arrangements. Almost to a woman, the teachers refused to "board around." Mary S. Adams gave three reasons why she would not board with a school director in Calhoun, Missouri: he lived too far from the school, expected her to do her own washing, and had four teenagers who attracted company, especially on Sundays. Upon arriving in Georgetown, Illinois, Sarah Quick was told by one of the directors that she must board around. He "said with an oath if I was unwilling to do that I should go home." She stood firm. "I told them I would like very much to please them, but I felt that it was not my duty to board around, and I would not do it."[30]

Teaching on the Frontier

How did the women handle sickness, loneliness, the lack of church privileges? How did they handle relations with men that might lead to marriage? What was their role in community building? How much autonomy were they able, or did they even want, to exercise? Finally, the key question of all: How many of the pioneer teachers were able to leave the East behind and assume new lives without kin and with people who were once strangers? Readers will want to make their own discoveries about the quality of the teachers' western lives as reported by the teachers themselves. The women's western experience is also illuminated by examining common themes as revealed in the entire body of letters from the West. More than two hundred letters from 130 of the teachers describe their new situations. The letters not only help to characterize the frontier towns or settlements where they taught

29. Perkins Diary, pp. 125, 127.
30. Sarah Quick married and settled in Georgetown, Illinois, and Mary S. Adams married in Clinton, Missouri, but died within a year.

but also reveal how local controversies affected their success in meeting their goals. Different solutions to personal problems are presented as well.

On their way back to their western schools following a home leave after three years, Martha Rogers and Caroline Wilkinson met again as they traveled with the new class of teachers just leaving Albany. Upon comparing notes, they decided that "Missouri and Tennessee are almost *twin sisters.*" Caroline Wilkinson was moved as she thought about the new teachers. "Oh! how it brought to mind the scenes of 3 years ago! How little I then knew of what awaited me—and I trembled involuntarily for the young ladies who were just going to try the *realities* of a *life among strangers!*"

For the women teachers who moved into fast-growing towns and trading centers, the West they entered was the West of the entrepreneur: in real estate and business, school building, and even church founding. In this collection, Martha Rogers's letters describe the competitive spirit in a Missouri frontier town.

Delia Hosford found the business spirit of Ottawa, Illinois, a hindrance to her goals. "Ottawa is emphatically a business town," she said, "and the greater part of the people are so engrossed in their business that they have no time for anything else." Although the town was sixteen years old, it had built only one schoolhouse. On the other hand, Mary E. Adams found the people of Neosho, Missouri, friendly and anxious to educate their children. In addition to her school, she wrote, "there are seven stores and a Court House, beside the dwelling houses which are neither very numerous or very magnificent." Virginia Smith was worried about the future of Sterling, Iowa. When she arrived, it consisted of a church, schoolhouse, hotel, store, blacksmith and carpenter shops, and fifteen or twenty private houses. "But they are beginning to bring liquor into the place," she told Nancy Swift, "which is an apple of discord wherever it is introduced." Whether or not Virginia Smith named the actual cause, Sterling did not survive as a town. Smith moved to Illinois, where she married.

As the persons essential to the operation of a school and as individuals vitally interested in churches, however, the women often contributed unwittingly to the entrepreneurial spirit. Their school plans sometimes fell victim to promoters who used new academies as a way to advertise their towns.

Mary Parsons and Lucy Ordway, who came from adjoining towns near Newburyport, Massachusetts, and knew each other at Mount Holyoke, waited in Greensburg, Indiana, for the building of a Presbyterian Seminary on the plan of Mount Holyoke. Mary Parsons knew that part of the goal of the school's enthusiastic sponsor was to raise the value of property in the town. "It looks a little dark but I mean to be patient and wait," she admitted to Nancy Swift. A year later she noted that the sponsor "does a great amount of business, consequently the school business is often delayed." Lucy Ordway gave up and returned to teach in New England, but Mary Parsons had her piano shipped from the East and continued to teach in the basement of the church for two years. She finally left to teach in the new Western Female Seminary in Oxford, Ohio, and in a select school in Crown Point, Indiana, where she died in 1860.

Maria Dunn found herself in a small family school in Perry County, Illinois. When she learned that she was to be paid by public money and read "extraordinary puffs . . . in the county paper" about her school, she concluded that "the motive in bringing me down was to make money," and soon left. A few teachers had trouble with discipline because the patrons were afraid to lose business. Elisabeth Hill left the young ladies' seminary in Lexington, Missouri, because she believed the administration's method was "to indulge all [the students] through fear of losing them, or losing the influence of their friends."

Following the model of the East, the schools of the antebellum West were entirely under local control. There was no assurance, however, that a western town would support a stable district school like the ones the women grew up with in the Northeast. The controversy over who should pay for schools, the broader community or only families with students, was at its peak when the teachers arrived. Schools often closed when money from public funds ran out and the teachers had the choice between continuing the school as a subscription school or leaving for a new situation.[31] Although Maria Freeman and Celia Sprague decided to continue to teach their former public school in Huntington, Indiana, as a select school, they expected attendance to fall off. Many of the people, they explained, "do not have the means or desire to send their children to school unless it is free." While Maria Barrett was teaching a public school in South Bend, Indiana, the state law requiring communities to raise funds for schools was declared unconstitutional. Because each township would now decide whether or not to raise public money for schools, she said, her free school was about to end.

Petty power struggles caused some teachers to lose their public school positions. By the time Mary Chase arrived in Savanna, Illinois, a new school board was in power. Because the new members had not been consulted about her appointment, they caused her to be dismissed. The family she boarded with helped her set up a select school in the Methodist Church, where she soon had thirty pupils. Her letter is included in this collection.

31. For the point of view of a contemporary supporter of public funding for schools in Indiana, see Gayle Thornbrough, Dorothy L. Riker, and Paula Corpuz, eds., *The Diary of Calvin Fletcher, 1817–1862* (Indianapolis: Indiana Historical Society, 1972–80), hereafter cited as *Fletcher Diary*, vol. 4, pp. 5, 8, 13, 42–43, 59; vol. 5, pp. 23–24, 63–64. The best general discussion of the school funding crisis in the Old Northwest is Fuller, *The Old Country School*, pp. 22–51.

See also Ronald E. Butchart, "Education and Culture in the Trans-Mississippi West: An Interpretation," *Journal of American Culture* 3 (Summer 1980): 351–73.

Several communities, however, were anxious to start public schools. Cynthia Bishop in Lafayette, Indiana, and Lucinda Beach in Columbus, Ohio, each found positions in new graded public schools. Bishop reveals some of the special problems of the new public schools in her letter included here. State superintendents of education tried to encourage good teaching by offering institutes. Four of the teachers met at an institute in South Bend, Indiana, where Cynthia Bishop won a prize for her essay on the construction of schoolhouses. While teaching at an institute in Geneva, Illinois, Harriet Tucker met Mary Arnold and Nancy Kidder. Fanny Warner believed her Wisconsin community wanted good schools, and was proud to keep records for the state superintendent.

It was in the smaller farming communities that many of the pioneer teachers seemed to find the most opportunity to take control over their own situations. In letters printed here, Mary Hitchcock explains why she left the Beardstown, Illinois, academy for a school in Princeton, a new settlement twenty miles into the country. She had considered the young ladies in the town spoiled and now appreciated her mixed class of thirty-seven students, many of whom walked over two miles to her school. Within a year of her move she married. Agnes Goulding preferred her country schoolhouse in Indiana to the seminary in town, saying that students "will learn just as fast in a log schoolhouse as in a brick one."

Whether women teachers from the East could successfully control mixed classes was questioned by many westerners. Ellen Lee, aged twenty, had been the eldest daughter at home of a large family of a Princeton, Massachusetts, shoemaker and his wife. Most of the adults in her small Indiana settlement had not had the opportunity to learn to read and write. Her log school, consisting of fifty pupils between the ages of fourteen and twenty-two, had always had trouble before. "They thought, of course, if a man could not govern their boys, a woman could not," she explained to Nancy Swift, "but I was allowed to take my course, and I gave them only one rule—do right & by awakening their consciences to a sense of right and wrong and other similar influences, I have succeeded much better." Calvin Fletcher, a school trustee in Indiana, observed Ellen Lee's school and stated that she had "revolutionized one neighborhood" by convincing thirty young men to sign a pledge not to use tobacco.[32]

The pioneer teachers held school in a variety of places, ranging from two-story brick seminary buildings in new western towns to log schoolhouses in frontier settlements and the one-room frame schoolhouse in farming communities, whose basic design traveled West with the settlers. In Peoria and Paris, Illinois, Sarah Matthews and Nancy Harris taught in new brick buildings; Nancy Harris's was three stories high, complete with a

32. *Fletcher Diary*, vol. 5, p. 11.

cupola and bell. Aurilla Cross found a "very comfortable frame schoolhouse," in White River Township, Indiana, but there had been no school for two years. The community was so glad to have a teacher that they made new seats and desks and even a blackboard, although she had to paint it. Even though Martha Boynton was not expected when she arrived in Wisconsin, the community built her a frame school in five weeks, furnishing it with a blackboard and a globe. It opened to thirty-three students, aged four to twenty.[33]

Teachers with log schoolhouses complained the most about their buildings. Roxanna Ellsworth watched the men in Parke County, Indiana, complete her log schoolhouse, which had stood unfinished for a year waiting for a teacher. They chinked the logs, added window frames, hung a door, and made new seats. "I will not allow myself to think," she said, "about the outside door opening directly onto the school-room." In Iowa, Mahala Drake had to stoop to look out the two small windows of her log school, and the only dry spot was behind the door. The roof of Martha Rogers's log school in Missouri leaked so much that the students had to keep moving to different spots when it rained.

Eunice Cole's small frame building stood next to the road in southern Indiana with no yard at all, while Catharine Fortner's new frame school was situated on an open Iowa prairie. Schoolyards may have varied, but not stoves; they were constant problems. Martha Rogers solved her stove problem by sending to St. Louis for a new one with her own money. Arozina Perkins had particular trouble with the old stove in her school in Fort Des Moines. One night she dreamed she saw "a beautiful bright star beaming in the clear daylight." When she arrived at school that morning she found a new wood stove waiting for her.[34]

Fanny Warner introduced new teaching techniques in her Wisconsin school to satisfy her "ever buoyant hope" of developing "an interested school." She borrowed bones from the local doctor for teaching physiology, had a blackboard made, and introduced singing. When she had a globe sent from the East, she found her students had thought the world was "'round like a wheel rather than an orange." Cynthia Bishop introduced a "Post Office box" for questions on any subject that interested her Indiana students. When one of the students dropped in the question, "What do men get drunk for?", she borrowed a neighboring teacher's drawing of a "drunkard's stomach" for the next class.

33. Sarah J. Matthews taught in the Girls' Stock School in Peoria. Her students were girls ranging from age seven to eighteen who were, she said, "the daughers of the first and wealthiest gentlemen in the city." She married Alexander McCoy in Peoria. Martha Boynton returned to Massachusetts and married. H. W. Wells, *The Schools and the Teachers of Early Peoria* (Peoria: 1900), pp. 96–97, 102–03, reference supplied by Charles J. Frey, Bradley University; John and Caroline Boynton, *Boynton Family* (n.p., 1897), p. 186.

34. Perkins Diary, p. 131.

The traditional New England schoolhouse of the first half of the nineteenth century. Its design followed the settlers west.

The Girls' Stock School in Peoria, Illinois, was an example of the brick seminary buildings in growing western towns. Sarah J. Matthews, National Board teacher from Lee, New York, taught here. When it became a public school, it was renamed the Irving School.

A frame schoolhouse on the Wisconsin frontier, built in the familiar style of the East.

Log schoolhouse in Allen County, Indiana, built between 1840 and 1850. Former students gather for a reunion in 1900.

Although Cynthia Bishop did not have to resort to the rod, Mary Arnold explained that she "was driven to corporeal punishment" in her Illinois school after "the wicked boys got the upper hand." She said that it "produced a good effect." In Portage Prairie, Indiana, Martha Brown was determined "to rule by love," but she secured her goal by using a classic teacher's method. "I govern a great deal by the eye," she said. "If I can get a scholar's eye, he can read at once what I desire of him, and will not often fail to do it." She encouraged the writing of compositions by promising to answer any letter a student wrote to her.[35]

Because the teachers were entirely self-supporting, questions about salary were raised often. Although a reasonable minimum salary acceptable to the National Board was $150 a year with room and board, many teachers averaged less. Louisa Bean, a New Hampshire native, wrote from Wyoming, Wisconsin: "My school is larger and my salary smaller than I expected." Classes in public schools were generally larger than in select schools. Mary Johnson, who taught the girls in a public school in Higginsport, Ohio, recorded an average daily attendance of nearly eighty students. She found her pay of $28 a month, from which she deducted the cost of her board and $2 for her assistant, to be "very low for the amount of labor to be performed." Cynthia Bishop's salary for her new public school position was $300 a year without board. She vowed she would not accept so small a salary another year, because her board was so high.

Teachers in subscription schools often had to determine and collect their own fees. When Rebecca Clark, a native of Concord, Massachusetts, decided to leave a select school in Tipton, Iowa, for a young ladies' school in Delavan, Wisconsin, she collected her fees on horseback. Not until a family of German settlers paid their bill would the Yankee settlers comply. Determined not to leave until everyone paid up, she finally collected $150. Harriet Hills was not so fortunate—the school treasurer lost the money collected for her by speculation. The money was loaned, she explained to Nancy Swift, "as they thought they could do better by making friends with a man who could help them to more money in two weeks."[36]

Most of the teachers organized Sunday school classes and many sent for Sunday school libraries. They all missed the preaching they were used to at home, not yet available in the new communities. Sunday school was often held in their schoolrooms, and, in small places, the schoolhouse doubled as a church on Sundays for traveling ministers. One of the happiest moments for Ellen Birge, a Vermonter, was the new sound of the first church bell in Batavia, Illinois.

35. Although Martha Brown was eager to continue in her school she returned to Massachusetts and married four years later.

36. Harriet Hills eventually returned to Vermont, where she died without marrying at the age of thirty-six.

Church groups were often anxious to have the women take a larger amount of the responsibility for church meetings than they were ready to accept. Harriet Tucker and Martha Rogers were each troubled with the problem about the propriety of women leading prayers or giving talks at mixed church meetings. Each independently compromised by reading aloud prayers and lectures published by men. Harriet Tucker, who started a ladies' society in a successful effort to substitute singing for dancing parties, felt no qualms about leading her own prayers in front of the women.

Perhaps the most frequently mentioned problems were those caused by conflicts among the many different religious sects who competed for members in the new western communities.[37] The women were expected by the board to be open-minded toward any evangelical Protestant church. As can be seen in her diary, Arozina Perkins, like many others, was used to visiting different New Haven churches. Fanny Warner was careful not to show favoritism between the Baptists and Methodists, who alternately preached on Sundays, for fear of arousing jealousy and losing the support of her frontier community for her school. "Though now I am slighted by both," she said, "at least I am not the 'lion' of either sect." The seriousness of the sectarian issue is illustrated by the letters in this collection of Mary Augusta Roper, who had to close her school in Mill Point, Michigan, because she took the losing side in a sectarian controversy. So distressed was she by the experience that she returned home to Massachusetts. Dismay at Sabbath breaking and intemperance were mentioned by nearly every teacher.

Yet a new self-confidence was revealed by many teachers. Asenath Hammond, who had lived in the home of a minister in Maine after her parents died, was surprised at her success in Indiana. "I never thought I was anything of a teacher until I came here and here they almost think I am perfection." Annie Wilbur, who had returned to Massachusetts because her father was ill, wrote from her brother's house in Albany that she would leave for Michigan as soon as the lakes were open for navigation. "If any of your teachers *wish* to *go* out sooner than the 29th of April," she told Nancy Swift, "I consider myself well qualified for an escort having been over the ground twice and meaning to pay my own travelling expenses."

The teachers demonstrated a great deal of mobility. Nearly all of them moved at least once and found new positions by themselves. Martha Rogers moved to three different schools in as many years, and Emma Farrar reported five changes before she finally started her own select school in Illinois. That the continual moving was not always by choice is evident

37. See Gary Topping, "Religion in the West," *Journal of American Culture* 3 (Summer 1980): 330–50.

from a comment by Almira Hudson, who was disappointed when she had to leave a school in Michigan because her health failed. Before she became sick, she had seen "the prospect of remaining a year or more."[38]

As the pioneer women teachers grappled with their professional problems of where and what to teach and how much to be paid, many of them took actions that demonstrated a sense of personal autonomy. Because they acted while serving as teachers, a woman's role acceptable to the broader society, the model so many of them presented of a woman as an independent individual capable of acting on her own was more easily accepted. In her description of the influence of Emma Willard's Troy Female Seminary on the role of women, historian Ann Firor Scott notes that feminist values of self-respect and self-support were more apt to spread when linked with acceptable views of women.[39]

Problems as Single Women in the West

On the other hand, even though they were professional teachers, they were also single unattached women and somewhat of an anomaly in their communities. Like men, they went to work every day and received a salary. Most of them hired out their washing and either paid for their meals or received board as part of their teaching salaries.[40] When the wife in Mahala Drake's boarding place in Iowa expected her to do the sewing and take care of the baby after school, Drake refused and found a different place to stay. In New Durham, Indiana, Laura Maynard's room was so small and so cold that she could not sit in it. It was also "entirely destitute of *earthen* furniture," she said, but she reassured Nancy Swift that she had "secured a two quart tin basin and one other *article* rather indispensable." Jennette Pitkin lost her trunk on the journey to Boonville, Missouri, in the fall. By the time it arrived, six months later, she had had to make all new winter clothes.[41]

---

38. Almira Hudson taught in Michigan and Indiana for the National Board. She died in Michigan, still single, in 1906.

As the public country schools developed in the Midwest using indigenous teachers, mobility continued to be the norm, with teachers moving "from school to school as if they were playing musical chairs," according to Fuller, *Old Country School,* pp. 215–17.

39. Anne Firor Scott, "The Ever Widening Circle: The Diffusion of Feminist Values from the Troy Female Seminary, 1822–1872," *History of Education Quarterly* 19 (Spring 1979): 3–26.

40. A study of a township in Iowa in this period reveals that all the single women in that place were widows. The ratio of single men to single women was less than 2 to 1. An Iowa County in 1850 was characterized by a preponderance of family groups and the relative scarcity of single men. William L. Bowers, "Crawford Township, 1850–1870: A Population Study of a Pioneer Community," *Iowa Journal of History* 58 (January 1960): 1–30; Mildred Throne, "A Population Study of an Iowa County in 1850," *Iowa Journal of History* 57 (October 1959): 305–30. See also Joan M. Jensen and Darlis A. Miller, "The Gentle Tamers Revisited: New Approaches to the History of Women in the American West," *Pacific Historical Review* 49 (May 1980): 189–91; Jeffrey, *Frontier Women,* p. 56.

41. Jennette Pitkin eventually returned to Massachusetts to marry; Laura Maynard married and settled in Iowa.

The teachers often found themselves without a network of support. Although members of a given class at Hartford corresponded with each other at first, they were scattered over so broad a region that only occasional visiting was possible. The resolution of problems of where to live, discussed earlier, of sickness, and of the all-important question of relations with men and marriage could contribute to the pioneer teacher's final decision to stay in the West or return East.

Health was of major importance, but fewer than half of the teachers brought up the subject in their letters. Only a third of those who did described long illnesses. "Chill fever" (probably malaria), which changed Mary Wilkinson Covel's "florid N.E. complexion to a sallow hue," typhoid, and the ever-present "ague" were among specific illnesses mentioned. Another third of the teachers mentioning their health commented that it was especially good. Cynthia Bishop said she had "not a sick day in Indiana" and was "rather gaining in flesh." Some western communities were proud of their salutary conditions. Writing on behalf of Louisa Bean, who thought her salary was so small, William S. Richardson, treasurer of the school board, said: "Sister Bean has quite an interesting school and a very comfortable school house. . . . She looks considerable Better since she came on here. I have no doubt but she will enjoy good health in this Cuntry."[42]

Still, the pioneer teacher did not underestimate the risks to her health. Sarah Getchell of Hallowell, Maine, nearly refused to go West for fear of cholera. Sarah Shedd, from Pepperell, Massachusetts, died of tuberculosis on the Wisconsin frontier after only seven weeks of teaching. Martha Eddy, who filled her position, explained that a cold caused an inflammation of Sarah's lungs, which were already diseased. The alumnae record of Arozina Perkins's classmate Jane Holbrook, a young graduate of Albany Normal School and one of the teachers to go South, has a terse statement beside her name: "Taught in Mobile, Ala., until she returned in the spring of 1852 with failing health to die, Oct. 1852." In the last report to the National Board, made in 1858, Governor Slade noted a total of twenty-one deaths among the teachers.[43]

Some teachers wrote of their loneliness. Although Ellen Lee felt "content and happy" in her school, she said, "I am entirely deprived of sympathy and good society." Her boarding place was a log cabin with only one room, but she explained, "My log-school house and my own secret place in the grove . . . are places peculiarly dear to me." Although Ellen Lee went West again to teach in Indianapolis after a home visit, she eventually returned to Massachusetts, where she married.[44]

A number of teachers noted the heterogeneous nature of their new communities, a sharp contrast with their home towns in the East. Both Lucy

42. William S. Richardson, Wyoming, Wisconsin, to Nancy Swift, 31 December 1852, with Louisa J. Bean letter, letters folder, NPEB Papers.

43. *Eleventh NPEB Report*, 1858, p. 6.

44. *Fletcher Diary*, vol. 5, pp. 209, 344, 445, 497.

Bell in Grand Haven, Michigan, and Sarah Dudley in Iowa County, Wisconsin, said they had a representative from nearly every nation in their classes. As the 1850s progressed, more teachers commented on the slavery question than had before. The teachers in the classes that were given copies of *Uncle Tom's Cabin* made positive references to it and to Harriet Beecher Stowe. Both Ann Forbes in Avon, Missouri, and Mary Lyon in Louisville, Kentucky, told of teaching black children in Sunday schools. The slavery question complicated the teachers' relations with community people in slave states. When Martha Rogers was suspected of being an "Abolition teacher" in Missouri, she sent a message to her prospective employer that the National Board teachers were expected to "*know enough* to mind their own *business.*" Inquiring about a new position after she returned to Chester, New Hampshire, from Tennessee, Emily Haseltine said she would consider going back to the South. "I like the people at the South very much indeed," she said, ". . . and would be willing to make it my home should I do so without being connected with slavery."

Because western society was constantly changing, there was no guarantee that even a new friend would remain in the community very long. In Dodgeville, Wisconsin, Augusta Greves complained that nearly all the officers of her church had left for California. The minister, who had to ring the bell and make the fires in the church all winter, was thinking of joining them. After H. M. Hurtin conquered the problem of whispering inside her Iowa school and fighting outside, she was discouraged by the continual entrance of new students. She felt her work had "to be done over and over again." Fanny Joslyn, a Vermont native, summed it all up for Nancy Swift. "Society has little permanence here—multitudes have emigrated to California but there are just as many left behind. It does seem to me that the West is the most changing part of the changing world."[45]

Other teachers shared adventures with new friends. Annie Perry, en route to a new teaching position in Missouri, was in a steamboat wreck on the Ohio River in which several lives were lost. She and her companions chartered an unfinished boat to take them on its trial run to the junction of the Mississippi, where they boarded a regular steamer. Augusta Allen took great relish in telling her story of being scared by a panther while on an excursion up the Missouri River, and Arozina Perkins and her new friends liked to fish so much they called themselves "The Hook & Line Co. of Fort Des Moines."[46]

In the East women were accustomed to driving a horse and buggy, not riding horseback. Both Abbie Rogers in northern Alabama and Fanny Warner in Wisconsin wrote of their new pleasure in learning to ride, undoubtedly using a sidesaddle. When she wrote Nancy Swift, Abbie Rogers was about to

45. Augusta Greves returned to Marshall, Michigan, to marry. After the death of her father in Onondaga County, New York, when she was eleven, her mother had moved the family to Marshall.

46. *Fletcher Diary*, vol. 5, p. 336; Annie Perry, Point Pleasant, Missouri, to Calvin Fletcher, 28 December 1854, Calvin Fletcher papers, Indiana Historical Society; Perkins Diary, p. 145.

take a forty-mile trip on horseback with friends. Fanny Warner found riding
"a relief from school cares." Although Elizabeth Miller never got used to
riding horseback, she was allowed the use of a two-wheeled chaise and a
"well-broken horse" by the family she boarded with in Pacific Grove,
Oregon. She felt a sense of independence as she drove hundreds of miles over
river plains and on mountain wood roads.[47]

Several teachers described the beauty of their new locations. Mary Augusta
Roper, troubled as she was over her school problems, called the sunsets over
Lake Michigan "magnificent in the extreme." When Frances Nelson told
Nancy Swift about the pleasure she felt in making sketches of western
scenery, Swift sent her a drawing book.

No issue faced by the pioneer teachers so reveals their vulnerability as
women as that of marriage and relations with the opposite sex, or so
distinguishes them from the men who also went West as professional
workers. Three letters in this collection deal with this complicated issue.
Mary Chase, while at the institute at Hartford, received an offer of marriage
from an old friend who had completed his training as a minister. She was so
unhappy at the thought of losing him that she wrote from Illinois hoping to
be released from her pledge not to marry within the first two years.[48]

Augusta Hubbell's letter demonstrates how easily a single woman's
reputation could be damaged in a new community. Owing even more money
than when she left the East, she fled back home to North Bergen, New York,
and poured out her story in a long, anguished letter. Her problems began
when the husband of the couple she boarded with in Iowa was attracted to
her by her singing in the parlor on Sunday afternoons. On the other hand,
Sarah Ballard's letter tells how she married a "pious" man who was superintendent of the Sunday school. By then she was thirty-six and looked forward
to holding a permanent school in their house in Wisconsin. She also told of
the marriage of her classmate Fanny Warner, who went home to Massachusetts for her wedding. Her husband was a trader from Fort Atkinson and they
returned to Wisconsin, where she continued to teach.[49]

The question of marriage was an area of great disagreement among the
pioneer teachers. Some teachers who married before the end of two years met
with disapproval from others. Mary Wilkinson, who went out to Ohio with
her sister, Caroline, in the spring of 1850, married Emerson Covel, a young
lawyer from New England, the following October. She wrote Nancy Swift
that he "prevailed" upon her "*to be actuated by the Golden Rule!!*" Her

47. Abbie Rogers eventually returned home to New Hampshire, married, and had a daughter.
Elizabeth Millar Wilson, "From the Old Home to the New, South Argyle, New York, to Albany,
Oregon," 7 December 1899, copies in the Archives, Pacific University, and the Schlesinger Library,
Radcliffe College, A-144, Manuscript Collections.

48. *Fourth NPEB Report*, 1851, p. 6.

49. Fanny Warner Morrison's husband, Alonzo, is listed as a lumber dealer in Jefferson County,
Wisconsin, in 1860. By then they had a child, Seth, named for her father. U.S. Manuscript Census,
1860, Jefferson County, WI, p. 422.

classmate Mary Washburn told Swift she hoped Mary Covel would "continue to be useful." She added: "It is not impossible that more than one of us may think it best to make permanent homes for ourselves in the *West*. But I hope that no more will think it best until they have been here at least one year." Writing from Illinois of another early marriage, Nancy Harris felt that "no other fault" had "done so much to dishonor the society & cause unpleasant remarks" as that of those who could not "resist the temptation to marry especially of those who marry before they have taught two years."[50]

Several teachers suggested to Nancy Swift that future classes be told not to display superior attitudes. "People do not like to hear 'the East' praised too much and will manifest contempt of the speaker," Agnes Goulding wrote. Elisabeth Bachelder sent a similar warning to new teachers: "Western people . . . dislike any appearance that shows superiority or indicates that we feel they are inferior to us in intelligence. . . . They treat me as a sister. I think I shall never regret leaving home."

Becoming Pioneer Settlers

Two-thirds of the pioneer women teachers agreed with Elisabeth Bachelder and were converted into pioneer settlers. Each used teaching as a way to achieve mobility that was acceptable to society. Women's professional options, however, were virtually limited to teaching. The pioneer teachers who remained single either continued to teach or worked in the developing social service professions. The teachers who married and became members of new communities generally left teaching and turned to voluntary service. Unlike young men who taught, the women did not parlay teaching into the more highly respected professions of the ministry, law, or medicine. On the other hand, teaching provided them a route to take in their search for new lives.[51]

50. Nancy Harris added: "I hope that public opinion may change its views of its enormity. And I pray you to exercise charity to us, and remember that we are unwise girls." She herself soon married in Paris, Illinois.

51. Alumnae records were supplied by Mount Holyoke College; the State University of New York at Albany; Oberlin College; and Framingham and Westfield (Massachusetts) State Colleges. Vital records were searched in each eastern state capital, and published town, county, and family histories were used in the New England Historic Genealogical Society and the Boston Public Library. Indiana records were checked by the staff of the Allen County Public Library, Fort Wayne. For the far West, information came from the Oregon Historical Society, California Historical Society, California State Library, and the Nevada Historical Society. Finally, mailings to county clerks and historical societies in midwestern states and historical societies in New York state provided some answers. The U.S. Manuscript Censuses for 1850 and 1860 were searched, and the 1850 index checked for the name of each teacher.

Teachers who went West from Ipswich Seminary appear to have followed a similar pattern. Zilpah Grant kept up a correspondence with her teachers. By 1839, thirty-seven of the fifty-seven Ipswich teachers were still there and ten were married. *Ipswich Catalogue,* 1839, p. 35; Guilford, *The Use of a Life,* pp. 183–204. Two accounts of Ipswich teachers who married and taught in the West are: about Mary

Nearly 80 percent of the women teachers who have been traced married, significantly more of them in the West than in the East. In the final National Board report, Governor Slade noted that nearly half of the women who remained in the West were married. He was not disappointed, but saw the women as continuing to serve in the role he had envisioned for them. They had become, he said, "fixed centers of efficient intellectual and religious influence."[52]

A number of the women spent their entire lives as single professional teachers moving about in the West and South from one position to another, interspersed with short visits to relatives in the East. As select schools and small seminaries lost pupils and public schools offered short sessions, large classes, and low pay, the teachers would move, hoping that the next position would be better. For these teachers, the search for community never ended. Since leaving Vermont thirty years earlier, Susan Griggs had taught in one southern and four western states. Rebecca Clark returned from Wisconsin to her native Concord and briefly taught in the district school. After the Civil War, she joined her brother Levi in Kansas, who, as a veteran, had received land. According to family tradition, when he died, she left Kansas on foot and walked all the way back to Massachusetts. Jane Chamberlain went on to become a missionary teacher in Turkey, where she served for ten years.[53]

Several of the pioneer teachers responded to the call to teach the freed men, women, and children in the South in the 1860s. By then they were in their forties and fifties. Elisabeth Hill joined the effort by Abolitionists to aid and educate black people in Port Royal, South Carolina, one of the coastal islands occupied by Federal soldiers early in the war. She died there after teaching six years. With many years of teaching behind her in Ohio, Kentucky, and Arkansas, Amy Chapman of Palmyra, New York, went to North Carolina, where she taught newly freed slaves for ten years. Rebecca Veazie returned from teaching for the American Missionary Association in Jamaica in 1864 and tried visiting relatives in Massachusetts. She felt uncomfortable with that arrangement and applied to the AMA for a position in the South, citing her twenty years of experience, many in the West. After

Longley, Stephen Return Riggs, *Mary and I: Forty Years with the Sioux* (Chicago: 1880) and about Eliza Paul Capen, Labaree, "Zilpah Grant," pp. 349–50.

52. *Eleventh NPEB Report,* 1858, pp. 6–7.

The percentage of teachers who married may be high. Only 71 percent of the twenty-four Mount Holyoke alumnae who were included in this study married. It was most possible to find marriage records in the western sources for women who married in the county they first entered as teachers. After the teachers moved, as so many of them did, they became difficult to trace. Eastern sources and alumnae records, however, are less affected by the women's mobility because they are more apt to be connected with the family and place of origin.

53. "Susan Griggs," *Vermont Historical Gazetteer,* Abby Maria Hemenway, ed. (Montpelier, VT: 1882), vol. 4, p. 191; interview with Gladys Clark, Concord, Massachusetts, 18 November 1982.

teaching for the AMA in Virginia and Louisiana, moving because her schools closed, she taught in Florida, where she died at the age of fifty-six in 1870.[54]

. The women who chose the West Coast, as well as the women who traveled to Minnesota with the earliest classes, achieved legendary status in their new communities. During their entire lives, the Oregon women were identified as pioneer teachers. As Mary Gray McLench reports in her reminiscence printed here, each married a prominent man. One became the second wife of the governor and another married a judge. Sarah Smith was married twice, both times to a widower with six children, the first a Methodist missionary. Soon after Elizabeth Millar Wilson was widowed, she became postmistress of The Dalles. She was the first woman in Oregon to receive a presidential appointment and held the office for twelve years. In California, Susan Lord helped establish at least two schools. She was the principal of the Young Ladies' Seminary in Benicia when it opened and later started her own female academy on the mining frontier in Butte County. She eventually married a judge who became active in Nevada politics.[55]

Harriet Bishop, a Vermont native, has long been honored as St. Paul's first teacher. Her portrait hangs in the Minnesota Historical Society. A member of the first class trained by Catharine Beecher, she was thirty when she left her teaching position in New York state for the frontier settlement. Despite an unsuccessful marriage, she remained in Minnesota all her life and published two books urging Easterners to migrate to her adopted state. Elisabeth Backus from Franklin, Connecticut, is remembered as the first teacher at the Falls of St. Anthony, now Minneapolis.[56]

54. Ronald E. Butchart, who has collected the names of more than five thousand teachers of the freedmen, checked the names of the National Board teachers included in this study and came up with these matches. Personal information and handwriting samples confirmed his findings. One other probable match is Sarah Parker, who taught for the Natioanl Freedmen's Relief Association at Port Royal, South Carolina, from 1862 to 1863. See also Ronald E. Butchart, *Northern Schools, Southern Blacks, and Reconstruction: Freedmen's Education, 1862–1875* (Westport, CT: Greenwood Press, 1980). Information on Amy Chapman was also supplied by Marjory Allen Perez, Wayne County, New York.

Letters from the American Missionary Association Archives, Amistad Research Center, New Orleans, used to confirm the matches are: Elisabeth Hill, Teacher's Monthly Report, December 1866, No. H6315; E. Hill, Hilton Head, South Carolina, to Rev. E. P. Smith, 5 June 1867; No. H6337; Rebecca B. Veazie, Quincy, Massachusetts, to Rev. Mr. Whipple, 23 March 1864, No. 56480; Rebecca B. Veazie, Portsmouth, Virginia, to the Rev. Geo. Whipple, 8 October 1864, No. HI-6183; Samuel C. Veazie, Randolph, Massachusetts, to the Rev. George Whipple, 6 December 1870, No. 63261.

55. Mills College considers the Benicia Female Seminary to be its direct predecessor. *Catalog of the Young Ladies Seminary, Benicia, Cal.*, 1865, supplied by Mills College; *Daily Alta California*, 17 September 1852, and *Butte Record*, 13 November 1853, from the California State Library; vital records from the California and Nevada Historical Societies.

56. Harriet E. Bishop, *Floral Home; or, First Years of Minnesota* (New York: Sheldon, Blakeman & Co., 1857); Harriet E. Bishop, *Minnesota; Then and Now* (Saint Paul: D. D. Merrill, 1869); Electa Backus and Harriet E. Bishop, Delta Kappa Gamma Society biographies, Minnesota Historical Society. See Winifred D. Wandersee Bolin, "Harriet E. Bishop, Moralist and Reformer," in *Women of Minnesota: Selected*

Harriet F. Bishop, from Addison County, Vermont, National Board teacher in Minneapolis, Minnesota, as portrayed in a painting.

A few of the pioneer teachers became interested in the Indian people in their new communities. Although the women saw them as uncivilized and

Elizabeth Millar Wilson, from South Argyle, New York, National Board teacher in the Oregon Territory, shown about the time of her marriage to Fred G. Wilson in 1854.

believed that Christianity presented the only hope for their survival, Elisabeth Backus and Elizabeth Millar Wilson both expressed a sense of common humanity with Indian people. Backus became a missionary teacher to the Choctaw Nation in Oklahoma. In Oregon, Elizabeth Wilson learned to speak Chinook and always remembered an expression of sympathy from the Chinook people after the drowning of her son, Albert; when she visited their reservation, one of the men, knowing of the recent death, sent to a nearby house to get their only rocking chair for her to sit in. Harriet Bishop, however, lost her sympathy for the Dakota Nation after the Sioux uprising of 1862, and published a book condemning them.[57]

Although few details are available of the lives of most of the pioneer teachers after marriage, the evidence that does exist suggests that they preserved greater personal independence in their marriages than more provincial antebellum women. More than three-quarters of the pioneer teachers were over twenty-five when they married and nearly a third were over thirty. A trend toward small families is apparent. More than half of those for whom information can be found had only one child or none. None has been identified as having more than four children.[58]

Several of the women increased their social standing by marrying professional men. The most desirable husband was a minister, and the largest number of women whose husbands' occupations are known did become ministers' wives. Two Vermonters married missionaries after teaching in Indiana: Ann Child served with her husband in India and Joanna Fisher in Turkey, where she organized a day school for girls. After teaching in Illinois, Martha Harris married a missionary to Persia, and died while teaching there.[59]

Several of the teachers became second wives of men established in the community. Two of the Oregon women married widowers. In Illinois, Elvira Powers married a minister with three small children. While teaching in Mobile, Martha Andrews became the second wife of a sea captain. They settled in Minnesota. Two teachers from Maine became friends after marrying widowers in Indiana; Abby Killgore's husband was a successful merchant and Keziah Price Lister's husband a prosperous farmer and lawyer.[60]

The diary of Keziah Price Lister's husband, Calvin Fletcher, sheds light on

---

57. When she described the incident, Elizabeth Wilson was "reminded of that touch of nature that makes kinships of copper-color and white." Elisabeth Backus applied to the AMA to teach in Nigeria in 1859, but it is not known where she went next. Elizabeth Millar Wilson, "My Early Life in Oregon," copied by Lucy Wilson Peters, 24 March 1913, copies in Pacific University Archives and the Schlesinger Library; Ethel McMillan, "Women Teachers in Oklahoma, 1820–1860," *Chronicles of Oklahoma* 27 (Spring 1949): 28; E. M. Backus, Bolton, Connecticut, to Rev. Mr. Whipple, 9 August 1859, No. 6638; 13 August 1859, No. 6641, AMA Archives.

Harriet Bishop's book was published under her married name, M'Conkey: *Dakota War Whoop; or, Indian Massacres and War in Minnesota* (St. Paul: D. D. Merrill, 1863).

58. Although the age of marriage has been determined for fifty-eight of the seventy-six married women, the number of children from those marriages is known for only twenty-six.

59. Thirteen of the teachers are known to have married ministers and eight lawyers. Joanna Fisher White obituaries, Grinnell College Archives; *Eleventh NPEB Report*, 1858, p. 6.

60. Lee Powers Hynes, *The Ladder of Hope* (Greenville, IL: 1964), p. 15; Emma Hynes Riggs, "Our Pioneer Ancestors," Greenville, IL, 1941, p. 46, supplied by Winifred Huffman of the Greenville Public Library; Carlton E. Sanford, *Early History of the Town of Hopkinton, New York* (Boston: 1903), pp. 526–27, supplied by Doug Welch of the St. Lawrence County Historical Association; *Fletcher Diary*, vol. 7, p. 518.

Elvira Powers Hynes of Morristown, Vermont, National Board teacher in Greenville, Illinois, from a daguerreotype taken in 1854, three years after her marriage to the Reverend Thomas W. Hynes.

the role a pioneer teacher assumed when she married a widower with nearly grown children. Keziah Liser came to Indianapolis to teach in a newly organized district school of which Fletcher was one of the trustees. Fletcher, who was born in Vermont and had started his career as a teacher in Ohio, had been responsible for the first teachers sent to Indiana by the National Board. His house was a stopping place for teachers on their way in or out of Indiana. He took a great deal of interest in the welfare of women teachers, even preventing a man from being paid more than the women. From the beginning, Fletcher valued Keziah Lister as a teacher and was moved by the affection he saw between her and her pupils. His first wife, who had come with him to the Indiana frontier from Ohio and borne him eleven children, died after twenty-three years of marriage. A year later, at the age of fifty-seven, he married Keziah Lister, who was then thirty-nine.[61]

The marriage was built on genuine affection and mutual respect. He always referred to Keziah as "my best friend." Once when she did her own housework instead of hiring a maid, she presented him a bill of $130 for her services, partly in fun, and he willingly paid it. In the evenings she read aloud from a variety of reading matter ranging from *Harper's Monthly* to inspirational sermons to *Jane Eyre*. They made several trips back East to visit his family in Vermont and hers in Maine. The price of her entrance into an established family, however, was high. Fletcher's children never accepted her and resented her living the comfortable life they believed their own mother had earned and never enjoyed. After eleven years of marriage, Fletcher died and Keziah Fletcher returned East to live a lonely life as a widow in Maine and Boston for more than thirty years.[62]

Who Stayed and Who Returned?

A final question might well be asked. Is it possible to isolate any factors that differentiate the women who settled in the West from the women who returned to the East, or was it purely a matter of luck, of being assigned to a western community made up of compatible people who offered acceptable religious privileges and dependable support for schools?

The majority of the women returning East were younger and had less teaching experience than the women who stayed in the West. What is more, most of the women who chose the East were women with families, including both parents, waiting for them. Although Agnes Goulding, the young

61. When the first National Board teachers arrived in Indianapolis in June 1847, Calvin Fletcher wrote in his diary: "Here we witnessed a scene I never expect to behold again—9 young ladies voluntarily left their friends & relatives to become teachers in the West." *Fletcher Diary*, vol. 3, p. 389.

Keziah Price Lister appears to have led people to believe she was a widow. In fact, her first husband, a doctor, had deserted her and lived in Texas. Calvin Fletcher went to a great deal of trouble to secure a divorce for her so they could marry. References to Keziah Price Lister are easily obtained from each volume's index. Some of the most important references include: vol. 1, pp. xii–xix, 11, 15; vol. 4, pp. 285–86, 342, 363, 435; vol. 5, pp. xvii, 262–64, 342, 473–75.

See also letters from National Board teachers to Fletcher expressing their thanks for his advice and hospitality: Abigail Kies, Fort Wayne, Indiana, 28 August 1847; Delphia A. Dean, Pendleton, Indiana, 10 April 1849; Annie Perry, Point Pleasant, Missouri, 28 December 1854, Fletcher papers.

62. *Fletcher Diary*, vol. 5, pp. 476, 494–95; vol. 6, pp. 15–16, 267, 313, 564, 600, 648; vol. 7, pp. 362–63; Will of Keziah P. Fletcher, Suffolk County (MA) Probate Court Docket #111407, and Depositions, 7 July 1899, 4 November 1899, supplied by the Indiana Historical Society.

The Washington School in Hancock County, Illinois, built in 1854, was in use until it burned in 1914. The pioneer teachers trained members of the coming generation of country teachers in the Mississippi Valley, who then continued their traditions in the same school buildings.

Mount Holyoke student who could not find a teaching job in Massachusetts, was successful with her log school in Indiana, she returned to her family and became well known for her work in reformatory schools for women. She never married and lived until 1907.

The women who settled in the West were older and had more previous teaching experience than the other group. The majority of them had lost either a mother or a father or both, or were already older professionals on their own. It appears that the teacher who stayed was predisposed to remain in the West. If she did not like her first teaching position, she found another. She did not return home to stay because she no longer had a home to return to. The pioneer teachers who later taught the enfranchised slaves in the South also appear to have made early decisions to leave home.

Emily Haseltine's brothers and sisters were kind to her when she returned to Chester, New Hampshire, but she asked the board to find her another school. "I would rather be far away earning my living if I could not be doing more good," she said, "than to be where my *home once* was, and *is not*." Sarah Dudley from Chelmsford, Massachusetts, who taught in Iowa County, Wisconsin, was converted to the West. "You may wish to inquire if I have ever regretted the steps I have taken in coming West," she wrote. "I reply—never."

Although a family claim did bring some of the teachers back East for a time, several of them reapplied to the board for western positions. Both Mary Coburn of Haverhill, Massachusetts, and Annie Wilbur of Newburyport were eager to return West. Each had come back because of her father's final illness. From her home in New Hampshire, Ann Sawyer appealed to Nancy Swift for a reconsideration of Governor Slade's statement that he could not find her a new position in the West that spring. She had originally served in Missouri and had refused recent applications to teach at home. Her plea was apparently successful, because she returned West and married in Michigan five years later.

The women teachers who found community in the West also became community builders in a wider sense than opening or continuing schools. More than thirty of the teachers who wrote letters taught in academies or small seminaries where some of their women students prepared to become teachers. Sarah Ballard was proud that four of the young women from her school were teaching. Abby Stanton, the widow whose husband had died in California, found a position in a seminary in Greenville, Kentucky, and asked the board to send "two of the best teachers." In her letter, Mila Walker enclosed an announcement for her new "Female Institute" in Georgetown, Missouri. Harriet Tucker owed the decision to build a new church in Jericho, Illinois, to the ladies' society she started there. "A spring was touched," she said, "a wheel was set in motion which would be no easy task to stop."[63]

In addition to establishing new families of their own, several teachers started new networks by encouraging members of their original families to join them in the West. Helen Landon's sister Jane applied to teach through the National Board, as did Catharine Paul's sister. In Indianapolis, however, Ellen Lee sent back directly to Massachusetts for her sister Elvira to fill a teaching position. Although Ellen returned East, Elvira stayed and married within the year. Parents of Emeline Eells, who married a lawyer in Albany, Illinois, and Emily Allen, who married in Indianapolis, followed their daughters west. In the last letter by Mary Hitchcock included here, she anticipated the arrival of her father and two brothers-in-law, who were encouraged by her enthusiasm to come to Illinois.[64]

63. Abby Stanton, however, died a year later in Concord, New Hampshire.

64. Emily Allen Coffman died soon after the birth and death of her first child and was survived by her father as well as by her husband. *Indianapolis Journal,* 22 July 1853, 2 August 1853, supplied by the Indiana Historical Society. *Fletcher Diary,* vol. 4, p. 326; vol. 5, p. 445; "Eells Family of Cornwall, Vermont," TPEEL20, New England Historic Genealogical Society; *History of Adams County, Illinois* (1879), p. 702, supplied by the Quincy Public Library.

The pioneer teachers represented a special group of antebellum women who were willing to take unusual risks because they wanted to build a better life. Compelled by Protestant evangelical religion, economic need, and their own literacy, they were able to envision a future for themselves far apart from the family and community of their origins. By using the teaching profession as their route to new lives, they achieved a significant degree of autonomy. Because teaching was an acceptable profession for women, they were able to attain a higher level of self-sufficiency than practically any other group of women in their time, almost unnoticed. By acting to take control over their own lives, they exhibited an independence of spirit.

The Individual Experience

The pioneer women teachers' decisions to go West cannot be entirely explained by the social, religious, and economic forces acting upon them. If they could be, all single women teachers looking for schools who professed Protestant evangelical religion in the Northeast of their time would have migrated West. Individual differences in personality and character must account for part of their motivation.[65] For that reason, the experiences of nine women are presented as they described them in their own words. Each woman's passage to the West was unique.

Cynthia Bishop, who earned money for her education by working in the Lowell mills, and Mary Hitchcock, who wanted to see more of the country, soon change schools. Martha Rogers's enthusiasms lead her to describe such events as a Whig rally, a knifing, and a school examination day without pausing for periods. Augusta Hubbell and Mary Augusta Roper detail the problems that caused them to return East within the first year, and Mary Chase and Sarah Ballard both explain why they chose to marry soon. Mary Almira Gray McLench tells the story of her journey by ship to Oregon from the perspective of fifty years.

The sensitive diary of Arozina Perkins makes up half of the collection. She carries the reader from her early thoughts of the West through to the resolution of some of the problems she found there. Her experience is the most poignant of all. A letter to Nancy Swift written a few months after the diary ends reveals that she transferred from Fort Des Moines to a position in the new Female Seminary in Fairfield, Iowa, and was apparently happy there. Sometime between late 1852 and early 1854 she returned to Marshfield,

---

65. While 71 percent of the National Board teachers known to have gone to Mount Holyoke settled in the West, only 20 percent of their Holyoke classmates left the East permanently. For a look at the life of the Vermont women teachers who did not leave Vermont in the nineteenth century, see Margaret K. Nelson, "Vermont Female Schoolteachers in the Nineteenth Century," *Vermont History* 49 (Winter 1981): 5–30.

Massachusetts, where she died, perhaps of pneumonia, in the spring of 1854, at the age of twenty-eight. Whether she returned to the East because she was sick or was on home leave is not known. She may have become disillusioned when she found that her vision of the West did not coincide with the reality she found in Iowa. In any case, it is not known whether Arozina Perkins, had she lived, would have completed her passage to the West.

Among the last letters to survive is one dated August 1854, from Lucy, symbolically the only unidentified correspondent. She was the first to write from the Territory of Nebraska. After describing the beauty of the bluffs and the surrounding countryside, she noted: "Society here is yet in an unsettled state." Although her present school was developing slowly, she was willing to wait. Two men "pleased with my enthusiasm," she explained, had promised her a lot for a seminary in Omaha City, soon expected to become the capital. As she ended her letter, she echoed the shared goals of the pioneer women teachers. "So you may soon hear of me as teaching a flourishing school—where so lately the red-man held sway—and chased the Buffalo—over the very spot, where I hope some time, my seminary will stand."[66]

---

66. Lucy ———— to Miss Ferry, Bluff City, Nebraska, 18 August 1854, letters folder, NPEB Papers.

PART II

THE DIARY OF AROZINA PERKINS

November 13, 1848, to June 5, 1851
(with a letter from Fairfield, Iowa,
August 30, 1851)

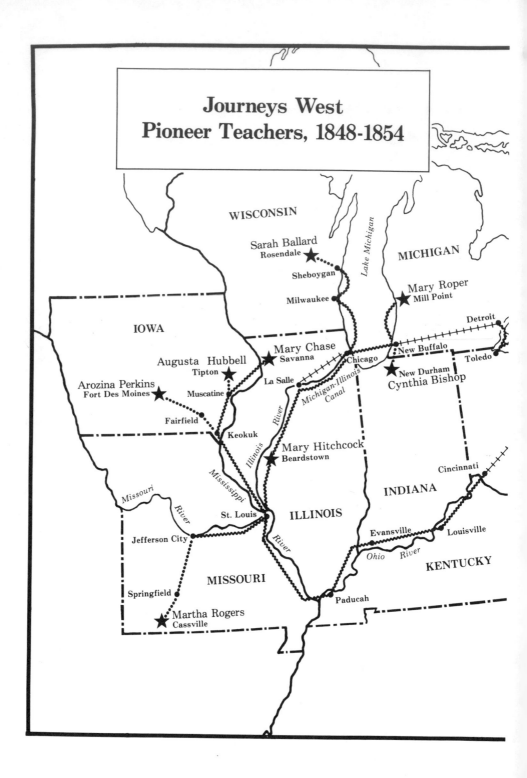

Journeys West
Pioneer Teachers, 1848-1854

WISCONSIN

Sarah Ballard
Rosendale ★

Sheboygan

Lake Michigan

MICHIGAN

Milwaukee

Mary Roper
Mill Point ★

IOWA

Detroit

Mary Chase
Augusta Hubbell ★ Savanna
Tipton ★

New Buffalo

Chicago

Toledo

Arozina Perkins
Fort Des Moines ★

Muscatine

La Salle

Michigan-Illinois
Canal

New Durham ★
Cynthia Bishop

Fairfield

Keokuk

Illinois River

Mary Hitchcock
★ Beardstown

Cincinnati

Missouri

River

Mississippi

St. Louis

ILLINOIS

INDIANA

Evansville

Louisville

Jefferson City

River

Ohio River

KENTUCKY

Springfield

MISSOURI

Paducah

Martha Rogers
★ Cassville

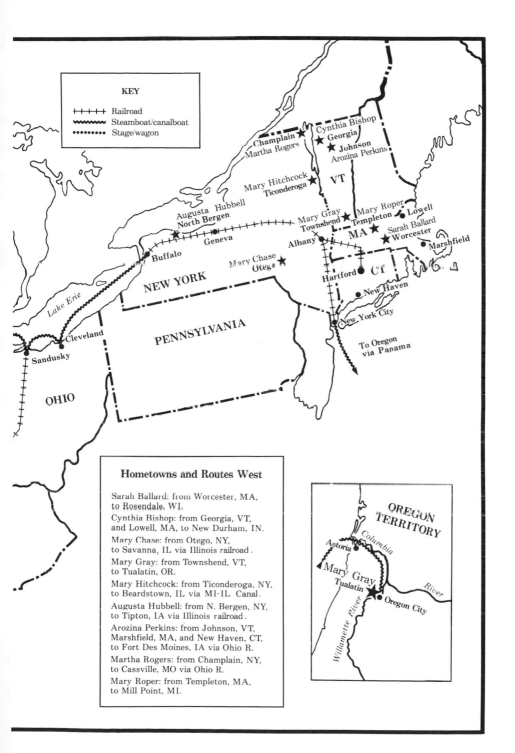

KEY

+++++	Railroad
∿∿∿∿	Steamboat/canalboat
•••••	Stage/wagon

Cynthia Bishop
Georgia ★
★ Johnson
Arozina Perkins

Champlain ★
Martha Rogers

Mary Hitchcock ★
Ticonderoga

VT

Augusta Hubbell
North Bergen

Mary Gray
Townshend ★ ★ Mary Roper
Templeton ★ • Lowell

Geneva •

MA ★
Sarah Ballard
★ Worcester

Albany • • Marshfield

Buffalo •

Mary Chase
Otego ★

NEW YORK

Hartford • **CT**

Lake Erie

• New Haven

Cleveland •

PENNSYLVANIA

• New York City

• Sandusky

To Oregon
via Panama

OHIO

Hometowns and Routes West

Sarah Ballard: from Worcester, MA,
to Rosendale, WI.

Cynthia Bishop: from Georgia, VT,
and Lowell, MA, to New Durham, IN.

Mary Chase: from Otego, NY,
to Savanna, IL via Illinois railroad.

Mary Gray: from Townshend, VT,
to Tualatin, OR.

Mary Hitchcock: from Ticonderoga, NY,
to Beardstown, IL via MI-IL Canal.

Augusta Hubbell: from N. Bergen, NY,
to Tipton, IA via Illinois railroad.

Arozina Perkins: from Johnson, VT,
Marshfield, MA, and New Haven, CT,
to Fort Des Moines, IA via Ohio R.

Martha Rogers: from Champlain, NY,
to Cassville, MO via Ohio R.

Mary Roper: from Templeton, MA,
to Mill Point, MI.

OREGON TERRITORY

Columbia

Astoria •

Mary Gray
Tualatin ★ • Oregon City

Willamette River

River

Shall I gather wild flowers on those vast prairies, and roam free amid the freshness and verdure of those charming vallies . . . or breathe another year the dust and smoke, and endure the formal ceremonies of the city?"[1] More than any of the other pioneer teachers, Arozina Perkins was enticed by the promise of the West and disappointed by its realities. A combination of innocence and spirituality led her to see the West as a kind of paradise where she could serve and suffer, and at the same time regain the freedom she remembered as a child in the Green Mountains of northern Vermont.

Arozina Perkins was born in Johnson, Vermont, on March 21, 1826, the youngest of twelve children. Although her grandfather, the Reverend Barnabas Perkins, had been a Baptist minister and attended Dartmouth College, her father, George W. Perkins, had chosen to pioneer in northern Vermont. When he knew his health was failing, he brought his wife, Elcy Thomas Perkins, back to her native Marshfield, Massachusetts, on the south shore of Boston. By 1846, when he died, most of the Perkins children had scattered, except for two of Arozina's sisters who also lived in Marshfield. Four years after her husband's death Arozina's mother married his brother, Asa Perkins, a widower, while Arozina was at home preparing to go West.[2]

In counterpoint to her deep convictions derived from evangelical Protestantism, two themes appear in the early part of her diary that combine to lead Arozina to make the decision to go West: a sense of loss of home and freedom, and a sensitive nature and a tendency to dream. Of her childhood in the Green Mountains she wrote, "I learned to love freedom from its gushing streamlets and beauty from its many tinted sunsets. My earliest recollections are blended with wild-flowers and stars and books." Her fantasies were fed by

1. Perkins Diary, p. 83.

2. George W. Perkins (1781–1846) and Elcy Thomas (1784–1861) were married in Marshfield in 1804. In the previous year, George's father, the Reverend Barnabas Perkins (1752–1826), described as a "missionary agent or evangelist," became the minister of the Marshfield Baptist Church. Among the founders of the church were Elcy's parents, Zenas and Abigail Thomas. The small white church, located nearly four miles out of the South Marshfield town center, still stands, although it has been rebuilt several times. The Reverend Perkins preached in New Hampshire and Vermont before and after his service in Marshfield.

Arozina lived with her sister, Elcy Perkins Holmes (1808–1864), and her husband, Thomas Holmes, when she visited in Marshfield. Their only child died in 1846. Arozina probably died in Elcy's house, remodeled and still standing at 88 Acorn Street. Their mother lived a mile away in the house now numbered 173 S. River Street, across from Arozina's other Marshfield sister, Eliza Perkins Williamson (1813–1892), wife of Elijah Williamson. The house of their grandparents, a quarter of a mile west on the same street, was occupied by their uncle, Isaac Thomas. The information on Marshfield and the Thomas and Perkins families was compiled by Janet E. Peterson of the Marshfield Historical Society using unpublished records from the Town of Marshfield and land records from the Plymouth County Registry of Deeds. See also *Vital Records of Marshfield, Mass.* (Society of Mayflower Descendants in the State of Rhode Island, 1970), p. 408; David B. Ford, *The Centennial History of the First Baptist Church, Marshfield, Mass.,* 1788–1888 (Boston: James H. Earle, pp. 16–18; U.S. Manuscript Census, 1850, Plymouth County, MA, p. 154.

her favorite books, stories of such women missionaries as Sarah Judson and Mary Moffat. Although she worried that she might be "impelled by a kind of romantic enthusiasm more than a true spirit of zeal and devotedness," she believed that God had planned a special mission for her in the West. She said, "I have been Providentially rendered homeless that I might fulfill a mission there."[3]

It was natural that her mission to the West would be that of a teacher. A graduate of Lamoille County Grammar School in Johnson, Arozina wrote in her biography at Hartford that she had taught more than five hundred different pupils since she was sixteen. She taught in Johnson, Marshfield, and Fair Haven, Connecticut, before teaching for a year and a half in a district school in the Mount Pleasant section of New Haven. She valued teachers, and in her diary wrote: "It is a sacred rule with me never to depreciate a school teacher by even the slightest word to their injury." She applied to the National Popular Education Board for a teaching position in the West in the spring of 1850. Although she had already resigned from her New Haven school, she found she was too late to enter the spring class, then preparing at Hartford.[4] She was obliged to wait until fall, and both her expectations and apprehensions continued to grow all summer.

At the institute at Hartford she was truly happy because she was surrounded by a group of women with similar goals. She later kept up a wide correspondence with them. After she arrived in Iowa, two events soon changed her mood, and she began to develop an anxiety about whether or nor she would be accepted as herself. One was the discovery that at first the community did not feel she was needed and questioned her motives for coming. "I seem to have been regarded as a sort of adventurer by the people here," she said. Nobody had heard of the board, she continued, and "it was the greatest mystery to the people how I got here so suddenly, and where I came from."[5] The other event was the breaking off of correspondence by the young minister she hoped to marry because he feared that the jail sentence of her brother Sullivan would hurt his career.

Near the end of her stay in Fort Des Moines, the pace of her diary quickened. As she enters the social life of the frontier town—even going fishing—its tone becomes quite matter-of-fact. Just as she felt the prejudices

3. Arozina Perkins, 2 October 1850, biography folder, NPEB Papers, Perkins Diary, pp. 67, 107–08.

4. Arozina is listed with twenty-two girls and thirty-eight boys, including her brothers, Silas and Isaac, in the School catalog for 1837. Each of the four terms cost $3 with $.50 more for languages and "higher English Branches." Books were supplied. About twelve of the students came from outside Johnson. The school building, many times remodeled and enlarged, still stands on the main street of Johnson, Vermont. Information about the school and its catalogs were supplied by Anna Dermody, reference librarian, Johnson State College. Perkins Diary, pp. 83, 91; Arozina Perkins, 2 October 1850, biography file, NPEB Papers.

5. Perkins Diary, pp. 140–41.

against "the Yankee stranger," as she called herself, begin to decrease, the realization that she could not make a living there forced her to leave. "Expect when I get what clothes worn out that I bro't with me," she told her diary, "I shall be obliged to wear a *blanket*."[6] Her tone changes from the romantic, self-conscious style of the early period to a final phase of real anguish as she realizes that she has not found what she is looking for in the West. She is still searching for a place where she belongs. Her vision of the future has lost its innocence.

In her last letter to Nancy Swift, Arozina sounded as if she were satisfied with her new position in the Fairfield, Iowa, Female Seminary. The Fairfield Business Directory of the next year, 1852, listed her as a teacher.[7] From then on the record of Arozina Perkins disappears until the notice in the Massachusetts Vital Records of her death in Marshfield on May 12, 1854, from "a disease of the respiratory organs," at the age of twenty-eight. Written beside her name is her occupation—"teacher." It is not known if she returned East because she was sick, as did several teachers, or because she finally stopped searching in the West for a replacement for her childhood home. How her diary survived is not even known. It was bought for $3 by the Connecticut Historical Society in August 1926, from an unknown source.[8] Although the diary ends with a completed volume, the narrative is discontinuous, raising the possibility of a lost second volume. Readers will also have to imagine for themselves what Arozina Perkins looked like. Although daguerreotypes are known to have been taken of her, none have been found.

The diary has been divided into seven chapters with explanatory titles. A minimum of new paragraphing has been added. Arozina went over her diary at a later time in pencil. Completed proper names have been filled in. Added parenthetical statements have been enclosed in parentheses and italicized. A notation has been made when a page is missing from the diary. In some cases, the narrative continues in the middle of a sentence, indicating that she may have removed a page simply to use it as paper. In the latter part of the diary, a few pages appear to be torn out perhaps

6. Ibid., p. 138.

7. Arozina Perkins, Fairfield, Iowa, to Nancy Swift, 30 August 1851, letters file, NPEB Papers, "Fairfield in 1852," *Jefferson County Records*, O. L. Prill et al., comp. (Jefferson County, IA, 1965), vol. 4, p. 120, supplied by Sarah Cartwright of the Iowa State Historical Department.

8. Massachusetts Vital Records, 1854, vol. 85, p. 210; Accession book #36329, Connecticut Historical Society.

Arozina's gravestone is next to her father's in the Old Burial Ground behind the First Congregational Church in Marshfield. The inscription reads: "AROZINA, daughter of George W. & Elcy T. Perkins, died May 12, 1854, AG. 28 years 1 mo. & 20 days. 'The storm that wrecks the wintry sky, No more disturbs her sweet repose, than summer evening's latest sigh, that shuts the rose.'" A carved rose is enclosed in a wreath above her first name which is engraved in large letters on a separate line.

because she felt they were too revealing. Except for a long lyric poem which opens the diary and three pages of religious reflections, the diary is presented in its entirety.

The first chapter of Arozina Perkins's diary chronicles her daily life in New Haven, beginning in the fall of 1848 when she was twenty-two and teaching in a New Haven district school. The activities of her life are intertwined with the church and school communities. She attends services in all the New Haven churches, including the synagogue, the Catholic church, and the African Methodist Episcopal congregation, in addition to Protestant churches of various denominations. She becomes more and more dissatisfied with her life in New Haven and begins to see herself as different from her friends and associates. Her early diary entries reveal the growth of her missionary spirit fostered by the lectures she attends and the books she reads and expressed by her service in Sabbath schools and her earnest attempts to distribute religious tracts in a district assigned to her.

Her interest in the West in particular as missionary ground may have been first aroused when she viewed the "Panorama of the Ohio and Mississippi Rivers" in the spring of 1849. As she begins her diary, she tries to sort out her thoughts about the past, symbolized by her lost "mountain home" in Vermont, and to open her mind to a new future.[9] She comes to identify the West with nature, freedom, and service as she prepares herself for her decision to teach in the West.

---

9. The diary opens with a long lyric poem recalling her youth in Johnson and describing her schoolhouse, mountains, and the Lamoille River. In the poem she has a vision of a holy man with a basket of flowers who "said he was my grandsire, come to bring those flowers from *Heaven* to me." The flowers faded and the vision disappeared. Her poem ends with her wish to gather "immortal flowers, that wither not, but e'er more lovely grow, throughout the cycles of eternity."

1

Teaching in New Haven, Connecticut
November 13, 1848, to September, 1849

New Haven, Ct. Nov. 13th '48.

Commenced teaching again in the south western part of the city.[1] I am going to try so to discipline my mind for the future as to think of school matters only during school hours. Not that I mean my interest shall in the least be diminished, but I think that I shall be able to discharge my duties better, if I do not allow the load of cares attendant upon a school, to weigh my spirits, as I usually have done.

Thanksgiving day.

I have been thinking of home today until I have grown quite melancholy. How my dear parents, brothers and sisters were accustomed to assemble there on this festive occasion, with happy, gladsome hearts. Now, how scattered is that once merry group. Some are at the far west, one here, and another there, and some are sleeping in the grave. Never again can we all meet together in this world.

My mother—sad must be her heart today as she thinks of all this, and many tears I know she will shed, and many prayers will she offer up for the welfare of her absent ones. And I have been thinking of the sad thanksgiving we had two years ago, and the fair young creature we buried then, and of the loneliness of that sister's heart, who then yielded up one of her heart's dearest, best treasured gems.[2] How many reminiscences crowd upon my memory. Methinks the remembrances of an aged person must be painful, at times almost beyond endurance. Oh "I would not live alway, I ask not to stay" any longer than I may be useful here, I would not survive all the friends and delights of youth, unless that life might be spent to the glory of God.

"That life is long that answers life's great end."

---

1. Arozina Perkins taught in the Mount Pleasant School on Putnam Street, near Liberty, a block from the waterfront in the southwestern part of New Haven. *Benham's City Directory, 1849–50* (New Haven: 1849), hereafter referred to as *New Haven Directory*, p. 158.

2. Arozina's niece, Eliza Holmes, only child of her sister, Elcy Holmes, and husband, Thomas, died of typhoid fever at the age of nine on 24 November 1846.

Dec. 4th.

Went into the Sabbath School at the school house this noon. There was a baptism at church today. In the afternoon the Lord's supper was administered.

10th.

Went to the Court Street Church this morning with C[aroline]. A very rainy day.

31st.

Christmas eve went to the Trinity. Rev. Mr. Pitcairn [Pitkin] addressed us from 1 Timothy 3:16—God was manifest in the flesh. Last Thursday I was present at the dedication of the College Street Church. Rev. Mr. Strong, their pastor, gave a discourse from Luke 19:45–46—And he went into the temple and began to cast out them that sold therein and them that bought: saying unto them, it is written, my house is the house of prayer, but ye have made it a den of thieves.[3]

Heard Mr. P[itkin] today. Text in the afternoon in Romans 13:11–12. I would like to attend church this evening but I am too tired. 'Tis the close of the year, and I suppose it would be

> "—greatly wise to talk with my
> past hours
> And ask them what report they have
> to Heaven."

and in the review of the past few months I might find abundant material for reflection, but I have not leisure to place half of it on paper. Nor do I wish to, for the human heart is so very deceitful, that I always find difficulty in attempting to analyze my feelings and motives, and so strangely inconsistent do they seem at different times, that a faithful record of them would be a curious mixture of contradictions and every day I have less confidence in my ability to judge of the operations of my own sinful and depraved mind correctly.

'49.

New Year's day and evening are here devoted exclusively to the entertainment of the gentlemen, and the ladies often make much preparation for the reception of their calls. Tables are set, ornamented with wreaths of flowers, and furnished with all the rare dainties their little heads can devise. Tea and coffee are provided, and, I am sorry to say, that the sparkling wine cup is sometimes offered, and I fear there are too many who are not possessed of firmness and principle sufficient to enable them to resist the fair temptation.

---

3. The Reverend Thomas C. Pitkin was the associate rector of the Trinity Church, Episcopal, in New Haven. The Reverend Edward Strong was the pastor of the College Street Congregational Society.

There were seven girls of us at Mr. Burwell's, four of them were guests, and we ought to have had a merry time. Perhaps the *others* did, but, somehow, I was not in the mood for enjoyment, and it seemed so ludicrous to sit there in the parlor so stiffly, and just be introduced to so many strangers, and to puzzle our wits what to say next that would be new or interesting, that I could scarcely keep my gravity, and gladly made my retreat as often as decency would allow, and my sleigh ride over in town with C.'s mad cousin I considered as really the best performance of the day.[4] In the evening we had a hollow pyramid, covered with evergreens and flowers with a light beneath. Several were present, and we had music and nonsense enough for the occasion.

13th.
A letter from Eliza, with news of the death of brother I[saac]'s wife on the twenty-fifth.[5]

15th.
Staid at Capt. W[right]'s tonight on account of the storm.

21st.
Went into the sabbath school at Mr. Phelp's church. Evening attended the Second Methodist.[6]

22nd.
Company this evening. Mr. Melan who is going to Africa as missionary, Mr. B. &c.

The committee called at school a few days ago. The scholars are becoming quite interested.

26th.
Called at Mr. ———'s. Was much amused with the ungrateful reception I met, as I made known my errand. I even laughed, as I turned away, to think what old ideas people will cherish. At another time perhaps it would have troubled me greatly.

24th.
Called at Dea. Luca's. He is deacon of the African church, and his is a very worthy family. His sons are distinguished musicians, and one of them, a lad only ten years of age, plays the piano with a rapidity and hearty of execution rarely if ever excelled in a youth of his age.[7]

---

4. At that time, Arozina boarded with the Burwells, whose daughter Caroline is probably referred to here.

5. Eliza Williamson, Arozina's other Marshfield sister, wrote of the death of the wife of their brother, Isaac.

6. Arozina belonged to the First Baptist Society, where the Reverend S. Dryden Phelps was pastor. The Second Methodist was probably St. John Street Methodist Episcopal Church. *New Haven Directory, 1850*, pp. 160–61.

7. Alex C. Luca was also a shoemaker in New Haven. *New Haven Directory, 1850*, p. 17.

28th.
Went to church. Took tea at Mrs. Burrough's. In the evening we went to the Second Baptist. How true it is that it is necessary to see people in many situations and under different circumstances before we can form a correct judgment of them.

Feb. 3.
Term closed.

7th.
Commenced school again.

8th.
Came to Capt. W[right]'s to board.[8]

10th.
Went down to Mr. B[urwell]'s.

13th.
Went down town. H. showed me some fine valentines, but I thought it too foolish to purchase them.

15th.
Visited at Mrs. Dewell's with Caroline B[urwell].

17th.
Teachers' meeting.

18th Sabbath.
Went to church. Exceedingly cold.

24th.
Called on several families. Spent the night at Mr. B[urwell]'s. E. there.

25th.
Snow and rain.

March 10th.
Saturday. Went in to see the Panorama of the Ohio and Mississippi rivers. The view of the scenery on their banks was almost equal to the reality, while the spectator could sit quietly and observe hundreds of miles glide along without experiencing one sensation of the fatigues of an actual journey. I have heard of a very wealthy Frenchman, who was also very indolent, and he used to take an artist with him in his excursions about the country to delineate the scenes they passed while he slept in this carriage, and merely

---

8. David Wright was a seacaptain who lived near the waterfront at 37 Putnam Street, not far from Arozina's school. In traditional seaman's fashion, he kept a parrot. *New Haven Directory, 1859,* p. 158.

had the *trouble* of looking at them on the canvas upon awakening. Were that same person living now, he might be spared even a jolting in his cushioned phaeton, if he would but open his eyes long enough.

There were many charming views in the whole, but one of the sweetest, wildest spots that I ever saw was that green, shaded lagoon with its cool streams, and luxuriant trees with their long, drooping fringes of moss. I even longed to tread the damp turf and stand beneath that verdant canopy.[9]

11th.
Heard Mr. P[itkin] this morning. Evening Rev. Dr. Hawes of Hartford.[10]

———

A few days since I saw the "Crucifixion of Christ. His trial before Pilate and the Last Supper" in wax figures like life. It was evening, and there were but few in the room, and, as we entered, a sacred awe seemed to pervade the whole place. So truthful was each representation that one would almost expect to hear each word of those solumn scenes; and the answer of our Savior as he sat there so meekly, bound, arrayed in mock royal robes, and crowned with thorns, seemed to be sounding still.—"And the high priest said unto him, I adjure thee by the living God that thou tell us whether thou be the Christ, the Son of God. Jesus saith unto him, thou hast said: nevertheless I say unto you hereafter shall ye see the Son of man sitting on the right hand of power, and coming in the clouds of heaven." I did even look at one of the scribes till I thought his breast heaved, and his hand moved along the page. I would have been glad to have taken several of my scholars in, for the scenes made a deep impression upon my own mind and I doubt not would have been highly instructive to them.

May 17th.
I caught a sweet little bird in the schoolhouse this noon. A strange spot for thee, little warbler, thought I.[11]

9. The panoramas consisted of oil paintings on huge rolls that were unrolled before audiences, accompanied by a narrative, producing an effect much like a movie.

10. Dr. Joel Hawes (1789–1867), the minister of the First Congregational Church in Hartford, was the president of the Board of Trustees of the Hartford Female Seminary and the Connecticut Bible Society. *National Cyclopedia*, vol. 11, p. 186; *Wells City Directory for 1850* (Hartford: J. Gaylord Wells, 1850), hereafter referred to as *Hartford Directory*, pp. 195, 198, 201.

11. A four-stanza poem, possibly written by Arozina, follows. The second stanza best expresses the theme:

> 'Mid books and papers thy place must not be,
> "But mid the wavings of wild rose and tree."
> Thou couldst not study here all the long day,
> "Bird of the greenwood, away, away."

May 22nd.
Went to the Catholic church this evening from curiosity to witness their marriage ceremonies. [12]

24th.
Went to prayermeeting after making a few calls.

25th.
Attended the morning prayermeeting. I think these are the most interesting and profitable meetings I ever enjoyed.

28th.
Made several calls, some among catholic families. Teachers' meeting here as usual.

27th.
This morning I went with Mrs. W[right] to the Jews' synagogue. It being the day of Pentecost, I felt curious to witness their ceremonies. But it was all unintelligible to us, the worship being wholly conducted in German. I saw several Hebrew Bibles there, and I tho't that christians too, ought to educate *their* children to read the original language of Scripture; and we should blush with shame at our neglect in this respect. [13]

29th.
Went to lecture this evening. A wedding—

30th.
It has been rainy a long time. How agreeable a pleasant day would seem.

June 3rd.
This morning I was looking from my window and a company of colored people passed. Presently another group came along, then another, and another, until I began to suspect that something was wrong in such a train on a sabbath morning. And as fights and affrays are no uncommon affairs in our streets, evenings, I did not know but some one might have been seriously injured in the last night's scuffle. Upon inquiry however we found there was to be a baptism down at the water, and we immediately prepared to join the company ourselves. Arrived there, quite a collection of dusky countenances were already waiting to witness the ceremony. Rev. Mr. [William] Thom[p]son officiated, a colored pastor of one of the African churches here. He first gave quite a lengthy argument in favor of his doctrines, which, perhaps, might as well have been omitted, and after an appropriate hymn, led into the briny wave three very neat looking females

12. The Catholic church was Christ's Church, whose pastor was the Very Reverend Philip O'Reilly. *New Haven Directory, 1850*, p. 161.
13. S. Zunder was the rabbi of the Mishkan Israel Temple held in rooms on State Street. *New Haven Directory, 1850*, p. 162.

and a lad. I was much interested in the Rev. gentleman's appearance, and would like to make his acquaintance.

10th.

Sabbath. Went to the College Street Church this evening. Addresses were delivered in behalf of the Christian Union Society by the Rev. Messrs. Sortelle, Lathrop, Strong &c. Very interesting.[14]

13th.

Went to morning prayermeeting. I much regret that I cannot attend them all. I did make the attempt to be regular but it seemed to be quite too much for me. The distance is so great.

The subject last sabbath morning was the great results that often arise from seemingly trivial causes—even the slight acts of our every day lives. Text. Gen. 24:16-19, Rev. Mr. Guernsey from Charlestown, Mass.

Walked down by the railroad towards West Haven. Found a few wild flowers on a sunny hillside. The little girls were with me, and the Botany class. I love children so well, and have mingled with them so much in their little sports, that I even enjoy their frolicks heartily, and am often charmed by their simple and frank expressions of feeling, so different from what I meet with in other circles.

16th.

Saturday. Last evening brother [Barnabas] and I went out in the country a few miles, and returned this morning. I do not know as I ever enjoyed a ride more than this. L. went with us, early, around a beautiful pond, and B. took a boat and procured us some water lilies.

This afternoon I went with Mrs. W[right]'s family to walk, out to the new cemetery. It is very neatly laid out, with a triple heart in the centre, and a cold well, shaded by a pretty summer house, which will be covered with vines, and, in time, the shrubbery and flowers will render it very pleasant. The Ready place, near by, is occupied by two maiden sisters who seemed very jealous of our admiration of their pleasant grounds. We had a fine time, but it was very warm and escaped, for a while the noise of *that parrot* that so annoys us. What beauty is there in a Parrot?

24th.

Our Sabbath School was quite large today: indeed it seems quite encouraging

14. The Christian Union Society was dedicated to having Protestant evangelical churches work together for moral reform, an approach believed to be essential to the solution of social problems. Voluntary associations made up of church leaders and members were dedicated to specific issues and included such groups as the American Bible Society, the American Tract Society, various temperance societies, and, of special interest to this study, the National Popular Education Board. For a sample list, see *Hartford Directory, 1850,* pp. 192–98. See also *First NPEB Report,* 1848, pp. 9–10.

lately to witness an increase of interest among our scholars on the hill with regard to it.

30th.

Saturday. Yesterday was a fast on account of the approach of the cholera. I went to prayermeeting in the morning. In the afternoon the Evergreen Cemetery was consecrated, and a short address very fitting to the occasion was delivered by Dr. Bacon. [15]

July 1st.

Heard Mr. Gonsalves, a Portuguese from Madeira, tell his story. He was at first intended for a Catholic Priest, and commenced his education accordingly, but his brother returning about that time from the United States, caused a change in his sentiments, and after accompanying him back here, finally embraced the religion of Christ, and became His humble follower. He is now anxious to pursue a course of study preparatory to a return to his home and the preaching of the gospel to his dark souled countrymen. May he have God's blessing and then he will surely succeed.

5th.

Yesterday was a very quiet day, and I spent it in the most quiet, demure manner possible. The morning I celebrated by writing in my room. In the afternoon I called on old Mrs. Lanson a remarkably pious and devoted colored woman who lives all alone, and is nearly quite blind. I love to go in and read to her, for I feel that I derive benefit myself from her calm, christian conversation. In the evening I went with brother to Mr. N's. Had a very pleasant time, and altogether I think I never spent a happier *fourth*.

14th.

Went with a few of the sabbath school scholars to walk in the woods.

I wonder what Colton thinks of me. I certainly was never sensible of appearing so perfectly insipid in any one's presence as I do in his. [16]

15th.

Heard Mr. Phelps in the morning. In the afternoon Dr. Floy. His text was Mark 9:38–39.

---

15. Dr. Leonard Bacon of the First Ecclesiastical Society, Congregational, called the First Church. *New Haven Directory, 1850,* p. 158. Cholera came from Europe in 1849 to New York City and New Orleans. It spread throughout the Mississippi Valley and followed the Gold Rush migrants West. See Schlissel, *Women's Diaries,* pp. 58–59.

16. H. Colton was superintendent of a district Sunday school held in Arozina's schoolhouse because the neighborhood was so far from the Baptist church. Arozina was apparently the mainstay of the Sunday school. Her minister described her work as "the moral & religious instruction of neglected children & youth whom she gathered into a district Sunday School & taught the word of God." S. D. Phelps, New Haven, 5 April 1850, with Perkins application, applications file, NPEB Papers.

21st.

Have been reading this morning the account of Rev. Mr. Moffat's missionary life in Africa. I love well to peruse such histories. For me they have more interest than my other. I have read lately, too, Mrs. Judson's Life, by Fanny Forrester, which I have not chanced to meet with before. It was so intensely absorbing that I could not leave it till long after midnight and had finished it entirely. The events therein recorded are sufficient of themselves to awaken interest even in the unconcerned, but when described in the glowing style of the charming authoress they become truly captivating. [17]

I was agreeably surprised this evening to find one person who is not too much prejudiced against Vermont to render a little tribute to its praise. I could even almost forget my usual reserve and speak to him of the snow-clad hills and glorious sunsets of my dear native state without fearing to look up lest I might detect a smile of derision stealing over his countenance ★ ★ ★ W. S. Colton. [18]

September.

It is a cool and lovely morning and the pure breeze that streams through my chamber is so refreshing it seems to infuse new life and grateful emotions for so much enjoyment in existence. The unclouded sun is still on the borders of the sky, and the long shadows are so still and deep that a quiet awe takes possession of my soul as I gaze abroad. It has been long since I have visited these pages, and my poor Journal actually reproaches me with its *blank* countenance; but varied scenes have claimed my attention of late, and I must be excused. And now if I only had talent or *genius* to weave a little garland from the events and feelings of the past few weeks to atone for my neglect—but I'll try. ——

The fourth of August dawned fair and clear, and at an early hour I was transported to our beautiful Station house to take the cars for Mass. The bell from the tower had already begun to toll as I stepped into the carriage, which, for some unaccountable reason had been delayed; but rapidly we drove, almost flew—surely, tho't I, we shall be in time, here we are but look— with the most provoking ease and indifference the whole train was gliding on beneath the bridge, even without *us*. Pale and vexed B[arnabas] stood at the door, his lips compressed and his brow stern. I laughed outright

17. Robert Moffat (1795–1883) and Mary Moffat (1795–1871) were missionaries in Kuruman, South Africa. His book *Missionary Labours and Scenes in Sothern Africa* (London: J. Snow, 1842) went through several editions. Emily Chubbuck Judson (1817–1854), whose pen name was Fanny Forester, was the third wife of the Reverend Adoniram Judson, founder of the American Baptist mission in Burma. His second wife, Sarah Boadman Judson (1803–1845) died on her way home from serving as a missionary with her husband in Burma. "Fanny Forester's" popular biography of Sarah Judson was first published in 1848. *NAW*, vol. 2, pp. 297–300.

18. Willis S. Colton, who also taught in the Sabbath school, was H. Colton's brother.

at his disappointment, altho' I was secretly half as much vexed as he. We sat down in the beautiful accommodation room, and not a word could I draw from his determined mouth. Then I told him it was "all for the best," but he would not acknowledge it. I told him that perhaps there was a providence in it, that we might be preserved from some great *smash up* or, may be, we were reserved unto destruction. But this last was not very consoling, so I tortured my brain with all my might to discover some route whereby we might reach Marshfield without waiting till Monday. After several unsuccessful trials, I at length tho't that we could, possibly, and seizing his hand I drove him to the ticket office and ascertained, after looking at half a dozen plans, and so forth, that we might get as far as Kingston by the railroad, and trust to luck for the rest.

Then came the question, how should we spend the time till eleven, it being only five, six hours, horrible! But *I* did not think so, I had a variety of ways, some errands and calls, after which I went to a bookstore, selected a book and was going back to the depot to amuse myself and leave B. to his own vagaries. Then I tho't of my painting lessons which I have talked so much about. I'd go immediately and see Mr. Hunt, the celebrated artist, and look at his patterns, and engage his services when I should return. Mr. M[oulthrop] introduced me, and, to my great regret I found he was just about to leave for Europe, to remain some months.[19] Then it was my turn to be disappointed—but I could do nothing "all is for the best," sighed I, half disbelieving it. But time was rapidly passing, and after some refreshment at Mrs. B.'s it was the hour almost before we were aware to start.

I have forgotten what occupied my mind most while on the way, during that long uninterrupted ride of nearly two hundred miles, but I believe it was thoughts of the dear friends I was going to see, of my dear mother from whom I had been separated so many months, when, all at once, slam went the door of the car, and the clear, ringing voice of the conductor sang out "Kings—ton, Kingston." After taking ourselves carefully out, and shaking the masses of dust from our clothes, we looked about us. It seemed that we were at the end of the track, the very extremity, the "jumping off" place. I sat down on an old chair in the baggage room, while B[arnabas] went to procure a carriage to convey us the remaining nine miles. It was half past seven—the sun was just setting—it was just the time of our teachers' meeting. I thought how they were assembled, and were even now fervently praying for the united success of our beloved Sabbath school, and my heart was lifted too in supplication for the same; and that we might again meet, all of us, in safety and strength.

Soon were we rolling in the tedious wagon, and soon, soon were we in the arms of our friends. How joyous is the meeting of beloved ones. It seems worth being separated a long time to stand in their presence again, and listen to their

---

19. William Hunt was an artist with a studio near daguerreotypist Major Moulthrop, who was a deacon of Arozina's church. *New Haven Directory, 1850,* pp. 34, 161.

tones of love. And now, day by day sped as if it were borne on wings. Visits were planned and we made them—frolicks tho't of and accomplished, calls were made, and whortleberries stripped greedily from their dry stems, fresh fish were fried down to the shore on a rock—jokes went round, news was told and replied to—friends had been greeted, there had been quiet and joy and sorrow and tumult—and now must come the parting. I'll just pass over this, for I like not partings, be they in anger and despair or in love and hope.

We were again whirling towards the city—and S[ullivan] was with us.[20] All the past seemed like a dream, and now arose tho'ts of forgotten scenes which were to have been related, forgotten witticisms to have been repeated, and forgotten friends to have been visited—no, not this, friends it was impossible to see, and, the changes which had been wrought during my absence, and many more which would probably be effected before I should visit again those scenes rendered dear by association with the houses of loved friends and acquaintances.

At Boston we strolled to the Common, sat down on a bench and enjoyed awhile the delicious freshness about, then went to the State house, and after writing our names in the visitors' book to render ourselves "*distingué*" we commenced a pilgrimage upwards to the dome. Round and round we circled, and up & up we went, till my head grew dizzy and my foot faltered, when lo, we stood—high, and lofty, at our elevation, and on all sides of us masses of brick, and steeples, and sea, and towers, and we gazed till my eyes ached, and I heartily wished I were quietly reclining on the moss beneath my favorite grove in my mountain home. *My home*, did I say? Ah it is mine no longer. Strangers now gather on that old hearth stone, and strange voices sound amid those walls and I—I have no home, none? Yes there is one above for earth's sorrowing children. I'll strive to live so that I may reach that home. —

In the afternoon we went out to Cambridge to the [Mt. Auburn] cemetery, and rambled about there for hours. I could have spent days there, and still have found something new—something to admire. But evening was approaching and we hurried back, went into the Custom house, Faneuil Hall, that old "cradle of liberty," the Museum, &c. and at eleven I was glad to find myself alone to rest from the fatigue of the day. But scarcely had I closed my eyes when a loud alarm of fire rang out above the clatter of trucks and carriages and all the confusion which ever and eternally reigns in the great Yankee city. For a long time I did not move till the rattling of glass and the noise of engines warned me it was near, and hastily dressing I sought the parlor and found there had been quite a scorch across the way in a brick tenement among some hats and boxes but it was soon extinguished.

The morning found me weary and unrefreshed nor did our parting with

20. Sullivan was one of Arozina's brothers.

S[ullivan] add at all to my pleasure. I had a tract which I had purloined from E[lcy]'s library to amuse myself on the way, and after perusing it, all at once found myself scribbling all over the margin to my dear H——— the following:[21]

———The cars—what a grand panorama does a ride in them furnish to the observer. It is a fresh and lovely morning. The profuse shower of a day or two ago has solidified every particle of dust, and the thick green leaves are dripping with the sparkling dew. What variety of scenery—winding streams, wooded vales—now a lofty mountain in the distance, and just by our side a fresh pond bright and clear, mantled with water lilies with their pure cups open to the dew and sunlight. Now a triangular field of buck-wheat, white as a snow wreath greets us. (I wonder, by the way, why farmers plant it always in a triangle.) now a little white cottage half concealed among the foliage, then a wild, rocky hill, fit only for pasturing sheep whose pointed noses might be nicely accommodated between the stones. Warren is a lovely place—the houses are all so dazzlingly white and the meadows and hills so very green. There is a clump of whortleberry bushes laden with fruit, there corn, and pumpkins with their large, yellow showy blossoms, now rivers, and stony brooks, patches of the familiar golden rod, gleaming like gems in their emerald setting of bushes. Oh, what are those flowers? stay, I cannot see them. There ever comes a tall, ragged fence of a yellow sandbank just as I am about to contemplate some lovely prospect.

Now let us look *within* a minute for we shall change cars soon. How various, and with what various feelings are we all actuated. Before me are two intelligent gentlemen. One is enjoying a snooze with his coat for a pillow and his hat for a screen. The next seat holds a conceited fellow, with a tall black hat supported on his bump of amativeness which is quite sufficient to support anything. Oh, look at those cattle standing in the noontide shade; how quiet they look.

Springfield. Crowded accommodations and a rear seat in the last car in the midst of a family party of southern gallantry and shallow love of display. We can view the course we have just flown over. 'Tis like the retrospect of life. A heavy cloud of dust nearly follows us and the farther we go the fairer does it look in the dim distance.

Hartford. Glad to get a free seat. And now, but a few minutes will elapse before we shall stop at our own city. But ah, the dust—it covers in handfuls from the window, and my sweet water lily which I have cherished so fondly from Brookfield is withering. The wicked dust has spoiled its brilliant, snowy petals, its stem is shrunken. How all that is lovely will fade. I almost feel melancholy to quite practical, but this theme has been sung so oft and

21. Her sister, Elcy Holmes, with whom she stayed in Marshfield. The expression is possibly "my dear *Heart*," demonstrating that she felt her diary was her true friend.

well, that I could think of nothing new till the spires of N. Haven should greet our view.

How very literary and industrious some people will be sometimes when they are observed. There sits a lady busily knitting a purse. I dare say she spends hours in idleness and gossip when at home, and there is a young pedagogue learning Geography from a map he has just hung up over his seat. For my part—I'd rather take a nap, or look at the different specimens of bipeds before me; or, for instance—take sketches; but in order to do so intelligibly I should have improved in and practiced my phonography better. Here we are wh——— goes the whistle. No, it's only Meriden, which by the way is not to be spoken slightly of. I can gossip a little longer if my margin holds out. "Oh, how I dread going back to the city—again" says a lady behind me. So do I, too, but I have come to the last leaf of my tract, and shall be obliged to wait till I can obtain a sheet of paper to finish; and with these hasty notes by the way, my love, &c. good by.

New Haven—Arrived here I was almost disappointed that I did not hear of some accident happening to that naughty train that ran away from us, altho' they were even so good as to wait three whole minutes—one hundred and eighty live seconds, and had we been Gen. Taylor himself they would have delayed no longer.[22]

The next day was the Sabbath a bright lovely sabbath, and I went to meet my class again but missed some of them whom I shall have to look up. At noon I was anxious to learn how *our* sabbath school has prospered since the superintendent and several of the teachers are absent. Attendance not quite as full as usual.

22. General Zachary Taylor was president of the United States from March 1849, until his death in July 1850.

2

Deciding to Teach in the West
New Haven: September, 1849 to March, 1850

[New Haven, September, 1849] Monday.

I met a throng in the schoolroom but owing to some difficulty—about the people refusing to pay their tuition fee, the committee were angry and would not open the school. And now I have a prolonged vacation. If I could only have spent it in Massachusetts—but I can find enough perhaps to be busy with.

Wednesday.

Went into Miss Hall's school with Mr. Day then went over to ask Mr. Lines when the school would begin again.[1] He said as soon as they wo'd pay their tickets. And when will that be? "I do not know." So I turned back quite as wise as before; and as I was walking along, troubled to conjecture where the matter would terminate, gloomy, discouraging thoughts began to arise in my bosom, and I felt perplexed and sad. I did not like to leave this school now, for the children had grown into my affection, and then perhaps I should remain here only thro' the winter, and it would not be advisable to commence a school of my own. I was quite unhappy. Just then I happened to meet Mr. B[enjamin] the city-missionary, and as I caught his eye, a cheerful, christian smile of benevolence spread itself over his features, and I immediately felt its influence, and gave care to the winds. I'll wait patiently, tho't I, meanwhile doing what I can and let the result alone.

Thursday.

The sewing circle met at our pastor's. I was quite interested, several pleasant ladies were there, and Mr. Gorham, and Rev. Mr. Phelps altho' he was quite feeble. He has been unable to preach for several sabbaths.

Wednesday.

The next week I called rather late at Mrs. B.'s where the sewing society met and remained to tea. But little work, and not so interesting as before.

---

1. Augustus Lines and Gad Day were members of the Committee of the First School District in New Haven, the district in which Arozina's school was located. Sarah J. Hall was the teacher in the Whiting Street School in the First District. *New Haven Directory, 1849*, pp. 158–59.

Thursday.

I started to visit the colored school, called to get Miss A[lling] to accompany me, found her alone and took off my bonnet and stopped till evening to chat with her.[2]

Monday, Sept. 10th.

I have become impatient, and have been to call on Mr. Day but he tells me to be quiet, and I have concluded to trouble none of the committee any further, but let them take their time. I walked above the green to find my music teacher, but she is out of town, and as I came back I had nothing to do but to admire the beauty and exquisite loveliness of the park now, and I wondered that I had not been over here often to walk thro' it, and resolved to come again very soon. Called on Mrs. Norton found her dispirited and unwell, promised to spend a few days with her by and by.

Tuesday evening, 11th.

Went to lecture this evening as usual. Saw Mr. Havens who furnished me with a host of tracts for distribution, and kindly offered to get me more when I should have given away all these.[3]

Wednesday, 12th.

Sewed this forenoon very industriously.

P.M. Went out, scarcely determining where. As I was passing the Catholic school beneath their church I felt a strong desire to enter. I did so, was politely received by Miss —— the teacher whom I nearly fell in love with. Can you be a catholic? thought I, as I contemplated her fine open countenance her soft hazel eyes, and smiling, dimpled mouth. I was as much pleased with the school as it is possible for me to be with anything catholic, and took my leave. I had in my hand some tracts, and in my zeal, I wanted to give one to every person I met. I called at the daguerrean rooms of Mr. Moulthrop then at Mr. Bakewell's, teacher of painting.[4] Saw and admired his copies, but was vexed that he would not give me lessons now: what does such a queer man as he want to enjoy vacation for? How unreasonable I am, but no one will accommodate me. Is not this what makes the world so selfish? All my time which I was going to devote to painting

2. The African School was also included in the First School District, with Mrs. Elizabeth A. Price as its teacher. *New Haven Directory, 1849,* p. 159.

3. Havens was probably the local agent of the American Tract Society, a voluntary association dedicated to moral reform supported by members of Protestant evangelical churches. The kinds of tracts Arozina would have distributed were inexpensive pamphlets promoting such virtues as temperance, honesty, and service to the poor. The morals were sometimes presented in story form, often addressed to children. A collection of nineteenth-century publications of the American Tract Society can be seen at the Connecticut Historical Society.

4. Robert Bakewell was a professor of drawing and painting with a studio at 47 Chapel Street. *New Haven Directory, 1850,* p. 161.

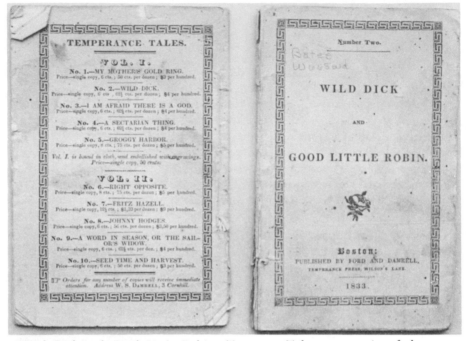

Wild Dick and Good Little Robin, *Temperance Tales, representative of the tracts distributed by Arozina Perkins in New Haven.*

and music will be past, just because it is vacation. Nobody can do anything during vacation: how silly an idea.

I called to see Miss P. who was my fellow laborer of *Hen-coop* memory,[5] but she was not at home. I met her for the first time since I left F. at the post office a few evenings ago and ascertained her address. Well, then I looked up a scholar of my class, gave away some tracts, found a little child crying in the street because her little playmate had struck her, and ran off. I gave her a book and told her to dry her tears; the naughty little one looked back longingly, but no, I shall give you none, to punish you.——

Last night I came into my room, looked under the bed and into the closet, and then sticking the scissors over the door latch as usual, sat down to finish a story I had borrowed of Miss B. the other evening. My old mania of reading seemed to return again with violence, and long I read, and leaf after leaf I turned of the "Neighbors,"[6] till I was almost spellbound, then, as the

5. She is referring to her school in Fair Haven, in the eastern section of New Haven, where she taught earlier.

6. *The Neighbors, a Story of Every-day Life,* by Swedish author Frederika Bremer, was part of the "Library of Select Novels" published by Harper & Bros. Translated by Mary Howitt in 1843, it was a sentimental novel told in epistolary form. Lucy Larcom also enjoyed *The Neighbors.* A copy is available in the Connecticut Historical Society. Lucy Larcom, *A New England Girlhood* (Boston: Houghton Mifflin, 1889), p. 244.

lateness of the hour was tolled by the busy clocks, threw it down with one strong effort, and retired.

13th.
This morning I have finished it. I'll never read again till I can learn to control myself—which reminds me of the grandmother who told her little son "never to go into the water again till he knew how to swim." But I am called.—"Miss Clark sends her compliments and desires your company this afternoon." "Certainly, here is a *tract* for you, Josephine."

I shall become as enthusiastic in the distribution of tracts as I was the other day about going West. The other day! I ought to have said *as I am now.* The fact is, I have been in a perfect fever for several months about it, but of late my excitement has been alarming. Probably it will reach a crisis soon. I hope if it should turn, to be calmer. But it shall *not* turn. I *must* go out in the Spring class of the National Board, and my dear mother *must* give her consent and blessing, and I *must* improve my time till then in learning painting and music, and oh frenzy—it is now two o'clock, and I have not practiced a note today, therefore I must not write a word more, but to my task—and then with my bundle of tracts start to make that visit.

——— The other day I went into the colored school. Was much interested in the appearance of the pupils, one little girl especially. She was fair as any daughter of Shem, with only the slightest possible tinge of olive, and a *fashionable* curl in her jetty locks, and, as she sat there so familiarly and meekly between two mudcolored faces, I wondered how *one* drop of African blood, and that diluted to nothing, could *so degrade a person* and place them on a *level with brutes!* 'Tis *even the same* in the eyes of the *creator,* as if every vein were filled with the sable fluid which has received its coloring matter from the God of Nature.

Wednesday, 26th.
Had a leisure afternoon and a benevolent streak and thought I would devote them to the sewing society. Perhaps my prejudices against such societies may be dissipated, but I never considered them in a very favorable light. Some of them are little more than nurseries of scandal and displays *of very great* benevolence. I choose to bestow my charities in a humbler manner. I read in a paper the other day that there was started somewhere a "very benevolent society for the purpose of making oiled cloth overalls for *whales!*" I laughed —and honored their *motives* quite as much as those of several of my female acquaintances that I'll omit to mention.

Sabbath afternoon, Sept. 30th.
It is a rainy, dismal time. I have been to church this morning. Mr. P[helps] was present, but unable to address us. I thought last Sabbath he was outdoing himself. His sermon in the afternoon was something very rich. My class of little boys has become very interesting. I intended to train them to

self-denial, to strive to infuse into them a missionary spirit, and have labored to interest them accordingly with gleanings of anecdotes from the lives of those faithful ones. Next Sabbath the school will be changed from morning to noon, and as that will bring it to the same hour with this one at the school house, I shall be obliged to give up one or the other of them, as I do not possess a spirit of ubiquity sufficient to render it quite convenient to be present at both at the same time, which I regret exceedingly. I hardly know which it is my duty to remain in. I am not aware that I am of any use in either. I'll ask Mr. [H.] C[olton] if some one else would not supply my place quite as well. He may *wish* to exchange for he has looked quite sober since he returned. Willis [Colton] was pleasant as usual last night. He must be very persevering and devoted, or he would not thus cling to our feeble school.

It is very dull—and the sky looks like an old drawing that has been half rubbed out.

——— I have taken my treasure of daguerreotypes from my trunk, and opened and grouped them on my table. I talk to them, and look at them, till I fancy they are real, and almost expect their lips to move in answer to my questions. Mother, dear, mother. I have a request to prefer, and it may be quite as favorably listened to by your picture as by your own dear self. Now be lenient, and kindly permit your daughter to go out and devote her life to the cause of education and truth and religion in the far west. Who knows what she may the means of accomplishing with the blessing of Heaven—at least the *motive* will be a sacred one, and may, like Abraham's faith, be imputed for righteousness.

I had a dream the other night about it, and indeed my dreams lately have been all about going, when I do sleep; but one night I counted every toll of the clocks till two in the morning before I could dismiss the subject so as to submit to slumber. We had been talking in the evening, and as usual I was called "enthusiastic," "*visionary*" &c. I retired but the word "visionary" had made a strong impression upon my mind, and as if determined to *be* so in reality. I dreamed I had three eyes—one new one in my left cheek just below the other, and it seemed to be a perfect match for my pair, in size and color. I looked in the glass, and thought about having the lashes pulled out, and sewing it up. Then I shut my old ones, and found the sight was far more perfect, everything around me appeared in its true light and lovely beyond expression thro' my new orb, and I concluded that this must have been intended for use when they should have decayed, and I wondered that I had not known before that I possessed this eye, for it seemed that I had had it a long time, and I speculated much upon it, and finally concluded that this accounted for my seeing things differently from some people, or in other words for my being "*visionary*."

Evening. Mr. Johnson called this evening all fresh with the newly invested dignities of his office as one of the superintending committee of

schools, and wished to make arrangements concerning the opening of the
school tomorrow, as "he is obliged to be away to his business early in the
morning." Now he may have tho't me scrupulous and superstititous, but I
certainly could not conscientiously attend to it tonight, and requested him
to appoint as early an hour as he chose in the morning and I would see him
then, and give him my answer and views. He looked displeased but made an
apology and withdrew.[7]

If I was *overnice* it must be attributed to early training and after practice;
but I am alarmed when I think how slack I am becoming about my
conversation on the Lord's day. Insensibly I am drawn into it and all at once
discover myself all engaged about something which I ought not to think of
on such a day, and then to save *myself* I rush precipitately to my room—often
leaving some one in the midst of a story, contrary to all *politeness* or
ceremony. Some time ago I was present where several young persons
happened to be in, and there was some singing and much talking, many
jokes and a host of new fashions discussed. I leaned back in my rocking chair,
and tried to imagine that I was somewhere else, when one very kindly, and
with much sympathy, as I was a stranger among them, inquired "if I were
ill?" Being assured to the contrary, another "thought I must be very
taciturn." I quietly remarked that it had never been "fashionable" to spend a
Sabbath evening thus at my father's hearth. "Oh," said one (with a sneer at
my *country greenness* as I translated it) "*we* keep *Saturday* nights." I opened my
eyes, and it must have been that the new one I have discovered lately
unclosed too, for I *did* remember that the evening previous work was laid
aside, and a book of light romances read for amusement; and I wondered that
I could have been so deficient in tact as to have even hinted at the
impropriety of spending this evening so unceremoniously!!

I have even offended several times by remaining silent on such occasions,
and with my strong desire to please it would be very natural for me to rather
fall in with the views of the others, sometimes, did I not strive to guard
much against it, and even then I am often guilty.

—— Mr. Havens has just been in to ask me to become a tract distributor
in his society, as some have left, and others have died, and there seems to be
a need of some one's services, and if mine will be the means of accomplishing
anything surely I do not feel disposed to withhold them.

Saturday, Oct. 6th.
A dull, drizzly day, and the whole week has been one of unusual depression
to me. Monday morning I went into school again, and have been toiling hard

7. Arozina "kept" the Sabbath. She believed the day should be spent in meditation, prayer, and
serious reading and not in visiting or work. D. F. Johnson was a member of the entirely new Committee
of the First School District in September 1849. Other members were George F. Smith and John W.
Mansfield. *New Haven Directory, 1850,* p. 178.

ever since with sixty restless, unquiet spirits, and trying to lay for them a stone or two in the foundation of their fabric of life. An Association has been holden the past four days at Second Church, and Thursday evening Mr. G. W. Gorham was ordained a missionary to the far west.[8] I never was present on an occasion when such deep solemnity seemed to sink into my very soul. There was something so high and holy in the idea of a life consecration to so laborious a cause—in leaving home, and all the associations that cluster about the friends and joys of youth, for the single hearted service of our great Master, that the impression lasted long, and nearly unfitted me for the duties of the succeeding day. May the God of strength give him zeal and firmness and encouragement to fulfill every duty of his mission of love to those destitute, error bound regions of our native land.

(*What vague ideas I then had of the West!*)[9]

[One page was torn out of the diary here.]

Nov. 3rd.
Ten o'clock, Saturday evening. Another cluster of weeks has fled into eternity—weeks of toil, busy, anxious toil—of care unceasing, and of exertion unwearied, but interwoven with the memories they furnish, is a brief tissue of pleasure, as pure, and transient too, as aught we gather from the fleeting hues of life. Why is the faint sunlight of joy, which, so cautiously breaks upon us here, so quickly obscured by the cold, dull, leaden clouds of reality? Why are we just learning to prize sympathy and friendship when they are suddenly withdrawn from us forever! Why do we not shut within our souls every stream of devotion, and mingle its tide only with the great Fountain of Love Divine, in the bosom of our God? 'Tis wrong, methinks, to bend our thoughts at an earthly shrine; idle too are human friendships—for duty may separate—death will divide, and the shadows of sorrow then dim the radiance of the heart, and darken the clear serenity that reposed there.

4th.
Today has been soft, bland, dim and hazy, and so still and calm that an oppression has seemed to rest upon the very soul.

Rev. Mr. Ketcham spoke to us this morning from Matt. 26:69–75. In the afternoon Brother Phelps from Luke 23:42–43.

In the evening I heard Dr. Poor, an aged missionary from Ceylon. He was very zealous, & the accounts he gave of his first labors there, and the etablishment of schools, &c. were very interesting. He first went there in 1815.

---

8. Probably the Second Baptist Church. *New Haven Directory, 1850*, p. 161.

9. This particular statement is significant because it reveals that Arozina went over her diary either after she returned from the West or while she was still there.

5th.

Monday morning. Another week is just entered upon, with all its duties and trials and responsibilities in perspective, and I feel that I need much divine assistance to enable me to labor effectually and devotedly for my great Master. One week ago my school was divided by taking out all the very small scholars, and thus a very great relief was afforded, for I had become well nigh discouraged with such arduous toil, and most thoroughly wearied both physically and mentally—

A short time ago Father Mathew, the great Irish Apostle, spent a day or two in the city. I had the pleasure of seeing him administer one pledge and his blessing; and it is hoped that his efforts will prove successful in carrying forward the cause of temperance among his countrymen here. [10]

— Last Friday evening Dr. Baird gave an address at the Centre church, and Rev. Mr. Gonsalves with several Portuguese exiles were present. Mr. G. produced the Bible from which Dr. Kally explained the truths of the gospel in Madeira; and his persecuted brethren and sisters sang a hymn in their own language, which sounded so plaintive and breathed out such clear and holy strains that I was affected even to tears. Rev. Mr. Stoddard, from the Nestorians was present, and occupied a slip near ———, but he did not address us. But is is quite time for me to go into my schoolhouse and prepare for the duties of the day. —[11]

Nov. 15th.

Eight o'clock. P.M. Alone by the kitchen fire this evening. I have been trying to keep the house from walking away; and I wonder, by the way, how any one should dare to intrust any thing to *my* care, who am so shamefully careless. Only night before last I took a *leap in the dark* which I do not intend to repeat very soon. I had been out to call on a couple of scholars of our sabbath school, one of whom is a pupil of mine also, who had both been badly injured, one by a fall into a cellar, the other by being thrown from a horse. I was in something of a hurry (and I do not remember the time I have *not* been, since I saw the light,) and instead of stepping down the door steps properly, as a lady ought to have done, I plunged off the end of them and alighted rather unceremoniously upon a flight of stone stairs leading to a basement. Yesterday I found myself unable to go into school, and, today, have scarcely been able to move my stiffened limbs about.

I have been amusing myself this evening by reading some pages of French. I fear I shall be unable to go out tomorrow evening. I want very much to hear Ka-ge-ga-gah-bowh, the Ojibwa Chief, who is giving a course of lectures

10. The Reverend Theobold Mathew (1790–1856), known as the Apostle of Temperance, toured the United States in 1849 and collected 600,000 pledges of abstinence before he returned to Ireland. *New Catholic Encyclopedia* (New York: McGraw-Hill, 1967), vol. 9, p. 461.

11. Arozina later heard the Reverend Mr. Stoddard speak in Hartford.

relative to the Indians, and his tribe in particular. He was present Sabbath afternoon and spoke from "Ye are our witnesses." Towards the close he displayed most pathetically some of the eloquence for which his race are so celebrated. His appeals in behalf of this dark browed brethren, "whose cabins are yet unblest by a knowledge of the gospel," seemed certainly sufficient to abate "the intensity with which the white man at the East hugs his Bible," and to cause him to share the Word of Life with those unfortunates upon our western borders.[12]

Sabbath evening I heard Rev. Mr. Thompson, from New York.

Monday, Nov. 19th.
Last Monday evening I saw the Panorama of the Holy Land. The scenes were beautifully colored and even the shadows reflected from the surface of the waters looked like nature. The garden of Gethsemene is a shaded, lovely spot, and the mountain views were very interesting—the pools—lake of Tiberias, tomb of Mary, & of the kings, vale of Sychar, Jacob's well— Cesires, and lastly Jerusalem were some of the principal scenes, and all of them were instructive to the student of the Bible.[13]

Nov. 25th.
Morning. Cloudy and unpleasant. I went out on a mission yesterday, after my drawing lesson Called on Miss R. then visited my Tract district. Spent nearly the whole day, and was much interested.[14]

———   ———   ———

Sabbath. 2 o'clock P.M.
It has been unpleasant today. A steady, copious rain has prevented me from attending church, and kept our teachers from the sabbath school. A few scholars came, and I was teacher, superintendent, chorister and librarian. I heard their lessons, told them stories of the Jews—we sung and were dismissed. But it is no merit for *me* to be present. I live so near there is no self-denial in it, even in the worst of storms. Nor do I feel that there would under other circumstances, for I so love to meet the dear children at all times.

12. Kah-ge-ga-gah-bowh, also known as George Copway, a chief of the Ojibway Nation, was educated in Illinois and became a Wesleyan missionary to his people. Frederick Webb Hodge, ed., *Handbook of American Indians North of Mexico* (Washington: Government Printing Office, 1907), pt. 1, p. 347.

13. A page was torn out between the words, *the* and *principal scenes.*

14. The equivalent of two pages of the diary are not used here. They summarize religious feelings that are also revealed throughout the diary. She describes the conflict between temptation and duty and concludes, "It is a *glorious* thing to live . . . to be tried in the furnace of affliction, and come forth purified—to feel that this world is not our house, but that our path leads to a brighter, holier region—the habitation of angels and just men made perfect—the dwelling place of the *Infinite.*"

It is warm here in the schoolroom, and to be quiet, I have come in to write a little. Yesterday I visited my Tract district. Had two or three interesting interviews. The families are mostly pretty well supplied with religious reading—most of them are members of the different churches, and all I believe in comfortable circumstances. In such a district the duties of the distributor are of a very different character from what they are in some other portions of the city which I sometimes visit. Monday evening I was present at the meeting of the Tract Society. About twenty members were there, and some of the reports were quite interesting. Mr. Benjamin, the city missionary, made some relations concerning the Catholics and Jews among whom he chiefly labors. It seems that the priest has forbidden his church to receive or read any protestant paper or book, and threatens daily to denounce some parents because they send their children to our schools (Perhaps he is not aware that I have nine of them.) While the Jews, on the contrary seem to be rather open to impressions of the truth, and one of them, lately from Germany, a man of great learning and abilities, meets him weekly to read the New Testament.—

— I have been encouraged lately to continue fervent prayer. It has seemed most sensibly that the Lord has heard my supplications, and will so order things in His providence that I may go west. I have sometimes been almost disheartened, and ready to give up, but I will doubt no longer, but trust and labor on.

All have spoken discouragingly to me—there is no one to whom I can tell my thoughts and wishes upon the subject without being derided. Even brother James whom I wrote to expecting to be much strengthened in his kind answer, ridiculed the idea, but I care not. It matters little *what* motives are attributed to me, provided I myself am conscious of being actuated by unselfish ones.—

Christmas Eve was passed in Fair Haven. Mrs. Dudley went with us to the Episcopal church which was very beautifully decorated with evergreens. Staid just long enough to hear the sermon. Text: "what came ye out for to see?"

Christmas day at ten o'clock we came into town to the Catholic church. After the services, there was a collection taken to defray the expenses of their sins the past year and for the benefit of the church, or priests, I do not know which. It was done in a novel manner. A clerk carried the contribution box, and the priest, dressed in his white tunic, and robe of embroidered lace, and tasselled mantel, followed him thro' every aisle, thro' the porch, and up into the galleries—for what purpose I could not divine unless it were to see that all his error-bound hearers paid punctually. He, certainly, lost much of his dignity, if he really ever possessed any, traveling around upon such business. I *came away* after this performance, but conclude that they all received full absolution except us poor heretics.

It has been sufficiently cold I think for a few days past to congeal the softest heart *almost*. I wanted a vacation this week, but could not *afford* to take it. Miss Jacobs, teacher of the little school, has been boarding here a few days—and perhaps will remain here all winter. I hope so certainly, for it is very lonely.

Last night I attended the sewing society, but it was so cold, and I went so far, that I felt all my sympathies frozen before I could get home—and shall wait for a thaw before I go again.

It is a great thing, and a difficult to learn to suffer in silence—to feel that the slightest murmur or complaint would be sinful and stir up strife if repeated.

Perhaps I look upon life too seriously, and attach too much consequence to things that others would consider unimportant. Perhaps it is not wrong to laugh *innocently* (?) at the faults of others or to indulge in witty (?) remarks at their expense. If so, then I am most unhappily constituted as not to take pleasure in such amusement, but to receive actual pain. But the fault is not mine. I cannot have sympathy with such deceit as I have discovered tonight—and I can not do otherwise than manifest my total dislike of it. O that I had a friend—just one, *truthful, frank,* pious soul, capable of entering into my feelings—but I am alone—utterly alone—B. is cold as the northeast wind—and every one else seems unapproachable. My dear Miss ———— is a good girl and I prize her above rubies, but intellectually there is want that I always feel with her. I do not deserve a true friend. I'll keep all my *griefs* within my own breast, and never look again for purity on earth. I'll make an effort to see things as others do—to call right wrong, and wrong right—and look pleased when others are whether I feel so or not—then possibly, I shall be less denounced as odd, singular and all those unpleasant names.

—— I had delightful dream the other night of Heaven and the Savior. So real, so glorious was it, that I could scarcely convince myself it was *only* a dream. I have thought a hundred times since I'd be perfectly willing to die at any hour could I know it would prove a reality. Dreams are a part of my existence—they form the dim, distant shaded background of the great view of life. They are the blending of the distinct present with the uncertain indefiniteness of Eternity—glimpses of the regions of spirituality beyond this cramped confined and mortal state.——

[*Late Winter, 1850.*]
Received a call from Mrs. Potter and Miss Morgan days ago. I have had so little time of late to think, that when I look back, everything seems a mass of confused events, and a hurried mingling together of heterogeneous attempts to accomplish impossibilities. I cannot see where my time all flies to—all of

it is occupied—and yet I seem never to do anything. About half—yes nearly the whole, I might say, is buried in the schoolroom—the trifling remnant is crowded and stolen, day after day, and now it is almost Spring again. The long cheerless season of Winter is fast ebbing away—a few days more, and the merry song of the woodland chorister, and the sweet up-springing breath of the early violet will bid me decide whether the West shall be my future scene of efforts, or whether I shall toil on here longer.

Shall I gather wild flowers on those vast prairies, and roam free amid the freshness and verdure of those charming vallies, where the clear-watered streams mirror forth the beauty of their flowery margins, or breathe another year the dust and smoke, and endure the formal ceremonies of the city?

Mr. B[enjamin] the city missionary called again at school this afternoon. I think he is one of the kindest, best of men. His whole time is spent in laboring among those, whom, many of them, no other means would reach. He did not stop long, but said he would call again soon.

Have been entertained (?) this evening by a history of my predecessors *in office*. Mrs. W[right] possesses quite as much *talent* in relating the faults and follies of others, and rendering even their virtues ludicrous, as any one I ever saw. I wonder what satisfaction it can afford her to pull down every thing that is considered estimable in another's character. Miss M. according to her, *must* have been the most eccentric specimen of poor persecuted school dames that ever existed, and then to have one even make fun of her cough, tho' she *was* queer—and even if she *did* put plasters on the children's mouths, and hurry to school an hour behind the time, brushing the flour from her dress, and tho' she baked pies in the stove oven, and unruly urchins eat out all the inside while she was kindly assisting some blockhead in his *cyphering*, and a thousand other irregularities—she wound off by saying— "still I could not help liking her."

And Miss Meiggs too, whom I heard highly spoken of, "she is an excellent person—but—." Well she had *need* to be severe even with Mrs. W.'s children, I knew where the shoe pinched. But that everlasting preface whenever she speaks of her is a very slight veil to conceal the motive of the narrator.

With a feeling of almost nervously unpleasant sensations I looked forward to the time when my own *euology* should be pronounced by the same— tongue, and eagerly did I seize upon every good trait developed in the story of each, to enlarge upon, and strive to make them appreciated by her, for it is a sacred rule with me never to depreciate a school teacher by even the slightest word to their injury.

Mrs. W. is a cold, stiff looking person, too dignified in her own esti- mation to bend to common things. Of course she places great value upon fashion and popularity—and *gentility;* but I never could see that her claims to the latter were any greater than they should be. Perhaps I am slandering—

perhaps I do not see her in the true light, but no one was ever more prepossessed in favor of a stranger than I was in my first interview with her, and my after opinion has been formed from my daily observation of her words and actions. I have fancied she acts a double part toward me, from appearances, but no matter. If others do not know her—if Colton thinks her a model—*I* never shall undeceive them. I'd never be so mean as to relate any household matter—any domestic occurrence for revenge. And tho' I write this here no one of her acquaintance will ever be the wiser for it.

I highly esteem Capt. W[right]. He seems above all those "trifles light—as air" which agitate the mind of his spouse, not is he aware of much of the meanness and deception practiced upon him. H[ester] is a lively girl of fourteen, and possesses naturally a frank, open disposition, tho' rather petulant, yet, if not spoiled by her mother, will make a fine girl. But the two little boys—I can give no idea of them nor of their management and I do not wish to. Their mother is a perfect amazon, a virago—a tyrant over them.

I do firmly believe that parents—*mothers* are answerable for the future well being of their children to a far greater extent than some ever dream of. She found fault with me a short time since for what she called want of firmness in punishing one of her boys. I explained the case to her, but all to no purpose—such a torrent of abuse as she poured upon my poor, defenceless head. I listen'd in silence after vainly attempting to vindicate myself—then retired to my own room and finished it up by a hearty *cry*. Mr. W. sat still all the while, and never raised his eyes from his paper, but hemmed a few times, and the next afternoon, when his benevolent-lady had gone to her sewing society—told me kindly that he could not see the least reason of attaching blame on me—spoke of the manner of governing children in different families, and the error of supposing that harshness could make a child gentle. I do not mean to entertain any unkind feelings towards Mrs. W. for she, doubtless, thought she was right, and I was wrong, still if she would have thought candidly about it, and had known all my thoughts and feelings of duty she would not have censured so.

— —

I have been reading History some in connection with prophecy, and have been much interested. Mr. W. and I have frequent conversations upon the Scripture, and I have profited by some of them. He is quite original in his style of thinking, and we agree so nearly that there is scarcely room for sufficient argument, for many of his ideas have been long entertained by me. The other evening he read one of Dr. Bushnell's sermons to us on the Trinity, & I have since finished the others. [15]

— A few evenings ago Miss Jacobs and I commenced attending the lectures on phonography by Mr. Thomas Ranny. She has become much

15. Arozina later heard Dr. Horace Bushnell speak at his church in Hartford.

interested in it, as I wished. Mrs. Baker and her sister also attend. Mrs. B. is certainly a lovely woman. I never see her without having my opinion of her more and more favorably excited. Martha is a good girl, I know, frank, cordial, and not so *excruciatingly* polite as some young ladies try to be. I shall endeavor to cultivate her acquaintance.

Miss Halleck called on me today just as I was about to commence school in the afternoon. I promised to see her in a few days.

Saturday evening.
Teacher's meeting, and because it is *stormy* or *muddy* "it is down to Miss A[lling]'s." How very dignified Colton must have felt when he appointed it. Jokingly I had said to him that I did not like to walk down there in the dark when it was so muddy, and the very next time he appointed the meeting "at Miss A's if it was stormy and at Miss Perkins if it was pleasant." I laughed [as] if I *was* in school, or smiled, but did not care. I believe he delights in teazing me, or in *trying* to.

March.
Saturday afternoon.
Mr. *Colton* called this afternoon and we had a long *chat,* tho' perhaps I should not use so familiar word as that, for I can seldom feel very familiar with him, or when in his presence. I know he is very good, and very useful and I will not magnify any little defects that may exist, even tho' *he* may think *me* a rude, uncultivated, careless person—as he evidently does. I esteem his brother W[illis] and feel at liberty to speak and act naturally when in *his* society.

Monday evening.
Have attended the regular Tract meeting. Heard some of the reports, but did not make any, for altho' I might have related many incidents which have come within my knowledge in going about, yet the imperious necessity— there is of *teachers* being prudent and guarded in their expressions, com- pletely sealed my lips, for even tho' my report might have gone no farther than those walls yet the *habit* has become so strong of confiding in few, and those whom I think will not injudiciously expose, that I thought it wiser to remain silent.

— —

D[avid] has been at home some time. He is the eldest of Mr. W[right]'s family. Was prevented from going another voyage at present by a severe cut on his arm. He is about twenty-six, a sober-looking, but fun-loving fellow—at first appearance very grave, and no one would suspect beneath the calm countenance of the young Capt. that so much mischief lies concealed. His drolleries serve to vary the scenes here considerably. Miss J[acobs] answers his jokes quite in earnest, while H[ester] laughs then pants, and finally winds up in tears. He says he has no business of his own to attend to, and sits quietly in his easy chair with folded arms and very kindly volunteers to attend to other folks' affairs.

A few evenings ago, his mother with Miss J. and H. were gone out. I was quite alone, trying to amuse myself with reading. It grew late when he came in, inquired "if his mother usually staid so late at the *sewing* society." I replied "that she did but seldom" but as ten, eleven, struck, I said "perhaps she has not gone there." I very well knew where she was, altho' she had been careful to conceal it from me, and Miss J. had said *she* was going to "call on the gentry." Last evening we were sitting by the stove talking familiarly of many things, when Miss J. spoke of something she saw at the—dancing school—H. checked her. I appeared not to notice it, and probably they tho't it very clever that I was so *dull*. It was all confirmed. Mrs. W[right] had been with them—frequently, but why they feel afraid of letting me know it I cannot imagine. To be sure I should not approve of it—but, what then? I have never told *them* so. I detest *shyness*. Why not act fearlessly, if consciencious? [16]

——— Oh it has been one of the loveliest evenings I ever saw. The moon shone so brightly, and it was so calm and pleasant. I had been to meeting and called for B[arnabas] to come home with me, when the company there proposed to accompany us. Accordingly Mrs. B[aker], M[artha] and Mr. Galbraith, a jolly, pleasant whole hearted gentleman formed an escort. We strolled over the beach, and around Mr. Halleck's beautiful grounds till we were tired all but the gay Martha, who was in her liveliest mood.

[A page of the diary was torn out here.]

Teachers' meeting. Mr. H. and W[illis] C[olton] and Mrs. F. and Julia present. Julia is a good girl. I love her better the more I know of her. She is kind, affectionate, zealous in her duties as teacher, and faithful in her domestic relations. H. & W. came before dark. It was a beautiful evening —the setting sun left the sky glowing with his departing rays. Miss J[acobs] had just been looking at it with me, when I remarked that it always makes me homesick to look at the sky at evening, and I judged it had the same effect upon her, for she instantly started, and said, "I'll go home to night. How long it has been, *four* or five weeks since I have been there," and hastily prepared for her six miles tour. I went into the house wishing I too might go home as easily—when presently H. & W. came in. W. spoke of the loveliness of the evening, in his usually agreeable manner. I remarked again that I loved to look at the sky, for it reminded me of home, where, in childhood, I used to sit at my window hours and gaze at it. H. thought it

---

16. Although Arozina disapproved of dancing, she appears to have minded Mrs. Wright's fabrications even more.

"very strange" and "wondered why it was so," asked me if it was in "idea of boundlessness." I said, no, and was going to explain further, when he interrupted me impatiently, with "Oh it's because you are not a poetess." Mrs. W[right] came in just then to look at the fire, and conversation ended. Mrs. F. and Julia stopped a while after meeting, then I retired, and tried to think why I could not love to look at the sky if I am *not* a "*poetess,*" and wrote the following—but it is not poetry, for I would not for the world have one think or call me a "poetess."

> I love the evening sky, for I can gaze
> Into its far, pure depths and dream
> That I am free—unfetter'd by earth's chains,
> Its sins, its follies and its cares. Ah, then,
> My spirit gathers fervor from its glow.
> And Love seems smiling from the rosy arch
> Upon the wearied mortal; and sweet tho'ts
> And mem'ries linked with childhood's dreams and hopes—
> Rush not my soul, and bid me see again
> My father's smile, my mother's kiss, my dear,
> Tho' humble, quiet home—the window whense
> For hours I gazed as I am gazing now.—
> But ah, how changed the lives, like fading tints
> Of rosebud's bloom, still beauteous tho' they are.—
> I see them pale—melt one by one away
> Into the soft cool night. O would that I,
> Life's journey, o'er, and all its labors done,
> Thus peacefully might fade to bloom *in Heaven.*

3

Leaving Family and Friends and the Past
New Haven and Marshfield:
April 1, 1850, to September, 1850

[New Haven]: April 1, 1850.
Yesterday I took leave of the Sabbath school, for I have decided, that, if it is not too late now, I'll go west this Spring. I have been waiting to use my little influence I may possess towards getting a new and convenient school-house here. It has been decided to build one in a pleasant spot, and Mr. J[ohnson] showed me the plan of it the other evening. It will be large enough for three departments. It seems that my work here is done now. The school numbers just double what it did when I came here, and, I think, may go on prosperously. For a year and a half I have met, almost daily, with these little ones, and closely have they twined about my heart. Some of the older ones, since I have been among them, have given evidence of renewed hearts, and for all of them have I prayed that the love of God may be the first and greatest principle of their lives. O may it be so. Lord forbid that the little good seed I have in weakness sown should fall on stony places, or by the wayside—but may it fall into good ground and bear fruit an hundred fold for heaven.

I closed at noon. In the afternoon I called on Mrs. Peter Phelps. Then went to see Mrs. Dutton relative to the class of teachers at Hartford. I introduced myself, and she must have thought my appearance very awkward, for my feelings were in a tumult of commotion from parting with my pupils—but she was kind and courteous. Then I called at Mr. Phelps'. Mrs. P. was in her easy chair, unwell. I staid but a short time for I could scarcely control my rising tears. At the door Mr. P. kindly offered to write me a letter of introduction to Miss S[wift] at Hartford, who takes charge of the class.[1] I went out thinking I'd go to Mrs. B[aker]'s where brother

---

1. Mrs. H. W. Dutton sent the letter to Nancy Swift, the superintendent of the National Board's institute at Hartford, that week. She wrote that Arozina had been a teacher in one of the district schools in New Haven "for about a year and a half & is warmly commended by the Committee for her success & fidelity." Mrs. Dutton explained that Arozina was a member of the First Baptist Church and that both the Reverend Mr. Phelps and his wife "speak in very high terms of her qualifications as to piety & ability for the work in which she now proposes to engage." She recommended that the board take Arozina at once

[Barnabas] boards; but, alone, I could no longer suppress my choking tears and walked on till I came to Mrs. N[orton]'s went in, and sat down to have my cry out. The cloud had been rising for several days and must now melt away. Some partings were over, and many more were to come; but I felt relieved and was able to go to Mrs. B.'s and appear quite calm.

Tuesday.
Went up to Mrs. W[right]'s, packed my things, and had them bro't to Mrs. B.'s. Made several calls. Evening went to phonography school with B. and Martha.

Wednesday.
Busy sewing. A bad headache.

Thursday.
Hurry—hurry—and waiting for a letter from Hartford.

Friday Evening.
Went to covenant meeting.

Sunday.
Went to church in the morning, to the second baptist afternoon, ours—in the lecture room, for they are repairing above.

This morning, before church time Mr. H., M[artha] and I went to the Jail, but they would not admit us for there is no room for spectators. (*Foote, the murderer was there.*)

Evening Mrs. B. started with me for the College Street church, but we were late, and the house was full. We went to St. Paul's, but there were no services; then we stopped at ours, where we had a prayermeeting. Went home tired out.

Monday morning.
H. C[olton] called said goodbye.

Tuesday.
Have been training with Martha, or she with me rather. Went over to Mt. Pleasant visited the Washington school house, but school was out; went into the Hospital and to the top of it. Saw the city roofs and spires, and many other things, then went nearly down to oyster point; called on two of my scholars, came back, called at Mrs. W[right]'s. Mr. W. & wife gone. Goodbye to Miss Jacobs, Hester, Minor &c. Henry and David came along to Mrs. H.'s—it began to rain and grew dark, and was obliged to go back without finishing my calls.

---

because she had already resigned her position "with the expectation of going West & it will be quite a disappointment if she is obliged to wait till the Fall." Mrs. H. W. Dutton, New Haven, to Nancy Swift, 3 April 1850, and S. D. Phelps, New Haven, 5 April 1850 with Perkins application, application file, NPEB Papers.

A night or two ago, B[arnabas] went with me over to the hill. We made about a dozen calls, among others at Mr. Burwell's where I boarded when I first commenced school here. Mr. & Mrs. B. are fine old people, but Huldah, their poor, foolish sister, is an odd specimen of the human genus as I ever met. She is about sixty years of age, nervous and excitable in the extreme. At times she would throw her arms around my neck and kiss me, and call me a *"dear cretur,"* then in ten minutes, scold me unmercifully; say I was more "pague tan pofit an wish my broder'd find me noder bordin pace." Sometimes she'd amuse me by some burst of surprise, prefaced by "Y Mit P. L. M.T. Purkee" and shake her long, bony finger ominously at me. She must be a great trial to her friends.

Caroline is of delicate health, and, when I saw her the other evening, was pale as the white lily, and too weak to be able to converse much. She teaches music, but is not strong enough to attend to it all the time. A few years since she was in an English family as governess. I admire her firmness, perseverance, talents and her every day appearance, and shall ever remember and esteem her.

Jane, the youngest, has been petted and spoiled like myself. She is near my age, and I tho't I should love her dearly, at first. But a slight misunderstanding arose between us. I tho't her selfish and proud, and she tho't me ugly and unlovely, and coldness grew and hardened into ice. No doubt I was most to blame, for I might have sought to win her love by fawning and fondness as some others do. But I could not act unnaturally. Then I unthinkingly showed my dislike to her kissing the cat—and, when the subject of ornaments was discussed one evening, unmindful of the bracelet on her arm and the rings on her fingers, denounced them all as in bad taste unchristian-like and sinful. I was certainly innocent of thinking that she was fond of them till I had spoken, but I *ought* to *have thought,* and not have expressed myself so decidedly. But let it all be forgotten now. I love her still—and wish her all the happiness her fond heart anticipates.— —

Last Saturday I called at Mr. Bakewell's room to get a box of prints. During my course of instruction under him, I have seen much in his character to admire as a gentleman and a christian. He had kindly accommodated me saturday mornings, and bestowed much attention upon my improvement in drawing, encouraged my feeble efforts, and pointed out all their faults as well as merits. I think his patience is inexhaustible. At parting he presented me another box of prints of a different kind; kindly wished me success in my western labors, and said when I should get located, with my little group of pupils about me he'd like to stand behind the scene and take a sketch of it. I told him I should paint all the flowers on the prairies this summer. He was too polite to doubt my assertion, whether he *thought* so or not.

B[arnabas] wanted my daguerreotype taken this morning, but *I* really did not, and was contrary. I tho't two copies of me were quite sufficient for him at present. He scolded, and I pouted, for I tho't it was silly, and I was in a hurry, and tired, and had not a dress to suit me, but he persisted, and I relented, and yielded. I ought to have gratified him, but I tho't him stubborn, and he was, and *I* too, but the weaker must obey the stronger, the women must submit to man—and *obey*.[2] So Mrs. B[aker] went with us to the daguerrean rooms and Mr. M[oulthrop] struck off an edition of my humble self and B. on the same plate, if I was so cross.——

When Martha and I got home that night—found Uncle Asa at Mrs. B.'s.[3]

Wednesday.
Tomorrow I shall start for Hartford. Visited my Tract District to bid them good bye, called on Miss Wood (*Judge Wood's daughter*) and resigned my pleasant mission in that society—made some calls, &c.

South Marshfield Mass.—April—1850.
Oh sweet is rest and quiet to the weary soul. How often have I tho't, in the brief intervals from care which I have enjoyed, of that still, calm resting place for the children of earth, and felt that soon its unbroken stillness would be mine. Oh I could be down in the grave without a murmur could the little remnant of my life be spent usefully.

As I had feared, I was too late for the spring class at Hartford and am obliged to defer going West till another class.

Miss Swift invited me to join the class of six for Oregon. I have never tho't of being qualified for such responsibility. It is a serious consideration, and sho'd not be treated lightly. I fear my health too is insufficient. Oh, I may never go at all. But there are others better fitted for the work than I, and perhaps they will be more successful than I could ever hope to be. Had I not hesitated so long between filial affection and duty—and had I not wished to remain in my school till measures were decided upon concerning the erection of another building—and had not my pecuniary means been so low, &c., &c., I might have been in time.

I left New Haven April 10th. It was a bright, beautiful morning, and I could not but be cheerful and happy as Uncle A[sa], Mrs. Baker, Martha, Barney, Mr. Starkweather & Baker conducted me to the depot. With many cautions from Mr. S. to beware of wolves, and from Martha to take care of snakes, and kind words and smiling looks from all, we bid adieu. The train commenced moving, and I was alone—alone in feeling, tho't, and friendship.

2. Arozina had crossed out the sentence between *but the weaker* and *and obey*. She later tried to restore it in pencil.

3. Uncle Asa was Arozina's father's brother, Asa Perkins (1786–1861). He married Arozina's mother the following month on 5 May 1850, in Marshfield.

At Hartford, I proceeded to the Orphan Asylum, had an interview with Miss Swift, heard a lecture to the class from Mr. Charles Beecher,[4] then, in company with two young ladies, returned to the depot.

As we were going towards Washington Street we met a man coming with great speed—our carriages came in contact, how, I scarcely know it was so quickly done. The man was thrown out, and fell upon his face on the sidewalk, blood gushed in streams, and, then I returned, my driver told me he lived only half an hour.

Thus suddenly to be hurled into eternity! how solemn! what a lesson to us to be prepared, for in such an hour as we think not the son of man may come to us also.

At Springfield I waited till the evening train for some of my baggage to overtake me, and started at eight. It was quite dark, and as I took my lonely seat in the car I shuddered at the idea of riding so late and unprotected. But Providence is ever kind, and I had not been seated long before a gentleman of genteel, modest, unpretending appearance, politely inquired if the next seat was occupied. Receiving a negative sign, he sat down, and, after a remark or two of trifling nature, and devoted attention to a huge news sheet, after a time, we were gradually drawn into conversation upon the all absorbing topic of my mind—the West. I learned that he was a Methodist clergyman on his way to W[eymouth] to deliver an address the next day, which was Fast. As we were going in the same direction he courteously offered his assistance and protection. It was midnight when we arrived in Boston and I gratefully accepted, contrary to my usual distrust of strangers. Tired and sleepy, my first tho't after reaching a hotel was to retire. Next morning I awoke at a late hour, breakfasted in my room, and went down into the parlor. A servant came in and told me it was time, nearly, for the train to start. I inquired for Mr.——— but he could not find him. Thinking he might have forgotten his charge of the preceding evening, and fearing I might be too late, I put on my bonnet and shawl and set off, the servant for guide, to the depot. I had proceeded but few steps when I heard steps closely following, and a pleasant "good morning." It was Mr.———. Said he went to seek me & I was gone, and, if I would go back to my room he would get my baggage changed and conduct me to the depot. With the greatest simplicity I *handed him* my *checks* and turned back. That was the weakest moment of my life. How did I know but he was a pretender, a graceless scamp. Well, I judged from his looks and appearance, and I have seldom been deceived in judging thus.

As I returned, I met the servant, he wondered, and said the cars would be gone, and Mr.——— was a rascal. Said he had not gone in the right

4. Charles Beecher was the youngest brother of Catharine Beecher and had recently become the minister of a church in Massachusetts. See Sklar, *Catharine Beecher*, pp. 229–32.

direction. I sho'd loose my baggage, &c. I cared but little for that, but I *did* really feel that I had acted foolishly and imprudently. I asked him to go and see that I sho'd be in time. We were soon there, and I could scarcely suppress a smile when my first glance encountered that of Mr.——— who, with the most perfect quiet, was getting my trunks transferred, without dreaming of my unfounded suspicions. It was a bright, cool morning, and it was not long before we stopped at W[eymouth]. I had told him honestly my unjust mistrusts, begged his pardon, tendered my gratitude for his kindness and we parted. Ours was the acquaintance of a day, but his calm dignity, and quiet modesty wo'd have excused, even a more timid person than I, from expecting to discover ought but truth in the clear eye and pale brow of the young divine. That the Lord may guide his steps and bless his ministry is the prayer of one who will long remember that brief acquaintance of the way.

Arrived at Cohasset about nine, but the stage for M[arshfield] would not leave till five, and as there was no hotel in operation there, I was accommodated at Mr. Smith's. Now I did not know that today was *fast,* or I should have waited a day or two longer in New Haven. We had had *our* fast there. Query. was it my duty to keep this too? I went to the Unitarian meeting, for there was no other, in the morning. Afternoon took a short ramble, then spent the remainder with the family, which is a very pleasant one; jolted to M[arshfield], and, thoroughly tired, threw myself into a rocking chair, and blessed in my heart the stillness and sameness of this old, unchangeable town.

—— ——

May.
Health is a blessing ever too lightly prized by those who enjoy it. Precious boon! I fear it is departed forever from my possession. The damp, unwholesome vapors of the sea have chilled my vitals, and if I linger long upon the coast, my stay on earth will be shortened. Then I'll improve the precious moments of the coming summer in making ready for my western tour. Friends may not detain me, for my duty lies *there.*

May 31st.
The whole of this month has been unpleasant, and I have scarcely been out. Brother H. and W. are gone, and I am sister's only *trial,* now.[5] It is lonely, but I care not, for it is quiet too.

June.
The month of roses, but where are they? It has been so cold they have not dared to unfold their sweet buds. Only one, of pale, snowy hue, has greeted

---

5. Arozina never mentions the marriage of her mother to her uncle. Of Arozina's brothers, the only names verified are Barnabas, Sullivan, Galbraith, George, Isaac, Silas and James.

us this season, and I bound it in a wreath and laid it on Eliza's grave.[6] And is she gone? she of the gentle eye and calm, meek brow, whose presence among us was so quiet and spirit-like that I always tho't of heaven when she was by!

O, would it were not so. But I saw her in her snowy shroud, and her eyes were closed, and her lips were colorless as the whitest marble. I looked, but she gave no answering glance. A youthful form bent over her, and sobs of anguish from the deep heart of manhood, as he gazed upon her whom he had so lately led to the bridal, and promised to love and cherish, broke the sacred stillness of the hour. But she moved not in sympathy with his grief. An aged father stood there, with tearless eye, and woe too strong for utterance, and an only brother severed from the companion of his early days, now sisterless and sorrow-stricken; but *still* she moved not, for her loving spirit dwelt not in the lifeless clay before us: it had sought that better land, where flowers fade and droop not, and "the inhabitant shall not say, I am sick." And they bore her to the churchyard, and committed her to the earth—"Ashes to ashes and dust to dust."—"I am the resurrection and the life."

Then we turned, saddened, to our homes, to mingle again in the unceasing duties of life, and to miss another smile upon our earthly pilgrimage, and another tone to cheer us on. "Death loves a shining mark," and the best of us was his victim; but rest, dear cousin, for ourselves alone should we weep, and prepare to meet thee in the spirit land. Thou (*thy memory*) shalt be another blessed link in the chain of love that draws our tho'ts to Heaven.

[Two pages of the diary were torn out here.]

June.
I cannot divine the cause of the sadness that comes over me so often, lately. Can it be a spiritual presentiment of an exchange of worlds, or is it only the result of physical indisposition? If the former, why sho'd it cause sadness, and, yet, it is rather a deep unaccountable solemnity, as I look abroad upon the green earth, the fragrant blossoms, with a heart overflowing with love to the Maker of them, and compare them with the briefness and beauty of life. The rich, sweet gush of music, and the full outpouring of the heart in prayer, can raise the heart still higher, at such times, and prepare it to engage again in earthly cares.

——

I have been over to sister E[liza]'s. An aged lady and her granddaughter live in the house with them. I am not much acquainted with Jane, but think her very patient and kind.

6. Eliza Williamson, who died on 23 July 1845 at the age of twenty-seven, less than three years after her marriage, was the wife of Aaron Williamson, a cousin of Elijah Williamson, husband of Arozina's sister Eliza.

July 1st.

We have had one of those frequent, sudden changes, today, which render the weather here so disagreeable and unwholesome. At ten o'clock the heat was almost insupportable, and I sat in a loose dress, with short sleeves, my hair thrown back, and the doors and windows open. At two, it was cool enough for a winter dress, and now, while I am writing, half past four, I am enjoying a good fire with a delaine dress and woolen stockings on, and the sky is clouded like November, and a chilly northeaster howls drearily without.

How people can like the climate of Marshfield with its damp, foggy seaturns I cannot determine. I should never wish to be obliged to spend my days here, tho' they would, of necessity be short. Give *me* the pure air of the *mountains* to *live* on. I'd never repine tho' I might *not* enjoy a ramble on the shore occasionally.[7]

[S. *Marshfield, Mass. Sept. 1850.*]

Remembrances of long ago.

"Look at that child's bare feet and tattered garments! How *could* you kiss the little vagrant? That is a new coin for charity, methinks!" Hush, hush, friend, you forget that we ourselves were once children. Think of the guilelessness of your own heart then, and how the fount of your warm affections was stirred up by a kindly look or a loving word, and chilled by harshness and neglect. That child has a *soul* struggling within that humbly clad form, and beaming from her bright, blue eyes—we may not know the richness and beauty of the gem—the delicate "shading of its ever varying lustre: its fleeting lines lie all too deep for mortal gaze, but, dim it by unkindness, and you leave a rust that will forever mar its shape and clearness."

Has the memory of a look never haunted you thro' long years, and as the same brow may beam upon you now, will not the remembrance of the cloud of long ago not cast a shadow over it? Oh, childhood's heart is deep, and impressions made at that early period, when the judgment is not strong enough to suggest reasons and weigh appearances, will often endure, and mould the character to coldness and distrust when all else, save the careless eye that gave the glance of scorn and the tongue that uttered the bitter word, is forgotten. Could we recall all the incidents of our childish years, the little wounds our sensitive natures then received, traced from these seemingly trivial causes thro' long years of tho't and action and feeling, might perhaps teach us the vastness of their effects upon our past and present conduct and sentiments. Would parents think of the delicate workings of their own spirits in childhood, how cautious would they be in word and example, and how prayerfully would they strive to lead their young charge aright. And

7. On 12 July 1850, Arozina submitted a new application to Nancy Swift in Hartford after receiving a letter from Slade. In the letter she mentions that she does not feel she could fulfill the demands of going to Oregon and asks to be sent to Minnesota or Iowa.

The Lamoille County Grammar School in Johnson, Vermont, attended by Arozina Perkins. The Greek Revival front was added a few years later, in 1847.

teachers too, would *they* but sometimes smile upon the child of poverty, 'twould wake to life a host of affection's flowers, and cast a sunbeam far into the future.— —

You have often chided me for my reserve. Do you know any of the causes of it? I could tell you a little tale that might bring a smile to your lip, perhaps, you would deem it so insignificant, but the results have been too grave and lasting to myself to raise a tho't of merriment.— — You remember Mr. [E. M.] T[oo]f, who was preceptor in our little village Academy.[8] He was, no doubt, a good teacher, and his sternness might have

8. E. M. Toof was the principal of the Lamoille County Grammar School in Johnson, Vermont, in 1837. *Catalogue of Lamoille County Grammar School.*

The view from the Lamoille County Grammar School includes the Baptist Church Arozina Perkins joined. The drawing was made in 1847 by Dr. S. L. Wiswall.

had a salutary effect upon the minds of some of his pupils, but upon mine it had a fearful influence.

I was a child, and had been told by partial friends that I was a *grand reader,* and consequently, my first day under his tuition, I went confidently through my sentence in the class—did my best—and looked to him for his approbation. But instead of bestowing one word of praise upon my childish endeavors he turned them into ridicule, and provokingly said I "read like a rabbit eating beans," which caused such a laugh among the grown up young ladies and gentlemen around me that I bent my head to the desk and wept.

I know I read rapidly, and should have been corrected, but in a very different manner; and had he told me so kindly, and shewed me how to improve, I would have strained every nerve to have complied, but I was from that time a changed being. As reading was the first exercise in the afternoon I ever after had an excuse for being tardy till the forty minutes devoted to it had expired. Had I not possessed a perfect mania for study, this circumstance might have made me hate the sight of a teacher, or school-house. As it was, I went in determined however *never* to *read* again, and if I happened accidentally a few minutes too early, I always waited in the hall, till the rattle of slates, and steps of the teacher assured me that the dreaded task was over. No doubt Mr. T[oof] wondered, but I was invariably so punctual in the morning, and conned my lessons all so diligently that he ceased to reprove me for my tardiness. If I suspected the cause, he never mentioned it. Oh had he done so kindly, how much after suffering it might have prevented. For it was not till months, yes, years after, when, as that teacher was succeeded by others, that I overcame my fearful timidity sufficiently to get up in school and read a sentence without trembling. And, you may smile, but it was even the burthen of my childish prayers that this dreaded fearfulness might be removed. My friends were surprised that I, who had even been so fond of reading them stories heretofore, should so suddenly refuse to articulate a sentence to them from a book.

Do you think this strange? yet 'tis true, and may, perhaps, account for some of my oddities, for, tho' I eventually overcame my bashfulness in this respect, yet reserve and timidity cling to me, and ever will, and the want of confidence it occasioned in my own abilities; has been *the bane of my life.*

This little incident caused me almost to dislike that teacher, and when, a few days after, I placed my hand so as to conceal a bright, new *patch* on my old, faded calico dress, as I passed his desk coming in from recess, it was thro' fear of him, and not shame of my poverty.

— I could have loved Mrs. T.———for I always idolized my teachers, but the glance of her grey eye was cold and proud, and a dread came over me as the hour came around for reciting my daily lesson to her. And tho' she often praised my diligence and progress, I know she loved me less than my classmate, Alma, for the world's cruel distinction was between us. *Her* parents were wealthy—*mine* poor. But in the simplicity of our young hearts, *we* loved each other fondly. How shameful that republicans should attempt to play the aristocratic. (Mrs. T.'s mother was a washerwoman report said, yet the daughter, who if she behaved properly, would have derived honor therefrom, in my opinion, inasmuch as she had been able amid many difficulties to gain an education sufficient to place her in the responsible position of preceptress, still chose to act the lofty and dignified, and said "there should be two *classes* in *society.*" Which class she would place herself in, or me either, I did not inquire then, for I was a child.) *Now* I can only laugh at her airs, but then I was too young to perceive the ridiculous in it, and was only impressed with the *awe* her presence inspired. Perhaps my organ of reverence was developed earlier than that of mirthfulness, which may account for it.

Well, to proceed: among the poor, economy is a virtue that springs from necessity, and as I was the youngest born, the *mantle* of my elder sisters sometimes fell in my direction, and about this time a white dress had been made over for me. It was a bright, smiling morning in summer and the Phebe sang merrily in the tree that grew on the little island near the bridge in the middle of the stream as I took my Grammar and Fables and danced gaily to recitation: for I studied at home that I might have more time to assist my mother.[9] I had on the simple, snowy robe, remade in modern style, low, and with short sleeves, but the *material* was antique, and the skirt, which had been cut in *gores*, remained the same. Now I should have positively forgotten whether I had on a bark blanket, or a princess' purple, when I sat down to my lesson, had I not caught the eye of Mrs. T. roving in a curious expression over my new dress—and noticed a haughty curl on her proud lip which I shall never forget. With the lofty air of a martyr I went through the lesson while Mrs. T. smiled, and Alma wondered "how I could spell and pronounce those many syllabled, accented French words" which she missed, and was "sure she never could get thro' with."

My step homeward was rather more measured than it had been an hour before, and I made some resolutions in my little head which have extended to this day. One was, to *despise arrogance;* and another was to wear what I pleased, if it corresponded with my circumstances, and never to censure others for doing the same. Another was, to consider the adorning of the person nothing in comparison with the importance of improving the mind. And this last decision carried me thro' years of study in some old, worn out, faded calico, or the remains of a once handsome gingham, *fitted* to myself by my own unskillful hands, without a thought of discontent or envy of those whose fathers' means enabled them to appear in better garments; happy if I could only carry out the plan I had formed to get knowledge.— —

Faint, yet pursuing.

How much is comprehended in these three words. A volume of meaning, sufficient for the motto of a lifetime, lies folded up in them. That was a cheering discourse that Rev. Mr. Newcomb gave us from this text, and I tho't the speaker himself must have been actuated by the same active principles that he labored to imbue others with.[10]

Faint, yet pursuing, faint with exertion, toil, faint with the view of difficulties before and about us, faint with the strife to overcome our own sinful natures, faint with the reproaches of the wordling, yet should we press onward, heeding no discouragements, yielding not to our feelings of depression but continue steadily and unremittingly, if slowly, to follow the great line of duty that is marked out to us.

9. Like other young women of her time, Arozina did not attend school continuously but, during some terms, studied at home. Families were not only reluctant to spend money on tuition or give up their daughters' help at home, but they also believed they could guide their children's learning themselves. As more women went into teaching, their desire for more years of formal education increased, often simply for the purpose of possessing credentials.

10. The Reverend Newcomb was probably a visiting minister in the First Baptist Church in Marshfield. The church had no settled minister at the time.

Faint, yes, I am often faint, and feel my utter weakness and incapacity to accomplish aught that is good. I am faint, and falter in my efforts to discountenance slander, faint in attempting to explain my motives to the understanding of others. I am faint, wandering homeless in this cold world, often alone and without sympathy. Faint, when I look around and see the vice that is prevalent in all places, and *faint* when I consider the deceitfulness of my own heart. Still ought I to proceed, still speak and act for truth, still wander on and murmur not, for the orphan's God is mine. *Israel's* Guide will lead *me* too, if I trust in Him, faint yet pursuing, thro' every trial, every danger. Then shall this by [be] my device, and when, wearied, and sick and faint, and almost ready to sink by the way, I'll struggle on—yet pursuing.— —

The sunset. Most winning and beautiful did our pastor delineate the charactor of Christ tonight, and never seemed these words more full of meaning—Except Ye have the *Spirit* of *Christ* ye are none of his. And then, with holy fervor he told us of that Spirit of humility, of meekness and forbearance, of benevolence, of *Love,* till his cheek glowed and his eye beamed with the greatness of his theme, and tears sprang into my own eyes as I traced the contrast with my own wicked spirit. Thoughtfully I walked home-ward—the sun was just declining from the edge of the horizon, and a dark, purple cloud was heaving above it and stretched far away into the clear cerulean of heaven. It was edged with a fringe of the brightest silver light, and, as the orb of day rolled his car out of sight, there remained in his track a massy wreath of the most gorgeously colored hues that I ever beheld, and, as gradually those golden billows changed and mingled into one, they assumed the form of a large, most intensely brilliant **T**, pictured out in fine relief from its richly tinted ground. Long, broad streaks, of pure, pearly white, centred, like the spirit of Love and Union, in that far, western point, and the sky above was dashed with tiny touches, delicately shaded as the inner surface of the sea shell. I never witnessed a more beautiful scene, and I fancied that immense, cloud wreathed **T** the very embodyment of *Truth,* high, sublime, glorious TRUTH![11]

As this evening drapery faded, the moon gained lustre, and threw fair light and soft shadows round, and the sad toned Whip-poor-will repeated his mournful song with unvarying monotony.

— — L. A. Tilden has been with us a day or two, and we were busy in remembrances of the summer we spent together.

— — I have just been thinking of the *West,* and, unconsciously, I confess

11. Arozina's interpretation of the sky is not unlike the popular paintings of the day by Albert Bierstadt and Thomas Cole, who inspired people to go West by their art.
A page is torn out between *the edge of the* and *horizon.*

that a moment of weakness came over me, and for the first time a shudder spread thro' my frame at the idea of going *alone*. But it was soon passed, and altho' it would be pleasant to have friends accompany me, yet we cannot expect to have all we wish for here—and *faint* yet pursuing I'll go on.

— — Jane saw a rainbow last night made by the *moon* against a very dark cloud, and *white* in its curve: it must have been beautiful. It was about eight or nine o'clock in the evening. Don't know that I ever heard before that the moon *could* make rainbows.

Finished my drawing class. They have seemed very much interested, and progressed finely.

— — Every day proves to me that there is nothing of an earthly nature worth living for—hopes and anticipations all what are they? but the shadow of the sunset cloud, bright and beautiful, but passing away.

Partings again—how can I endure them? Here I have just learned to love some whose acquaintance I commenced the first few months I spent in Marshfield, and now is to be broken off again abruptly, and perhaps never again be resumed. My life seems like a strange, bewildered dream. 'Tis like the zephyr's harp. I just begin a strain of low, sweet music, when a sudden blast will sweep the chords, and, ere the echo dies away, 'tis broken by the tones of many high and lofty strains that tremble, blend, then die. My harp is waked by every breath, stirred by the tones and words that scarce could move the vibrations of other strings. There seems a struggling to express the music of the spirits and if some gentle hand calls forth an answering strain, a rougher one will drown the harmony and cause a discord there.

— Now, the time to which I have been looking forward is come. I go to meet the class at Hartford, preparatory to labors in the West.—A fond farewell to friends, and prayers for their happiness.

S. Marshfield, Mass. Sept. 1850.

〰〰〰〰〰〰〰〰〰〰〰〰〰〰〰 *4* 〰〰〰〰〰〰〰〰〰〰〰〰〰〰〰〰

Training to Be a Western Teacher
Hartford: September 5, 1850, to October 2, 1850

Hartford, Conn. Sept. 5, 1850.

At length I am here! I am really here myself! After all my toil last Winter, my sleepless nights and weary days, my late application to the Board then, and the summer spent in "inglorious rest" in consequence I have been blessed with health and sustained courage to meet the class at present assembled. I found it just as hard to leave my mother as it would have been last Spring, and she is perhaps but little reconciled to my scheme— But I pray for health, and the blessing of Heaven upon my feeble endeavors, and then I fear not failure.

I arrived here the 3d. inst. The class were to come the 23d. ult., but, owing to some other arrangements of my own, some pecuniary embarrassments, and a little instruction to a lad in painting, I could not be punctual.

The morning was cloudy, but I had no idea of the drenching rain we were going to have, till I arrived at the boat in Hingham. A young lady from M[arshfield] was going in company with me as far as Boston, and we had concluded to take the boat for the *pleasure* of it, but were glad enough when it touched the wharf at B[oston]. Arrived at the depot I made a few notes which I will transcribe.[1]

Worcester Depot, Boston, 1½ P.M.

Just parted from M. and after two excursions from the boat, had a *jam* in a pint measure of a carriage with 20 other unfortunates; and am now seated here with one hour and half of leisure. What shall I think of that will be pleasant? A lady near me is humming a tune to amuse herself or others; and I feel damp and anything but agreeable. My parasol is wet, and veil, and I have opened one and spread the other on it to dry. My head aches sadly, but I will try to forget self, or I shall render myself and others unhappy.

After twelve hours of travel, and most thoroughly fatigued, I arrived at the Orphan Asylum Washington St. just as the sun had thrown his last rays

---

1. Arozina could have taken the train to Boston. A regular stage ran from Marshfield to Cohasset where the train stopped.

The page from Arozina Perkins's diary announcing her arrival at the National Board institute in Hartford on 5 September 1850.

above the horizon. Introduced myself to Mrs. Grosvenor, who, I found, has taken the place of Miss Swift in consequence of the illness of the latter.[2] Took off my bonnet, and was immediately ushered into the presence of the class who were assembled in the parlor to listen to a lecture upon insanity from

2. Lucy Tappan Grosvenor had superintended the third class in the spring of 1848, before her marriage to the Reverend Mason Grosvenor. She was called back to direct Arozina's class, the eighth class. Arozina got to know Nancy Swift, the regular superintendent, better than her classmates did, because she traveled West with Swift, who went to spend the winter in Tennessee, with her sister Lydia. Because the letters in the NPEB papes are mostly addressed to Swift and were collected by her, Arozina is one of the few members of the eighth class whose letters survive. *Fifth NPEB Report,* 1852, p. 13.

Rev. Mr. Gallaudet chaplain of the Retreat.[3] I should have been much interested in it, had I not been so tired and hungry, and was glad to have the opportunity to take a cup of tea and retire.

Slept very little, arose dull, and passed the day in a confusion of exercises. First, after the important duty of rising and dressing, we had breakfast, at seven; immediately after, family worship in the parlor, then, after a short space, at nine, instruction is given in music, one hour, by a young lady with a glorious voice. Three minutes recess; then spelling, after which the ladies practiced calisthenics, and I was spectator. At one we had dinner of beef steak, bread, butter, potatoes, onions and cold water. Then calisthenics in the hall, and nothing more, as general, till tea, then worship, and the evening to ourselves. I wrote a letter to B[arnabas] and finished one to Mrs. Potter and retired after 11 o'clock.

This morning I feel more rested. I forgot to mention the lecture yesterday Upon "Mechanical Letter Writing" by Mrs. Grosvenor. And another thing too—as I arose from the table the night of my arrival, Mrs. G. told me I had been recognized by two Misses Stephens [Stevens], and they wished to speak with me. My surprise was great when I found them to be U[rsula] and A[ugusta] Stephens from Hardwick, Vt. They were the last ones I had dreamed of finding here. Miss U.S. was a teacher of mine nine years ago in Johnson. What curious events time will bring forward.[4]

I was scarcely settled yet, and have made few observations of my fellow teachers, but was struck the first night with the somewhat singular appearance of a young lady, Miss Bates, from Washington, D.C. Her accent sounds to me like Irish. She seems to have great kindness of heart but, perhaps I ought not to indulge the idea, yet I have imagined that she is a Catholic sent here to gather what she can concerning our expedition. I have read Hogan's developments, and perhaps am more suspicious than I should be.[5] She presented herself for Oregon, but is not accepted at all, and will return in a few days. I have had a little conversation with her, asked her if she had considered the responsibility of the situation. The answer was, in effect, that "they wanted persons to teach religion and morals, and she knew she was famous for that." She is rather singular and causes much amusement for us.

3. The Reverend Thomas Gallaudet (1787–1851), who was chaplain of the Connecticut Retreat for the Insane, was a particular favorite with the teachers. He was a cofounder of the first school for the deaf in America, the American Asylum for the Deaf and Dumb in Hartford, and supported virtually every educational reform in antebellum America, including women's education. *DAB*, vol. 4, pp. 111–12.

4. At forty-six and thirty-three respectively, Ursula and Augusta Stevens of Hardwick, Vermont were considerably older than Arozina. They went to teach in Albany, Illinois, on the Mississippi River.

5. William Hogan was a former Roman Catholic priest who aroused anti-Catholic feelings by asserting that the Catholic Church believed the Pope possessed the divine right to rule the world. See his *A Synopsis of Popery As It Was and Is* (Boston, 1845).

6.

Passed a restless night, and this morning feel dull enough. My room was with Miss Humphrey, the assistant, but the arrival of a stranger last evening rendered it necessary for me to give place to her, and I roomed with a dozen others in the great chamber.

7.

Miss Bates took departure yesterday. She has gained the affections of all, from Mrs. G. to Bridget the servant.

It was extremely warm in the afternoon, and, having no exercise, I sewed very industriously. After tea a few of us took a walk, visited the Charter Oak, that venerable memorial of the enthusiasm of our ancestors in the cause of freedom. Next to the Plymouth Rock, I consider this to be the most sacred relic of our land, and it seemed like sacrilege to thrash its branches so rudely to procure leaves for our Herbariums. [6]

Our exercises today have been few. Music at the regular hour, and calisthenics. We were going to visit the Atheneum but were prevented by the weather.

9.

Yesterday was the Sabbath, and in the morning I heard Dr. Turnbull. Text Ps. 1:1. P.M. Dr. Bushnell, from Acts 20:21–22.

Music this morning, calisthenics, physiology. I wrote the forty test words in spelling—missed one. A lecture this afternoon by Mr. Samuel S. Greene, which was very interesting. Subject, Language. His personal appearance is very pleasing, and his manner of communicating, clear and intelligible. [7]

10.

A lovely day. Was pleased to meet my brother [Barnabas] who arrived in the morning train from N. Haven.

We had two lectures in the morning by Mr. Greene. After dinner we visited the Atheneum, Wadsworth Gallery of Paintings. Beautiful, beautiful, I would write beneath them all—but nature's own has charms above them. From the dome of the State House, we had a lovely view of Hartford with its roofs, steeples, shrubbery, and its broad, blue river as it wound along and was lost in the distance.

6. Connecticut's original charter was hidden in the Charter Oak in 1687 to keep King James II's governor, Sir Edmund Andros, from seizing it and taking control of Connecticut. A famous tourist attraction, the tree fell in a storm in 1856.

7. Dr. Robert Turnbull (1809–1877) was a Baptist minister in Hartford from 1845 until his death. Dr. Horace Bushnell (1802–1876) was a liberal Congregational minister, who integrated human experience with religion. He was a proponent of the Christian nurture of children. Samuel S. Green (1810–1892) was the superintendent of schools in Providence and founded the Rhode Island Normal School in 1853. *National Cyclopedia*, vol. 8, p. 349; vol. 10, p. 499; *DAB*, vol. 2, pp. 350–54.

Yesterday we had the pleasure of being shown thro' the rooms of the Insane Retreat of Dr. Butler. He told us familiarly of his method of dividing his patients into families according to their tastes, habits of life, and species of insanity. There were some who were beautiful young ladies, some of them quite young. But we were particularly amused by a little, old woman called Aunt Sophina, who thinks she is only five years old, and Dr. B. says she is no older in intellect. Dr. B. made some remarks upon the causes leading to insanity which will be very useful to us if we remember them. We then assembled with the inmates for prayers in the chapel. They were very orderly, and, as their voices arose in a hymn of praise, I could scarcely restrain my tears as I tho't of all the unfortunates so various in their distractions and maladies.[8]

This evening Rev. Mr. Gallaudet spoke to us about deaf mutes. He has taught in the Asylum many years, and married one of his pupils. His lecture was exceedingly interesting. He told us of the method of teaching this interesting class, how to commence and proceed with them, and also some anecdotes about them. He said he once told a celebrated painter that he could communicate any historical fact to a pupil merely by the expression of his countenance and motions of body without the usual signs by spelling words. He folded his hands and commenced. The circumstance he wished to convey to the mind of the mute was the sentence Brutus pronounced upon his two sons. He began by looking back, back, till he had made him understand the fact was far in the past. Then he made an undulating motion with his head towards the east, to intimate it happened across the ocean. Then made a peculiar Roman nose, and strutted forward, looking on each shoulder for the epaulets of a commander—looked around, as if surveying an army, exhibited a stern countenance and gestures of the face to denote the penalty to be expected for the commission of crime. He then made the signs for sleeping and waking—the discovery of two criminals, showed the sternness of the judge and the tenderness of the father, and he was understood.

11.

Forgot the morning exercises—we had some calisthenics. Miss P——— of the West Haven Seminary has been with us for a few days and rendered our exercises very pleasant.

I can scarcely settle my mind on any thing fifteen minutes at a time. We have been expecting Gov. Slade every day since I came here—hope he will come soon, or we shall not be able to accomplish anything. Walked to the Charter Oak with Miss P. and two other young ladies.

---

8. Dr. John Simpkins Butler (1803–1890), superintendent of the Connecticut Retreat for the Insane for nearly thirty years, was noted for his humane treatment of the mentally ill. *Yale Graduates, 1880–90,* p. 553.

12.

Music at a quarter past eight. Rev. Mr. Grosvenor gave us a lecture upon Western Life, and Our Expectations there, which was very interesting. This afternoon Rev. Horace Hooker and lady called, and Miss Day. Met with the class in physiology and practiced calisthenics with Miss Flint.[9]

13.

After prayers this morning we had some time for study, then were examined in Algebra by Mrs. Grosvenor. It is very cool, tho' pleasant. Gov. Slade has arrived in town and will visit us this afternoon.[10]

10 o'clock P.M. We were all much gratified to receive a call from Gov. Slade this afternoon. He spoke to us of Oregon—the trials and responsibilities a teacher there must necessarily endure. He is a noble, benevolent looking gentleman, and *is* really such.

Walked with Miss Flint. Hartford is a very pleasant place.

My chum was exchanged last night for Miss E. Miller—of N. Argyle, N.Y.[11]

14.

Saturday night. We are all seated around our table: some are writing, others talking of home and others of their hopes in far distant places. I am very tired tonight. Have been down town with Misses Moore and Flint.[12] Went into the physiology class this afternoon; have written and sewed some, and Rev. Mr. Gallaudet lectured us again upon English composition.

15.

Went to the centre church this morning, but Dr. Hawes was absent at the meeting of the Board of Missions at Oswego.

P.M. Heard Dr. Turnbull preach a beautiful discourse from Heb. 11: 8–26. Subject, sacrifices—of those who leave their homes for a far distant land—of mothers; *they* are continually wearing out their lives for their children. Christian faith naturally produces sacrifices. The greates *sacrifices* are those of feeling. (*How true!*)

I have sometimes tho't it would be no sacrifice for me to leave *my friends* and go to a distant shore I had so great a desire to do good, and the idea of going to those places was so pleasing that I feared I might have been impelled by a kind

9. Sarah C. Day was a member of the Committee for Selecting Teachers, and the Reverend Horace Hooker addressed some of the classes. Annie Flint, who was twenty, was from North Anson, Maine.

10. William Slade, governor of Vermont from 1844 to 1846, was the paid agent for the National Popular Education Board.

11. Elizabeth Miller, one of the teachers who went to Oregon in March 1851. See chapter 10 of this volume, "From Pioneer Teacher to Pioneer Settler: Oregon Territory."

12. M. Augusta Moore, who was twenty-four and from Bangor, Maine, taught in La Salle, Illinois.

of romantic enthusiasm more than a true spirit of zeal and devotedness. And I have tho't upon it, and prayed about it, till I feel willing, I think, to be placed in any position that Providence may assign to me.

16.

Arose early, swept some, and after breakfast was busy in arranging matters and things. Sewed, had calisthenics; then Mrs. Grosvenor gave us an exercise in Letter Writing. We were to write upon any subject and to whom we pleased. I scribbled mine to H. as I usually do.

Two more ladies arrived. Commenced receiving instruction in Monochromatic Painting. Calisthenics. Gov. Slade favored us with his company at tea. After prayers Mrs. G. opened the *mail* and read some of our communications that were written this morning.

17.

A delightful day—Miss M[oore] and I arranged a large hair (this word is the effect of being in a room with a dozen chatterers. Julia just asked if any one could braid *hair* prettily as I was about to write) *desk* for our especial convenience. [13] What a fine cupboard it makes! thank you Miss———— for the suggestion. Our room looks quite pleasant now. Indeed I can hardly think a more sociable, lively dozen of girls can be gathered from the same number of states. I can think of nothing but *duodecimals,* for all consider ourselves *primes*.

We had a general exercise in spelling, after which the class in monochromatics met, then calisthenics, and time to write a little before dinner. [14]

P.M. A few of us visited the Historical Rooms. I was very much interested, of course, how could I be otherwise amid such eloquent records of the dim, distant Past. What a volume each of those ancient relics is capable of unfolding to the curious antiquarian. There were Indian relics—a coat of buckskin trimmed with beads, a twine of rushes or something else, pestles, axes, tomahawks, braided moccasins, &, &c. Among other things those old shoes had a peculiar interest. What home tales could they not tell? and that wreath of flowers made of birds' feathers by an Indian heathen girl; a piece of the tree on which the Salem witches were hung, and and the first sentence sent by the Electric Telegraph from Washington to Baltimore, which was: "What hath God wrought!"

Shewed the two ladies that came yesterday the Charter Oak.

13. Julia E. Bassett, who was twenty-two, attended the seminary in Castleton, Vermont, where she lived. Her father died and her mother remarried the year before Julia Bassett went West to teach in Paris, Illinois.

14. A monochromatic painting was a drawing utilizing the different tones of one color. Like the view from the back of the Lamoille County Grammar School included in the previous chapter, monochromes were also executed in pencil.

There comes Miss Flint with a box cover full of peaches to treat us. This is our *study* hour.

Wrote to B[arnabas] about Oregon. Commenced a letter to Mother.

18.

Went into the kitchen and washed. The Society has very kindly furnished conveniences for the Class. Sick nearly all the rest of the day.

Miss Swift arrived in town yesterday, and we were pleased to meet her today. She is a fine lady—very benevolent in expression and her whole manner seems kindness.

19.

Ironed a little, lay abed a little, drew some in Monochromatics.

P.M. Physiology, Painting. Received a call from Miss Hubbard, a young lady who went to Ohio one year last Spring. She has come home on a visit and thinks of returning with the Class. She was my predecessor at Mount Pleasant.

Evening, went to the city with her; called on Miss Swift, and left Miss H. at the Eagle Hotel.

20.

We were all called into the schoolroom after Monochromatic painting, this morning, to be seen by a couple of ladies from the city. Gov. Slade and Miss Swift were present. I do dislike the idea of being set up to be looked at. It gives me the impression of a *caravan.* Yesterday the class of 16 in calisthenics were called into the parlor to practice before several schoolgirls! It seemed so perfectly ridiculous for such *dignified* personages as some of us *pretend* to be, to go thro' such girlish exercises for the purpose of *exhibiting.*

We assembled at three to attend the funeral of Mr. Hamilton's (*who live at the Asylum*) little adopted child who has interested us so much.

Rev. Mr. Gallaudet took tea with us, and spent the evening in talking to us about School Government. He said it was an excellent way to govern by the Bible, by texts. He mentioned several cases of the deaf and dumb, and his method of governing them. Laura Bridgman and Julia Brace can distinguish persons and property by the scent.[15]

21.

Finished my second piece of Monochromatic painting. Assisted Mrs. G[rosvenor] by copying a piece of writing during dinner. I do respect and love Mrs. G. more and more every day. The circumstances of Miss J.'s leaving us has rendered her still more estimable in our opinion while the duplicity of

15. Laura Bridgman (1829–1889) was the famous blind deaf-mute educated by Dr. Samuel Gridley Howe, director of the Perkins Institute for the blind in Boston. Julia Brace, who was also deaf and blind, was taught in the American Asylum for the Deaf and Dumb in Hartford. *NAW,* vol. 1, pp. 240–41.

Miss J. is exposed in such a light that we cannot but pity her and regret that she was ever numbered with us.

Was quite domestic an hour or two this afternoon, then shewed Mrs. Grosvenor a little in Perspective.

Enjoyed our Saturday evening prayermeeting much. Sat up late knitting, while Lizzie drew, and Augusta wrote. The former is my chum, the latter one whom I dearly love. She is a gifted being, and I love her the better because of the misfortune that in early life marred her unfolding beauty. Yes. August H. Moore will ever find in one heart, at least, an ever welcome place. (*She had the small pox.*)

22.

Sabbath. Staid in my room in the morning.

P.M. Went to Dr. Bushnell's Church and had the pleasure of hearing Rev. Mr. Stoddard, missionary from Oroomiah. His history of the Nestorians, and the commencement of his labors there and description of his "eastern home" were very interesting. I was particularly struck with his illustrations of the *simple trusting faith* of that peculiar people and their veneration of the Bible. [16]

Divided into groups for prayer, this evening.

23.

We had the pleasure of receiving a short call this morning from Rev. Mr. Stoddard.

Miss Swift was present, and distributed to us some books that were presented by the Tract Society.— Busily engaged in Sewing this forenoon. Derived much pleasure and instruction from a visit to Mr. Harris' School. The exercises were in Spelling and Geography, and so conducted as to reflect credit upon teacher and scholars. One class wrote the words on slates, another had a lesson of monosyllables, and as the teacher pronounced the word, gave the two letters that formed the diphthong in each. Mr. H. said he had taught there ten years. [17]

Dr. Butler, of the Insane Retreat, talked to us this evening. He is very familiar and easy in his address, and kindly answered many questions that the subject suggested. He warned us against late hours as one of the great causes of incipient insanity. But it is useless for us to retire early, there is so much to be said in our great "prairie chamber" that the idea of sleeping is absurd. I was awakened before light this morning by the somnambulish conversation of a half dozen about me. I tho't the young ladies were up and

16. The Reverend David Tappan Stoddard (1818–1857), a missionary in Persia, was on a three-year speaking and publishing tour in the United States. *DAB,* vol. 9, pp. 52–53.

17. N. Harris was the principal of the Hartford English and Classical Academy, a private school. *Hartford Directory,* p. 199.

busy about something. One on one side was making a most fervent appeal to some person "to go" West with her; another was repeating, in a very solemn tone, a truth that we have all experienced—"Verily, verily I say unto you, *there is no rest.*" Poor child, there *is* no rest below.

Found a letter at the office from B. He does not seem to think very favorably of my going to Oregon, and I do not know as I am a suitable person to go.

24.

Calisthenics. Gave myself a lesson in portrait painting. Worked busily at my *head* and sewing all day. Evening went with Miss Wilson on an errand for Mrs. Grosvenor.

Evening, Miss Humphrey, the assistant, gave us an exercise in History by cards.

Jane Holbrook left us this morning for home, where she is to stop a few days and then proceed to Mobile.[18]

Had some conversation with Mrs. G and Miss S. about Oregon—and came up stairs and cried because I could not decide about it.

25.

Helped the washerwoman by taking care of my own clothes. Drew some.

Rev. Dr. Hawes called this afternoon and gave us a short, but eloquent address. He told us that he wished there might be something to connect our thoughts with him, and therefore he was pleased upon this occasion to speak to us. He spoke of the responsibilities of teachers, their trials and rewards. Gave us a recipe for happiness which was tested many years ago: "I have learned that whatsoever state I am in therewith to be content." He referred to his own experience and feelings of weakness when he commenced preaching, and his favorite prayer, "Hold thou me up and I shall be safe."

Long shall we remember this affectionate warm hearted attention of the man whose years have numbered three scores in the ways of earthly wisdom.

26.

Finished my sketch in Monochromatic. There was a gathering of the deaf and dumb, today, who have been educated at the Asylum. Addresses were given them by deaf mutes, and translated by teachers. I *imagined* them to be very interesting from what I *saw*, for there was so much noise near the door that I caught but little of the spoken communications; And it certainly *was* so to

18. Mary A. Wilson, aged twenty-six, from Temple, New Hampshire, had taught most recently in Acton, Massachusetts. While a student in New Ipswich Seminary in New Hampshire, she heard a man from Lane Theological Seminary in Cincinnati speak of the need for teachers in the West and always remembered it. She taught in Mooresville, Indiana. Jane A. Holbrook, aged twenty, from Lima, New York, a graduate of the State Normal School at Albany, returned home from Mobile, Alabama, because she was sick. She died in October 1852.

witness those 600 mutes all filling the body of the Church and watching so
intently, their orator. (*A silver pitcher was presented on the occasion to Rev.
Mr. G. and another teacher, by the mutes.*)

27.
Today, the Class visited the Public High School, thence, we went to the
Deaf and Dumb Asylum, and there met a throng of sign-speaking people of
all ages and ranks. I confess I never tho't so much about this class of
unfortunates before, and never sho'd have guessed there were so many in our
country. Some of us communicated with a few of them by writing. Found
them very intelligent and polite. Long shall I remember that crowded group
with feelings of warmest sympathy and admiration.

28.
Went to New Haven. Miss Wooster, from Humphreysville, returned with
me. She has been with us at Hartford, but as she is not a professor of
religion, the society refuse to send her out; it being contrary to their rules to
do so. She has been educated in the Espiscopal belief, and says she never was
among pious people so long as she has been lately. I tried to get her to
promise that she would attend to the interests of her soul; but she said that
she was very anxious to go out West under the patronage of Gov. Slade's
Society, and should she now seek religion, it wo'd be said that her motive
would be to be accepted as teacher. I felt very sorry for her, and promised to
write to her. I think she is seriously inclined. [19]

In the evening I had the pleasure of attending the Union quarterly
Sabbath school Teachers' meeting. How much I have enjoyed those meetings
in times past. Met Mr. Colton there as ever.

29 *Sabbath.*
Went to our church. I had been anticipating hearing Mr. Phelps, but found
that he had exchanged with Dr. Turnbull of Hartford, and, had I staid
there, I might have seen him. It was quite a disappointment to me, but all
for the best, doubtless. Dr. T. gave us an excellent discourse in the morning
from Psa. 116:7. P.M. Eccl. 7:4.

I went into the Baptist S.S. in the morning. Saw Mrs. Phelps, Mrs. Butler, and many others. At noon, I went over to my favorite spot of labor on
Mt. Pleasant. The school were met in the new schoolhouse which is much
pleasanter than the old one, and I was gratified to observe the favorable
change. The children kept their eyes fixed on me, and when they were
dismissed, gathered about me with their little smiling faces to claim a kiss
and hear what I had to say to them; for they tho't I had *been West* and had now

19. Only women teachers who could testify that they had accepted Christ through a conversion
experience were accepted by the National Board.

come back to stay with them. They had not forgotten one who took so much interest in them so long.

Mr. C[olton] was there but not as superintendent. Took tea with Mrs. Norton who has been very kind to me. She is still alive, tho' very thin and pale. I fear she will remain on earth but a short time. Consumption has nearly done its work.

In the evening I went with brother B[arnabas] to the United Meeting at the Chapel St. Church. Rev. Mr. Love preached from 1 Tim. 1:19. Subject, conscience.

B. and I have harmonized pretty well, although of different beliefs. He goes where he pleases, and I do the same, and often we go together.

30 Monday.
Clear and cool. Read a letter from A. C. Baker, Mrs. B[aker]'s cousin, relative to the *Rochester rappings.*[20] It seems, that in spite of his professed infidelity, he has here found something which he cannot account for, which he believes.

Afternoon visited at Capt. Wright's. Mrs. W. *seemed* glad to see me, and I tho't perhaps I was unjust in my conclusions of her last spring. Capt. W. came in just as I was leaving. I was afraid I should not see him at all. Said he wanted to have a long *talk* with me, and I should have been pleased to have had one of our old *chats* on Scripture. I used to enjoy them right well. Told him what I had tho't about fallen angels since I saw him.

Evening, called at Mrs. Potter's. Mr. Coldgrove came in, and we had a *talk* about the Stratford mysteries, and *western difficulties.*

Tuesday.
Called on my friend, L.D.C.[21] Found him sick of rheumatism, but he kindly wrote me a *bundle* of letters of introduction, to his acquaintances at Burlington, Iowa, and Rev. Mr. Brabrook of Davenport. Received a letter from Marshfield, or B[arnabas] did, requesting him to prevent me going to Oregon. Spent the evening at Mrs. B[aker]'s. Havens called.

Wednesday morning.
Took leave of all there. left B. to pursue the "even tenor of his way," and came back to Hartford. Arrived here, found all the girls in great confusion *packing.* The Gov. was giving orders, Mrs. G[rosvenor] had on her bonnet to

20. Considered by some to be the birth of spiritualism, the Rochester Rappings started in March 1848 in the home of Margaret and John D. Fox, when they communicated with spirits by responding to tapping sounds. Their daughters, Kate and Maggie, gave a public demonstration in Albany in February 1850, before offering seances in New York City, attended by many prominent people. Cross, *The Burned-Over District,* pp. 345–48.

21. Possibly Mrs. Potter's brother, "friend Candee," who Arozina later claims convinced her to go to Iowa. See Perkins Diary, pp. 128, 137, 146.

Arozina Perkins's signature on a letter giving her personal biography written at Hartford. She concluded it by saying: "I feel that you know very little of my true feelings at present, nor will you be able to gather much from this paper."

start for Springfield and a letter came in from mother refusing to consent to let me go to Oregon and I laid aside my bonnet and went to work. Our baggage was to leave by noon, and it was now nearly eleven o'clock. No time was to be lost, and saying "nothing to nobody," I crammed my trunks, repeating all the while as difficulties occurred, Sir Isaac Newton's theory of matter and space; "that if all hindrances were removed the whole world might be crowded into a square inch." By the time dinner was ready I had completed the operation. The afternoon was rainy, but I traveled out into the city (*with Miss Johnson & her cousin*) to do some necessary errands—and in the evening, wrote my *autobiography* with a dozen about me, asking questions and busy with all sorts of preparations. It was in the form of a letter, addressed to Mrs. G., and mentioned the parents, their occupation, brothers and sisters, age, education, experience in teaching, religious history, motives in offering, & ties to prevent going.[22]

22. There were two Mary Johnsons in the eighth class. Mary Johnson, aged thirty, from Sodus, New York, taught in La Grange, Tennessee. She returned home because of the death of her last parent, and in 1855 requested a new assignment in the West. The other Mary Johnson, who was thirty-three, had returned from teaching in Ohio eight years earlier "to get more education" and applied from a teaching position in Athol, Massachusetts. She went to teach in Higginsport, Ohio, near relatives.

Our last gathering for family prayers was a solemn and interesting one; and as my feeble voice rose amid that group, it was with feelings that all would never meet again this side of Heaven.

Practiced calisthenics for the last time with Miss Humphrey—the dear, kind, mild creature whom we all love so well, and who has assisted Mrs. G. so faithfully.

Miss Griggs[23] slept with me as Miss M[iller] is sick, and we were much amused in the night by Augusta's lamentations as she came up stairs and found her chum missing and all the blankets "engaged."

After breakfast, Miss Powers and I started in advance for the depot.[24] On the way Rev. Mr. Gallaudet overtook us, with one of his pleasantly comical faces on, to pretend he did not think the present a serious occasion. As he took his leave, an old gentleman in the cars said to Miss P. "What! are you *all going?*" "Yes, sir." "So many of you?" "Yes." "That is Rev. Mr. G. is it not?" "Yes Sir." And probably the poor man wondered that "so many" had been discharged from the *Insane Retreat!!* (*Perhaps he regarded us as hopeless cases.*) Mr. G. is *chaplain* of the *Retreat*.

23. Susan Griggs, aged thirty-four, from Fayston, Vermont, had a long career teaching in the West—at the age of sixty-six, she was still teaching in Kendalville, Indiana. *Vermont Historical Gazetteer*, vol. 4, p. 191.

24. In 1851 Elvira M. Powers, who was twenty-seven, from Morristown, Vermont, became the second wife of the Reverend Thomas W. Hynes in Greenville, Illinois. She died in 1859, after bearing four children. Her picture is included in part 1, "The Shared Experience." Riggs, "Our Pioneer Ancestors."

Journey to Iowa
October 3, 1850, to November 13, 1850

[*Albany, New York, October 3, 1850.*]
Well, we were finally bound for *The West*. There were 26 accepted teachers. Three are to go to Oregon in the Spring, two are sent to Mobile, two to Wilmington, NC, one to Shaufferstown, Pa. and 18 to the West, Mrs. G[rosvenor] is to go as far as Geneva, and Miss Swift to Lexington, Tenn. to spend the Winter.[1]

We arrived in Albany about three o'clock, and were met by the city missionary and distributed in pairs among the best families in the place, as I suppose. Miss Bassett, my traveling companion, and myself, were accommodated at Mr. Boyd's.

Evening, we all met at the Delavan House.

Oct. 4.
At nine, we were on our way, but Gov. S[lade] was too ill to attend us. At Utica, changed cars, and some Indians came aboard with beautiful shell baskets and bead bags. At Syracuse, a few of us took a short, quick walk with Mrs. G. Arrived at Geneva about nine P.M. Mr. Squires and some others met us at the depot. Mr. S. came with his carriage for Gov. S. and inquired for a couple of *Vermonters*. Miss B. and I were sent home with Rev. Mr. Messer. He and his lady are kind, old people, and did all they co'd to make us comfortable. We arose late, and, after breakfast, met the others at the Medical College, and ascended to the top of it to obtain a view of the town. It is a lovely place, situated as it is at the head of Seneca Lake, and I wo'd like to ramble all over it.

Mrs. G. said there was one family who expected a couple of us, and were disappointed in consequence of two or three stopping on the way to overtake us Monday; And she said Miss B. and I must go to make up the deficiency. Mr. Sill is cashier of the Bank and has a pleasant house on the very edge of the Lake. He lost his wife a short time since, and his eldest daughter, Lillie,

---

1. Nancy Swift was going to visit her sister Lydia Swift Wright and family. Lucy Tappan Grosvenor came from Geneva, New York.

takes charge of the household. Susan attends school, and two little girls and a boy of five or six, complete the family. We were told they "were very genteel," and we must make ourselves *interesting*. We were very cordially received, and pleasantly entertained.

At three o'clock, we went to the depot to meet the Gov. but he did not come in till the evening train. Spent the evening in social conversation.

Oct. 6. Sabbath.

A.M. Heard the Rev. Wm. Hogarth.

P.M. Gov. Slade gave a short address. He made some very beautiful remarks in relation to our enterprise, and, closing said: "We come, not with the whirlwind or the storm, but with the still, small, gentle voice of woman."

7.

Class met at Mr. Lum's and sang the parting hymn,

> "Blest be the tie that binds
> Our hearts in Christian love;
> The fellowship of kindred minds
> Is like to that above." &c.

We then had prayer, after which Gov. S., Rev. Messrs. Hogarth and Currie came in. Jennie leaves us today for the South.[2]

Mrs. G. insisted upon my going to a dentist's as the other girls had done, and to please her, I went to Dr. Crane's and had my teeth examined. He told me some of them needed filling, and now was the time to have it done. I hesitated, for I had never been troubled with teeth-ache, and hence inferred I never should be. He looked into my eyes, and asked "*why* I did not have it done." My *means* were very *low* and for the first time that I remember, I blushed at my *poverty;*—yet it was rather because I could not tell him frankly so, without appearing to *solicit* his generosity. I went out and met Mrs. G. She *scolded* me, and next morning sent me there again, and went herself to be *sure* that all was right.

Well, my teeth all insured, it was time to be at the depot, where we all parted from our dear Mrs. G. and William G., and all our kind friends at Geneva, and were soon on our way. We were placed in a car with the funniest seats—such tall, queer backs, I concluded they were intended for sleepy heads, and took a nap. Awoke at Rochester, the place of rappings. Here the Gov. went out and got a handkerchief full of cakes for a luncheon. Arrived in Buffalo about nine, and after tea met in the sitting room for prayers with the family. This seems like a new thing for a public house.

9. Wednesday.

Wrote to Brother James. Wrote a card of thanks to Mr. and Mrs. Grosvenor,

---

2. Jennie is probably Jane Holbrook, who taught in Mobile, Alabama, and died in 1852.

which all signed. Walked down to the shore of Lake Erie; viewed the
waters upon which we were soon to be tossing.— Miss Flint has been very
homesick today, and came near giving out entirely. I really pitied the poor
girl, as she promenaded the room, looking so very sober, and heaving such
very heartbreaking sighs, and was rejoiced when she told me she had
decided she would go on.[3]

Tonight came the sad adieu to six of our number (*who took another boat for
Detroit*) and our kind, fatherly Gov. who are to take the northern route.
Miss Moore says she does love the Gov. so, "it seems as if there were some
of her father kind of mixed up with him." I was in a state room with four
others, and for variety, was most dreadfully seasick. At Cleaveland, in the
afternoon, Rev. Mr. Maltby came aboard to attend us to Cincinnati.[4] We
expected to land at Sandusky in the evening, but got aground and lay till
morning. Some of the girls found persons who lived near their destinations,
but I saw none who were bound to the distant Fort. And indeed, whenever
I spoke of my stopping place, people would open their eyes as tho' I were
going to the *Moon*.

We staid at the *Verandah* House thro' the day. In the forenoon Miss Flint
and I took a survey of this *beautiful* city, and we did not wonder that the
cholera proved very fatal here; we were even surprised that all of the 5000
inhabitants and the countless geese and pigs had not fallen with it. There
was more filth and old rubbish than can be found in a score of Eastern
cities.[5]

P.M. Miss Swift gave us a lecture on teaching. As we sat there with the
door opening into the street, we were much amused by the continual
transits of the gentlemen of the place, and their remarks as each of them
gave us a quizzing glance.

At seven, we were in the night train for C[incinnati] and in our jolting
lumbering cars crossed the whole state without being much wiser, only
that I noticed the light and shade looked like beautiful white rocks as they
played upon the tall banks beside us; and some other observations,
forgotten now. After day break, we followed the course of the Little
Miami, and the scenery was charming. The track here is very bad, and we
were rocked in every direction, horizontally, perpendicularly, laterally and
diagonally—and Mr. M[altby] told us we might be thankful that we did

3. Annie Flint died within a year in Georgetown, Illinois. For Arozina's recollection of Annie Flint's
homesickness see Arozina's letter to Nancy Swift, 30 August 1851, printed at the end of the Perkins
Diary.

4. The Reverend Benjamin K. Maltby of Cleveland, a member of the Executive Board of the NPEB,
was appointed an agent in the West for finding positions for teachers, raising funds for the board, and
escorting the teachers across Ohio. *Third NPEB Report*, 1850, p. 17.

5. Sandusky was among the new cities in the Mississippi Valley most affected by the 1849 cholera
epidemic. See Schlissel, *Women's Diaries*, pp. 58–59.

not find stakes and bars of iron protruding from the floors of the cars. And, as about noon, we paused at the Queen City we were the most tired, hungry and sleepy set that could be imagined. Dr. Weed met us, and provided places for some of us, while others went to the Walnut St. House with Miss Swift. I wanted to go there too, for I was too much fatigued to think of being agreeable to anyone, but was sent with Miss Bassett to Dr. Wilson's. We comforted ourselves with a cup of tea and a nap, then went below, as Mr. Maltby called to accompany us to the Mechanics' Institute. I never was sensible of feeling so perfectly stupid. Mr. M. laughed outright when he saw me; my head felt like India rubber.

We saw at the Fair a great variety of curious and beautiful things, proving that the West is not behind the East in skill and talent.

After tea, spent an hour in the sitting room with the family, then retired. Mrs. Wilson is at the East, whither she has gone to place her son at college and her daughter to school. A sister of hers is here on a visit;

[Three pages are torn out of the diary here. During the missing period, Arozina would have boarded a ship at Cincinnati and traveled on the Ohio River toward Louisville, Kentucky.]

breathed so loudly and fiercely that I almost felt fear. Morning stopped at Louisville; there we saw Miss Johnson who parted from us at C. to go alone to her place in Tenn.[6] Colporteurs came aboard; seemed very interesting to me, I have read and tho't so much of these faithful laborers. Mr. B. lent me "Layard's Nineveh," which I have desired so much to read.[7] Passed the evening at the door of Miss Swift's room in conversation.

17th.
Passed a boat partly sunken. Had some curious, muddy water for dinner, just from the canal. Had serious tho'ts of preserving some of it for a Historical Society somewhere.

18th.
Ran aground in the night.

19th.
Stopped a short time at Evansville Ia. Some of us went ashore and had a lively walk. Read, talked and knit. Boat aground again, and we walked on deck. We have made the acquaintance of Judge Balachth of Alton, and R. J. Harper from Yellow Springs, Iowa.

6. Mary Johnson, who was traveling to La Grange, Tennessee.

7. Colporteurs were traveling distributors of Bibles and religious tracts. They either gave their books away or sold them at low cost. Sir Austen Henry Layard's popular *Ninevah and Its Remains* (London and New York: 1849), telling of his archeological discoveries in Assyria between 1845 and 1847, went through many editions.

20th.

Sabbath, and such a one as I never experienced before. The morning was fair and beautiful, and as we lay quietly on a bar near the middle of the river, we could gaze either way. The foliage on shore was just tinged with the mellow hues of autumn, and every thing seemed calm and lovely, as it does ever on Sabbath mornings, but the restless spirit of man. The hands were at work all day, trying to start the boat; and amid the confusion of removing the men and freight to the shore to lighten it, a scuffle ensued between the mate and a deck passenger in which the former was badly wounded. All day the landed passengers were roaming about the wood on the bank, building large fires, and gathering nuts, like a band of savages. I retired at night wiser than if I had listened to three sermons in our quiet, steady New England. I learned some lessons which I shall never forget, and not to be gained in any other way. I never before knew so much of the continual employment of boat hands, their recklessness of life, disregard of truth, profanity and gambling; and I have learned sympathy for them. Only once have I seen cards discontinued in an evening, and that was on account of a *sing* got up by some of our company.

Monday morning.

Called at New Liberty, Ill. where we again took a walk; and the gentlemen gathered some Mistletoe for us—the first I ever saw. Sandbars all day. At two, the dear, good Miss Swift left us at Paducah, Ky. Stepped ashore again.

P.M. finished the first volume of "Nineveh." Scenery has been beautiful today. Evening, we walked on deck and made the pilot a visit. The moon rose, while there; the motion of the boat causing it to appear as tho' dodging up from behind the trees then back again to see what the world was about, before she would lend us her lamp. We saw the meeting of the waters, the union of the Ohio with the great Father of Streams. Slept little, and saw the sun rise, presenting the same novel appearance that the moon did. Drank the health of my Eastern friends in a glass of the Mississippi's turbid tide. After breakfast sat a long time viewing the scenery, which, on the Missouri side, is wild and bold. Those high bluffs rising in naked layers of stone, some wooded with every varied tinge of foliage, were new and pleasing to me. A child fell overboard, and, as the little fellow struggled to maintain himself above water in the foaming wake of the boat, the interest seemed intense. His little curly head was seen tossing above the waves, and, when picked up, he was lively as ever.

I sat writing last night at the table, when Mr. R. came along, and we had a long conversation upon religious duties and responsibilities, and the particular creed of the Baptists. Time passed very swiftly, and it was nearly eleven before I tho't of the impropriety of sitting there so long with him.

At Chester, Miss Peirce left us.[8] Sick nearly all the day. Wednesday

---

8. Catharine F. Peirce of Barnard, Vermont taught in Evansville, Illinois.

morning, arrived at St. Louis. Went ashore a little distance, then on board another boat for Keokuk. Here I parted from the last of our band, and as I looked on the noble Tempest that bore them away, I thought of what the Gov. said, that "they come not in the *whirlwind* or the *storm*" but I could testify they had gone in the *Tempest*. Mr. R. introduced me to Mrs. H. of Quincy. Were it not for his kindness and attention I should have felt very badly.

I stood on deck this evening and watched the long shadows crossing each other on the surface of the dark waters, and the showers of burning cinders, like falling stars, quenching in the waves, but I was *sad* and *troubled;* for *one* was by my side, who, the evening previous, had confessed his interest in my welfare, and now awaited my decision. What should it be? I tho't of every thing, almost, and, oh, how I longed to tell him of my brother; for I felt that it would relieve my unhappy heart, and, perhaps, cause him to forget the unworthy sister. But the secret was not *mine* alone, and I co'd not expose it. I retired, but not to sleep, and after tossing uneasily for hours, arose and went out on deck. I do not know as I shall ever be able to sleep again. Oh, Father in Heaven! teach me Thy will and pleasure and render me willing to obey Thee.

24th Thursday.
About nine in the evening reached Keokuk, and next morning was introduced to Rev. Mr. Williams, teacher, and Mrs. W. mother of Rev. Glen Wood, of whom the children of Mt. Pleasant S.S. had told me so much. Saturday, sick and unhappy. The miserable fare on the Ohio, and the wretchedness of the accommodations, in reality, affected me much less than the remembrance of the situation in which I had left S[ullivan].[9] Mrs. W. was very kind to me, but I could *not* be cheerful. I had already taxed myself *before others* till I could hold out no longer. I did not know but I was going to die, but she nursed me with such care that after a time I felt nearly well.

Here I heard that Judge McKay at Fort Des Moines, who made the application to Gov. S. for me, was dead; and deemed it advisable to write and ascertain the truth before continuing my journey.

Meantime, Mr. W[ood] came home and Mr. R. obtained a situation for me at Montebello, in case I should not go to Fort Des Moines. I attended the sewing society with Mrs. W.; heard Rev. Mr. Kingsbury of the Choctaw Mission give an account of the state of things during the 33 years he had been among that people—walked on the Mississippi's shore, and visited the presbyterian and baptist S. S., &c., &c.

Nov. 8th.
Friday morning; a letter from the fort stating that Judge McK. is neither sick nor dead, and *has not* been. Mr. Stevens, who was teaching when he

9. Arozina's brother Sullivan was apparently in jail.

wrote the Gov., and into whose school I was going as assistant, this winter, has closed; but the trustees of another township will give me employment and *certain* wages. I hardly know what to do, but, fearing lest the Society may blame me if I stop short of my destination, and having very indefinite ideas of the wants of that distant place, perhaps it will be my *duty* to go.

Saturday.
Was going with Mr. Williams and Miss L., his assistant, across the river to have a ramble and gather Geological specimens; but, for some unaccountable reason, he did not come near the whole day.

Sabbath.
The services of today have done me very little good, for my heart has not been right, and worldly tho'ts have not only intruded, but been *taken in* and encouraged. Oh, I have been very unhappy! and this evening the good familiar hymn "When I can read my title clear" &c. never seemed so new to me, and there was a depth of meaning which I never before felt so clearly, in this verse.

> "*There* I shall bathe my weary soul
> In *seas* of *heavenly rest;*
> And not a wave of *trouble* roll
> Across my peaceful breast."

Oh, how sweet is the anticipation of *that rest!*

Monday morning, Nov. 11th.
I bade adieu to Keokuk, and the kind friends there and started again on my pilgrimage.

I had been told that on Mondays and Wednesdays a good coach would run nearly thro' to Fort Des Moines. My surprise, therefore, when by the light of the lantern I discovered a large, lumbering mudwagon, may be easily imagined. I tho't, perhaps, I might be under spectral illusion occasioned by being so early awakened from my dreams, and "clumb" in, (as people say here) patiently waiting for the morning light to undeceive me. But as day eventually dawned, revealing slowly and gradually the faces of my fellow passengers, it also clearly demonstrated the nature of the vehicle, with its five, hard, hickory *ribs,* covered with patched canvas above me, while sundry jars and jolts of the *springless* thing had already convinced me of the inconvenience of nerves in this Western region. About nine o'clock, we drew up for breakfast at a low, log house, and were treated to a variety of *dishes.* Perhaps it was well that the room was rather *shaded* and our appetites keen by our long ride, or possibly we might have made rather of a *light* breakfast.

A merchant, Mr. Thompson, and a young disciple of Esculapins [a physician] going thro', a lawyer, Smith and lady from Oskaloosa, a returned Californian, and another gentleman, completed the *cargo,* saving a quantity of trunks piled on behind. And we *lumbered* on—over hill and across plain, all thro' the mud. The roads here are worse than anything of the kind I ever heard of, being *repaired* only by the *heavy rains,* and in many places the wheels were lifted some inches from the ground, causing the agreeable apprehension of finding ourselves the next moment at the bottom of some unseemly pond, or deep ravine.

The ideas I obtained of the country were very imperfect, being founded only upon the slight glimpses had while ascending a hill, on foot, occasionally; for our *curtains* effectually shut out all prospect. From three in the morning till 11½ at night—twenty live long hours—we were, going the first 60 miles, and when we stopped at Fairfield, I was too fatigued to feel hunger; and after an unsuccessful attempt to see Mr. B., who, Mr. McK[ay] wrote would attend me the remainder of the way, I "lay me down to sleep" the *remnant* of the *night*. About three or four again, I was ready for our *Western Stage;* when, lo, the long, narrow, fog-colored canvas wagon had disappeared, and in its place stood a comfortable, at least, comparatively so, coach. If people here call the *other* a *coach* I am at a loss for the *right* appellation to *this*.

Mr. B. slept so soundly that *this morning* he could not be *awakened,* either. I tho't he must have *some* very pleasant dreams, and felt sorry to disturb them. Altho' all earthly friends were becoming more and more distant, yet I still felt that I had the same Heavenly Protector that had watched over me thus far, and I was not *alone* with *such* a Friend.— When the sun rose upon us we were in the midst of a broad, level prairie, the *first* I ever saw, stretching away in the distance, like a vast ocean of land.

We passed now and then, a house with a "section" of corn of luxuriant growth, adjacent, and "few and far between" log schoolhouses were scattered, with long, narrow windows set in *sideways*. Where the scholars could be gathered from, I could not imagine, unless raised up by enchantment from beneath the dry leaves and withered grass.

We breakfasted at Mr. Ping's. He has lately been arrested for robbing the mail, but as nothing could be proved against him, was acquitted.

Ottumwa is a thriving little town. Some of our party stopped there for dinner; but I was so sick, riding so constantly, that I felt sensations very similar to the seasickness I experienced on Lake Erie, and chose to fast.

The country along here is very fine, in some places slightly timbered with Oak. Land worth from $5 to $10 per acre. In the afternoon, sometime, we called for entertainment at one of the dirtiest places I ever found. There was so much unnecessary accumulation about, indoors and out, that I could *not* have eaten unless half starving. Here I think we left the Des Moines, a beautiful stream, along whose banks our way had lain for miles the previous day.

As we approached Oskaloosa in the evening the sounds of the smith's hammer and the *cowbells* possessed a music peculiarly *sweet* to me; for *rest* was near. I always loved the dull, simple cowbell; and when I hear it now, it reminds me of other days, when at evening twilight all things and creatures seemed returning *home;* the laborer from his toil—the kine to be milked— and all was gathered in, from the innocent little chickens to the children in their trundle-beds.— If ever weary traveler, then, welcomed these village sounds, *I surely* did; and, after supper and a warm bath, slept the soundest and fastest I ever did in my life, and in the morning felt refreshed and vigorous for this our last day's journey. We rode now in "some hack," as one of the seven, crammed into it, remarked, while surveying our accommodations by the breaking light of day. He was a Kentuckian, and the rest were purely western, in their *phrases,* at least, and I was much amused in attempting to translate the meaning of them.

Another scene of interest too was opening upon my vision, and I found myself lost in surprise again in spite of my previous resolutions *not* to be astonished at anything I might meet with out here. I lifted up my eyes, and behold! before me were *houses,* but of no material of which I ever dreamed it possible for them to be constructed. They were, literally *earthly habitations,* being built thro' out of *sods,* and thatched with straw or grass. The fences, too, were of the same easily obtained article: the earth was thrown up to the height of a foot and a half, leaving a deep, handsome ditch on the outside of the enclosure, and the whole forming a barrier over which it would be impossible for a creature to jump. About the doors were clustered pig-stys and haystacks, and the large, ample, low rooms frequently adjoining the houses, or in front of them, I was told, were their *stables* and *cheese* and *milk* rooms. I was hoping all the while that our hack would break down in front of one of them, or something might happen to give us a view of the *inside* of these novel domiciles. I wished the class co'd be with me to admire the philosophy of these people in the "conformity to circumstances" indicated here. What could be their aims? For what object are they living? So far from society and religious privileges, they ought to possess in their own minds and hearts, and the love of their families sources of improvement and happiness.

Pella is a curious little place, and we saw people there with *wooden* shoes on their feet. How they are made I cannot tell; but when I return, I think I'll procure a pair for a specimen. [10]

The kind hostess here gave me a huge slice of cake for dinner on the way, for she said we would not stop again till night. We had some wild plums for breakfast, and some fine new cheese, fresh from the *Dutch stables.* The prairie along here is covered with a low growth of the crab-apple and hazel-nut. Six miles from Red Rock the mail was left for that place; and a little, ragged,

10. Pella was settled in 1847 by Dutch people who fled religious intolerance in Holland. The Pella Historical Restoration Site consists of sixteen restored buildings commemorating the original Dutch settlers.

barefooted lad, mounted on a lame old horse, started, off with it. I tho't *I* would not like to live there, and have *my* friends' letters borne in such a precarious plight; yet were they but to *reach* me *safely* I would never question the *manner* of transportation.

At a little distance, we passed another house of "Entertainment and whiskey," with a large Elk's branching horns set up on a pole for a sign. Soon we entered upon another of Nature's almost boundless fields, and for 18 miles there was not a house and scarcely a tree in sight. It had been burnt over on one side of the way as far as the eye could reach, and the variety of its dark brown hues contrasted beautifully with the pale, blue sky above; while in another direction, the smoke was curling in fantastic wreaths against the horizon. All was hushed as if some spell were upon the scene; not even the breeze sighed thro' the low, dry grass. I was deeply impressed with the stillness and solitude that pervaded the whole vast expanse. *Here* was grandeur—sublimity even; and, amid the luxuriance of Spring and Summer, there must be the strange, wild beauty too, I gazed and gazed upon the "circling vastness." It seemed

> "As if an ocean, in its gentlest swell
> Stood still, with all its rounded billows fixed,
> And motionless forever."

I was in the centre of a wide Western Prairie, and one of the many dreams of my early days was being realized; and for a time I was happy. I tho't how often, when a schoolgirl, I had traced out on the map the very spot upon which I now stood, while my mind was filled with imaginings of its wildness, and tho'ts of future devotedness to the cause of Truth and Education here. I was *happy* in the exercise of that foreshadowed *devotedness now*, and prayed that *it* might be *pure* and *holy*.

6

Teaching in Fort Des Moines, Iowa
November 13, 1850, to March 21, 1851

[Fort Des Moines, Iowa, November 13, 1850.]
About eight o'clock in the evening I reached my destination. C. McK[ay] Esq. was at the tavern and accompanied me to his brother's [Judge McKay]. I must have been *unexpected,* for I fancied there was much coolness in my reception; but *that* I did not heed much, for tho' I had been six long weeks on the way, and was wearied and worn with fatigue, and the warmth of kindness *would* have seemed cheering, yet I was not in a sensitive mood just then. I had been sped in the swift moving car, tossed upon the heaving, tumultuous bosom of Erie, threaded the windings of the Ohio and ascended awhile the broad stream of the Mississippi; I had been racked and *churned* nearly 200 miles in mud wagons and hacks, and *now,* as I was at the end of the race there were obligations of gratitude in my heart for my safe preservation too great to admit one tho't of murmuring because strangers did not *immediately* regard me with the love and affection of my friends at home. God has been exceedingly good and merciful to me; and when I reflect upon *all* His providences, and how many dear and kind friends, have been formed to me from strangers, hitherto, I'll not distrust him now.

The next morning C. McKay, called, and we went out upon a hill whence was a fine view of the town and surrounding country.

Mr. McKay lives in a brick house, pretty comfortable, too, for this region. It has three rooms, while the majority of dwellings here have but one. We had, for breakfast, wild turkey, cold, and warm. For dinner, turkey and squirrels. Next day a dish of venison.

Saturday, I wrote all day to B[arnabas].

Sabbath, attended Rev. Mr. Bird's meeting holden at the Court House. The room was filled. There is but one church here, and that belongs to the Methodists.

Monday evening.
Felt *lonely,* extremely so.

Tuesday.
A fine day, walked with Judge McK. to town.

Fort Des Moines, Iowa, in 1856, showing the Des Moines River in the background.

Wednesday.
Commenced a cloak for Mrs. McK.

Thursday.
C——— called; very kindly offered me his services.

Friday afternoon.
Judge McK. has just returned from hunting, with two, great wide-eyed *owls*. I wondered if they were going to make us *eat them*, too. *Guess* I could *see* into *dark* things *then;* perhaps be able to disentangle the snarl of my *school* prospects! Oh, yes, I might then be *visionary* in reality.

I have found matters here very different from my expectations with regard to the *wants* of the people. Mrs. Bird has a new schoolhouse just completed, and the only one in town, and a school of about forty children. Of this I was totally ignorant until since I came here. There is a district school three months in the year, usually during the winter, and one of the trustees commenced it at the Court House, but the other two objecting to his terms, and, determined to have a school on a cheap scale, hired another man, and turned Mr. G. out of the house. Upon examining their teacher, however, he proved a complete ignoramus, and they had to look about for another. The school where I expected, in case of emergency, to find *"certain"* employment, was engaged: by some mistake, or misunderstanding, *two* teachers were employed; one of whom, learning the fact, gave up, and offered his services here. The other had been dismissed unknown to the other, and thus *that* school was *teacherless. This* I did not learn however until *I* commenced. Well, the gentleman was examined, and Y. says he knew no more than the first one, only that he knew enough to keep his ignorance from the other two of the trustees. *He* would not sign his certificate, and if he persists in refusing to do so, I do not know as it can be considered that he is lawfully employed. Mr. Y[oung] called on me the day he was "unhoused," spoke very discouragingly of my commencing a school, and, certainly, I never have been so puzzled to determine what is duty. Had I known the state of things here I think I would have taken Mr. Williams' and R.'s kind advice, and remained [in Keokuk], or gone to Montebello.

But I was here now, and it wo'd be silly as well as impractical to get back; and after thinking and praying over the subject, I finally concluded to begin and teach this winter, at least, tho' tuition is so low, and board and all necessary expenses so high, that I may not even clear *them.* I went to Mr. Bird's on purpose to get his advice. He and his wife were very kind to me, but I could perceive that my coming had troubled them. They need not fear that *I* shall undermine *their* school. It seems that their friends have tho't this was my object, or the object of some one in getting me here. Oh Sectarianism! when will your votaries cease their dissensions?

I have almost been tempted to believe there is *no* regard for *truth* among the western people; and now, shall never expect when I am told a thing here, to find it *is* so, and I have almost come to the conclusion to place confidence in *no one* again, except in Him in whom all Truth dwells. I told Mr. B[ird] my circumstances, and that necessity alone compelled me to do something, yet if I should in the least interfere with Mrs. B. I would sooner return to Montebello (for I tho't I might perhaps *borrow* the means.) I wished that friend C[andee] who was instrumental alone in getting me here knew all the trouble I was in. I can blame no one but myself for coming so far with no other assurance than that contained in Judge McK.'s letter to Gov. S[lade] that, "if she will come I will see that she *does* want for anything while she remains." The omission was accidental, of course; but the class had quite a laugh over it, and I tho't very probably that it might be verified, tho' not in the sense in which it has been. That is, I did not expect to "want" for a *school.* [1]

---

1. Governor Slade enclosed Judge McKay's letter (now lost) in one of his own to Nancy Swift, saying: "The assurance in regard to a compensation is very indefinite, but there is not time to write and get a reply before the teachers should be assigned to their places. My belief is that Miss Perkins may go there with a reasonable expectation of obtaining a reputable compensation." William Slade, Middlebury, Vermont, to Nancy Swift, 31 August 1850, administration folder, NPEB Papers.

"Friend C[andee]" was the brother of Mrs. Potter, one of Arozina's friends in New Haven. Mr. Candee apparently advised Arozina to choose Iowa. See Arozina Perkins, Fairfield, Iowa, to Barnabas Perkins,

Yet it *may* be all for the best that I am here—the dealings of Providence are mysterious, and

"There's a Divinity that shapes our ends,
Rough-hew them how we will."

The morning after my arrival, I overheard the people in the kitchen talking of my prospects, and so forth, and some one remarked "She wishes she was at home, I reckon." No, I did not; I tho't there was a wise purpose, hidden to us, in it all, and resolved to go forward trustingly and meekly, and I knew that the Lord would sustain me.

I think Gov. S. and Mrs. Grosvenor would have been interested, and my Eastern friends, who tried to dissuade me from the "wild notion" of coming out here, would have laughed, to have witnessed the scene that morning of Monday the 25th of Nov. at the little Methodist church of Fort Des Moines. Judge McK. was industriously *kindling a fire* in a tall coal stove, and I, after *sweeping out,* sat down patiently *waiting* for *scholars. My* appearance then, I think, would have formed a grand subject for friend Bakewell's pencil; for if the countenance is an index of the mind and heart, every variety of curious & anxious and ludicrous expression must have characterized mine, *then.* He must picture me, too, *far from friends,* nearly 2000 miles from my Eastern ones, and make it appear *real* to give the true effect.[2]

The first day, I had nine scholars. At noon I went to Mr. H. Everley's to board. I have found them to be *very* pleasant and friendly. He and wife were formerly baptists, and are still so in principle, tho' they have united with the Methodists rather than lose all church privileges. They have but two children, Joseph and Mary, the first six, the other nine years old. I have a nice, comfortable room, with a bed, stove, sofa and carpet. I do love the quiet piety of this family, and am thankful that my lot has been cast with them.[3]

Buffalo, New York, 20 May 1851, used with permission from James S. Leonardo from a copy in the Connecticut Historical Society. Included in "Letters of a Pioneer Teacher," *Annals of Iowa* 35 (Spring 1961): 618–20.

2. Arozina's New Haven painting teacher, Robert Bakewell, had said he would like to paint Arozina with her students in the West.

3. Arozina described her room in more detail to her brother Barnabas. "There are *three* rooms, one of which the *parlor,* I occupy. Shall I describe it to you? Well, in one corner stands a bed, in another a table covered with books, a clock and my accordion, between the two windows, under the looking glass is a stand, no, I happen to have it pulled out by the stove just now, to write on. Behind me is a sofa, and beneath a carpet. My two trunks are part of the furniture, and my rough box which I obtained so quickly in my hurry at Hartford is under the bed, with my *go-to-meeting* bonnets in it. Mr. Everley has a great taste for pictures, for the walls are hung with them. I have just been up to see what they are—a portrait of Martin Van Buren and James Madison, hangs just opposite my bed. I happened to notice another very particularly, 'tis of Paul and Virginia in a most tender parting scene, a declaration of independence, a mother washing her hopeful son." Arozina Perkins, Fort Des Moines, Iowa, to Barnabas Perkins, New Haven, Connecticut, 2 January 1850 [1851]. Used with permission from James S. Leonardo from a copy

Fort Des Moines, Nov. 28th.

Went out this morning to school with only a hood & shawl, entirely innocent of how the wind blows here, and came home at night much wiser. Found the presiding elder here.

29.

Wrote to S[ullivan]. Have been severely tried all the week about my fire at school. The coal is so dirty, and it is so cold here, I tho't this is but a *beginning,* and I *must* have patience. More trials than this are doubtless in store for me. Wrote to Mrs. Wood [of Keokuk], today. Monday, eight more scholars, wrote to sister Eliza.

Dec. 6th. Friday Evening.

This, then, is the ultimatum of all my hopes and desires to do good at the west! Were I sensible that I am *needed* here, I should rejoice, even amid all difficulties. But Mrs. B[ird]'s school renders mine unnecessary now, and people consider it a *favor* to *me* to send their children to school. It certainly *cannot* be a *very great* favor to the poor children to revolve around that stove, trying to keep themselves from freezing by a fire that is so high and hot as to burn one side while the other is shaking with the ague. I claim the merit of having discovered a new law of attraction, not mentioned in any philosophy I ever studied—that of *heat,* which proves here completely irrisistible when exerted upon *certain bodies* coming within the sphere, of its influence. Very important, truly!

It is certainly sadly interesting to witness half my pupils suffering all the different stages of the ague and fever every other day. It almost gives *me* the shakes to see them. The little fellows seem to bear it with great resignation. I have been troubled with a severely sore throat—the result of my initiatory process, but think I shall, after this, become toughened to it. My *toes* too have been *frozen,* but will get well.

Dec. 8th.

Attended the Sabbath school at the Court House. An O[ld] S[chool] Presbyterian, Rev. Mr. Mason, of Davenport, preached this morning, and there was a communion season, and I felt as I have often felt before, that I wo'd *gladly* unite with them around the Lord's table. My heart is full of love to *all* christians. Oh, why can we not all agree?[4] There is *one* who would have

---

in the Connecticut Historical Society. Included in "Letters of a Pioneer Teacher," *Annals of Iowa* 35 (Spring 1961): 616–18.

4. Unlike New School Presbyterians, who joined in worship with other evangelical groups on the frontier, Old School Presbyterians were traditional and only allowed their own members to take communion. Arozina disagreed with their strictness and believed it contributed to sectarianism. See Sydney E. Ahlstrom, *A Religious History of the American People* (New Haven: Yale University Press, 1972), pp. 464–66.

been deeply grieved had he been there today. And perhaps the dear Savior whose presence *was* among them *was* grieved and wounded too. Oh, where and when will my troubles and trials cease? Where *is Duty?* and *what* is it? Teach me, oh, thou Infinite One who "alone hast the words of eternal life."

Evening. Twilight thoughts were ever sweet to me, but now that I know and feel another spirit mingling with mine in communion with our Maker, they are blissful indeed. Yet there is the shadow of a cloud resting above which cannot be all imaginary; and I scarcely dare to dream of *joy* on *earth*.

I have been reading one of Christmas Evans' sermons tonight. His life and writings have interested me much lately.[5]

Monday.
Dreamed I saw a beautiful, bright star beaming in the clear daylight, and went to school this morning and found a nice, wood stove in place of the odd thing I left there the other day. (Who'll say they do not have faith in dreams after this!)

14. Saturday.
A letter from Miss Flint. Glad to hear she is contented.[6]

21. Saturday.
Judge McKay and lady have spent the evening with me this week. I have had an increase of scholars, and my school now numbers 24. I sat writing one evening, and thinking of all the discouraging circumstances about me, I tho't how often I had complained, and tho't *mine* a hard lot, and even written my murmurings here, forgetful often of the countless blessings with which I have all my life been favored; and then I considered the pure, holy, spotless life of Him, who, when on earth, was so *poor* he had no *where* to lay his dear head, and *why* should I, an unworthy, sinful wretch, expect more. "The disciple is not above his master, nor the servant above his lord." True, I have broken my last dollar, yet *still* I'll trust His goodness who suffers not a sparrow to fall without notice of His eye. And I sincerely pray that these pages may never again be blackened by words of discontent, nor my heart rendered sinful by indulging them.

I tho't of Mrs. Bird, and how she wept, it is said, when a couple of *her* scholars were taken away and sent to *me*. They came one day, then went back

5. Christmas Evans (1766–1838) was known as the Preacher of Wild Wales. A Baptist minister, he preached to large gatherings all over Wales and published many sermons, noted for their humor and inspiration. *Dictionary of National Biography* (London: Oxford University Press, 1937–38), vol. 6, pp. 921–22.

6. Arozina told her brother that Annie Flint wrote, "The first question there is, after they found *out* a person's name, [is] 'how old is she?' She told them she did not intend to tell them until she found out what the age of *old maids* is there." Arozina Perkins, to Barnabas Perkins, 2 January 1850 [1851].

For an account of Annie Flint's death, see the letter from Arozina to Nancy Swift printed at the end of the Perkins Diary.

again, and the past week they have commenced coming to me. I was troubled, and almost tho't it best to send a note to the father saying that I did not *wish* to take them, on Mrs. B.'s account, &c. I cared not if I merely could pay my expenses here, and I tho't I now had scholars enough just to do that. That Being whom I love will provide for the future.

As all this was passing in my mind Mr. Everley came in, and gave me a letter. The writing was strange to me, and as I broke the seal and read, the kind, generous, christian spirit of the writer touched my heart, and I wept for joy and thankfulness that I had found another friend here in this distant land. It was from Rev. Mr. Gunn of Keokuk. He is pastor of the Baptist church of that city, and when he learned, after I left there, that I had been remaining so long without becoming acquainted with them, he was grieved, and, it seems, after reading the letter I wrote to Mrs. Wood, resolved to write me. He offered to pay my expenses if I would return there; and "if I would come, and had not the means," he could "send them immediately." How ungrateful I have been to harbor a single doubt of the watchfulness of the All-Seeing One.

Last evening C. Mc.K. spent some time here. Wrote, today, to Gov. Slade, and answered Miss Flint.

28.

Tuesday evening. C. Mc.K. called, with Mr. Allen, a young merchant here. Spent the time in talking of music, Aeolian harps, and the coming Christmas. C. left an invitation for me to *attend a cotillion party,* at the tavern, the next evening. Of course it was only intended to be complimentary, altho' C. said he would go if *I* would. He might have been in jest, and probably was.

Wednesday. Wrote to H.L.T. and Miss Wooster.[7] Walked down town in the afternoon and in the evening attended Rev. Mr. Birds prayermeeting at Mrs. B's. schoolhouse. It seemed pleasant to meet there for prayer, and I wondered I had not been there before, altho' I *knew* it was because I have had such a cold lately that I dared not go out evenings. Two letters tonight; one from B[arnabas]. It has been twelve weeks since I heard from him.[8]

Thursday evening, Mrs. and Miss Williamson visited here. Quite pleasant ladies. Called at Judge McK.s.

Friday evening, was spent at Mr. Keene's. A few young persons were present, and the evening was spent in nonsense. To wind off, we had a candy pull. I learned *one* thing however, that is, what *eggnog* is. When the refreshments were passed around two kinds of drink were offered. One I knew, but the other was a new name. I plead innocent of ever having heard

7. Miss Wooster was the teacher Arozina befriended at Hartford who was refused a teaching position because she was not a member of an evangelical church.

8. Arozina responded the next day with a long letter to her brother, saying it was the first letter she had received from the East since she left there three months before.

or know what *eggnog* is. Well, desiring to ascertain the nature of every thing *new*, I took a glass of it, smelt, tasted, and set it on the table, perfectly satisfied. The company must have been amused, tho' it may be nothing strange *here* for ladies to accept such a beverage. They *certainly* would have been, I think, had I told them this was something new to me, which I tho't of doing at the expense of a laugh, but considered that perhaps it might be tho't that I misconstrued the kindness of our host and hostess and I remained silent.

Saturday. A paper this morning from B. I wish I knew what to do. It is a long time since I wrote to ——— and I have tho't that I never would write again, for if I *do,* I must tell him of brother S[ullivan]. It would not be right. I am now satisfied, to let him remain in ignorance of it; for I am sure he would not wish to become connected with the sister of one who has been in jail, even tho' that one may be innocent. And I fear to confide the secret to any one on my brother's account, for I well know how uncharitably the world judges of such things. But it has worn upon me. I have tho't of it till I do not know whether it will be best to write the whole to *him* or never trouble him again. Just now I commenced a letter, thinking I'd do it, for I heed not any consequences to myself. I felt that I had done wrong in concealing it so long. I wrote nearly a page, then threw it aside. Oh what shall I do? I never was so troubled in my life as I have been since I started for the west. Every night I weep, and pray, and lie awake long, then go to sleep to dream of it all. One night I was heading S. over difficult places. His hand burning with fever was in mine, and I was consoling him with assurances that I *never* would leave him.

And now I will write to ——— and acquaint him with all the circumstances, and thank him for all his kindness and the interest he has manifested in one who is unworthy of it all, and should he even despise and hate me then, I'll find happiness in trying to aid and encourage S. in the path of rectitude and virtue. I'll follow him every where like his shadow, and devote all my energies to his reformation. I'll be near when evil companions shall tempt him, and, with God's blessing, he shall not yield to them. No, I will not write; I'll remain silent. It matters not what he thinks is the cause. He will soon forget our acquaintance, and should he ever afterwards be reminded of it, will thank Heaven that he was spared the disgraceful connection.

— I have just returned from Mrs. Bird's sewing society. Five ladies only were present, but it was interesting to be present at such a gathering, small tho' it be, so far at the West.

29.
Sabbath evening; spent in tears. How weak I am.

Jan. 1, 1851
Have written that dreaded letter at last, and an enormous burden seems removed from my mind. To-night I expect to sleep more soundly than I have done for weeks.

Have engaged in a variety of things today. In the morning opened to a hymn in memory of our custom at home, read a chapter, and prayed to be kept from all temptation and sin, and that all who are dear to me may be blessed and happy.

Afternoon made half a dozen calls; evening went to prayermeeting. A New Year's present of a Brother Jonathan,[9] and with it a letter from ————. Shall I open it, or not?— And this is probably the *last* expression of kindness I shall ever receive from this source.

Thursday.

Went to school this morning, found no fire, commenced kindling one, and, by accident, tipped the stove over. Down it came—pipe and all—sent word for aid, and the ever kind Mr. E[verley] came to my relief. This is a nice beginning for the New Year. But I don't intend to do so *every* day—it would cease to be variety.

4. Saturday.

Spent the morning writing to friends, the afternoon at Judge McKay's. Evening—read my Brother Jonathan through.

5.

Heard Mr. Bird, from Jer. 28:16— This year thou shalt die—. Evening Mr. Nash, a baptist brother, who has come on here with a view to form a church, addressed us from Ro. 15: 29.— And I am sure that, when I come unto you, I shall come in the fulness of the blessing of the gospel of Christ. May he have come in the same Spirit that Paul possessed.

6.

Called on Mrs. N[ash]. Found her fatigued with her long journey, and in a poor state of health.

6.

McK. and Mr. Y[oung] spent the evening here.

7.

Tuesday evening—attended the prayer meeting commenced by our Baptist people—at Judge McK.'s.

9.

Found Mrs. N. on coming from school tonight; she will spend a few days with us, perhaps board here, in which case I shall give up my nice, comfortable room to her and take lodgings in the bedroom, which I should be loth to do if she were not sick and a stranger.

---

9. *Brother Jonathan* was a popular weekly journal of stories, essays, biographical sketches, theater reviews, and some news items. It was published in New York City.

Last evening I sewed industriously, a thing I have not done before for a long while.

11.
Washed and ironed.

P.M. Mr. Rainking, lately from California, called; interested us by accounts of his journey across the plains to that place and some matters there. While on the way he said they crossed vast fields covered with salaeratis, and found many alkaline springs, of which it would be death to drink. While in the mines, they had a couple of pet snakes to catch rats and mice; and lizards were very common, which they would not allow to be kill'd because they would apprise them of danger from poisonous snakes when asleep by running over their faces and awaking them. Altogether, I think him a very amusing Dutchman.

Evening, attended a singing meeting at Mr. R.'s.

12.
Rev. Mr. Nash preached from Rev. 2:10— Be thou faithful unto death and I will give thee a crown of life. Two thoughts presented—the *exhortation* and the *reward*. Some very beautiful remarks on the second upon the different manner or the modes in which this reward is presented to be adapted to the various longings of the immortal soul—to the weary and worn it is said to be a place of *rest*; to the sufferer of disease and pain it says that "there the inhabitant shall not say I am sick," &c., &c.

Evening, was much interested reading the Journal of the wife of Lorenzo Dow.[10] What a life of toil, privations, suffering, journeyings and persecution was endured by that faithful couple, and all for Christ's sake.

13.
C. Mc.K. and Mr. Young spent the evening. — Was disappointed in not getting a letter tonight. I think if my mother and sisters knew just how I am situated, and how much good it would do me just to hear from them, they would not be so tardy in their communications. I received a letter the other night from S.'s lawyer at Cincinnati. O how anxiously will the time pass till he shall be at liberty.

14.
This is the greatest place for mud I ever saw—I have *waded* thro' it for several days. Prayermeeting here tonight.

---

10. Peggy Dow's "Journal of Life" is included in the Reverend Lorenzo Dow's *History of Cosmopolite, or the Writings of Lorenzo Dow* (Cincinnati: 1848). The eighth edition of this popular western Methodist minister's book was published in 1855 with a printing of 30,000 and is available in the Boston Public Library. Lorenzo Dow (1777–1834) was particularly opposed to the Jesuit influence in the West. *National Cyclopedia*, vol. 10, pp. 472–73.

15.
Read a sermon of C. Evans! A letter from ————. How kind; and yet it but aggravates my present feelings since I feel that it would not be so if *my* letter had been received.

18.
Two of the coldest, most tedious, days have passed that I ever knew. I never experienced such penetrating winds as we have—they seem to come all the way from the Rocky Mts. Found no fire yesterday morning, and was very nearly out of patience. This has happened so frequently and the boy who pretends to see to it is such a notoriously mischievous and wicked fellow that I decided to tell him not to come to school any longer. This morning I saw his father and he seemed to think it rather above the dignity of his son to make fires, or be a "lackey," as he expressed it, although I gave the lad his tuition for it; and, I tho't was offended because I dismissed him. Perhaps I ought to have had patience with him longer. I have tried kindness in my treatment of him, and hoped it might have a good effect, and had become almost discouraged. And, too, I was ignorant of the *aristocratic* notions of western people. I sho'd not think it any disgrace to attend to the fires myself, but I cannot chop the wood very well. Mr. E[verley] is the kindest man there is here. Were it not for him I should nearly give up.

19.
The wind was so strong going to S. School this morning that I was obliged to turn about and go backwards. It seemed nearly to take a person's breath away.

Yesterday evening the little band of Baptists here met and covenanted to form a church. I understand that one *was* organized a few years ago, but the pastor died and the church fell to pieces. May *this* one be built upon the Sure Foundation.

Brother Nash spoke to us this morning from Luke 12:32. Fear not little flock; for it is your Father's good pleasure to give you the kingdom.

The western custom of having no service in the afternoon leaves much time for meditation and prayer but I fear is not improved in this way, as I learn that it is quite common to make calls, and even go out to tea on the Sabbath.

20. Monday Evening.
Letter from S[ullivan].

Tuesday.
Studied the Bible, read Lorenzo Dow's works.

Wednesday.
A letter from my sisters.

Thursday evening.
Spent at Mr. P.'s. A mixed throng of 30 or 40 young persons present. I felt sad and joyless, and little like being gay or lively. Had quite a long conversation with Dr. C. a young man from Ind. while the rest were merrily engaged in an amusing play; and, at an early hour, went home.

Friday.
S. McSherry spent the evening. An answer to my dreadful letter came tonight, read it, then went to bed and cried all night. I cannot tell *why*, only that I *felt* like it.

Saturday.
Sick today, yet the face *must* wear smiles, and the heart crush down all its selfish feelings and *appear* to be interested in the serious and the gay—the important and the trifling—as ever. Wrote two letters one to Mrs. Potter, sister to friend C[andee] that sent me here. Tore up the other and burnt it.

Sabbath 26.
Went to church and sabbath school; at a suggestion that teachers' meetings would be the means, perhaps, of improving the school, for I felt that something of the kind was needed. Mr. Berkley made an appointment for the first one.

Monday evening.
Wrote a letter which I did not tear, not burn up.

Tuesday evening.
Commenced one to brother S.

Wednesday; eve'g.
Finished it, and wrote one to Dr. W. requesting him to visit him and aid him in obtaining employment till we could be together.

Thursday; eve.
Took my pen to scribble here—nothing very important to say. It has been so excessively cold for a few days past that we were all in danger of becoming walking icicles. Friend C[andee] was not so far out of the way, after all, when he said it was "so cold in Iowa that prairie chickens came into the house voluntarily to be roasted."

Feb 1. Saturday evening.
Went over to Mr. Birchenckie's to the "sing."

2.
Mrs. Nash was taken worse this morning and I staid from church to aid in taking care of her.

4.
Last night she breathed her last in a land of strangers.

5.

Brother Bird preached the funeral discourse from ———

Her remains, followed by *one* solitary mourner, were borne to the graveyard about a mile and half from town, and there strangers laid her till the last trumpet shall sound. We stood till all was finished; and *selfish* feelings crowded upon my heart, for I tho't what if *I* were to die here. There would not be even *one* to mourn for me. But I do not *wish* to have friends grieve when I am gone, and should it be the will of Heaven that I be covered with the turf of these western praries I shall sleep as sweetly beneath their wild flowers as if they were watered by the tears of fond and beloved friends. These were my reflections as we turned from this *first* burial I had witnessed in Iowa.——

Rev. Mr. Hare, the methodist minister of this place, with his wife spent the evening here.

8. Saturday.

Closed my term yesterday. Can't say yet whether I shall be able to clear all expenses or not. Expect when I get what clothes worn out that I bro't with me I shall be obliged to wear a *blanket*, for all things are so dear here that I never can make enough to clothe me decently. Paid out my last dime the other day for postage on the letter I sent to S. "The earth is the *Lord's* and the fulness thereof."

Brother Brabrook and Johnson came here yesterday: will spend a few days.

11. Tuesday.

Elders B. and J. left today. May their faithful labors among this people be blest—and the little church they have recognized be like a city that is set upon a hill in its works of benevolence and righteousness. The ceremony was very solemn and interesting to me, being the first of the kind I ever witnessed. In the morning of the Sabbath, Brother B. spoke to us from Acts 20:28— The church of God which he hath purchased with his own blood.—Then the Articles of faith and Covenant were read, and the charge, was given to the church, and right hand of fellowship extended to the pastor in behalf of the church, in a most affecting and impressive manner. Yesterday, arrangements were made to settle Brother N[ash] and it was deemed advisable to commence raising funds for the erection of a house of worship. Feeble yet, only 14 in number, nothing can be done speedily, but by the blessing of God, we can do a *little*.

I have just returned from a visit to the jail. A poor young man, not twenty years of age, is confined in the dungeon, awaiting his trial for the murder of another, in a fit of intoxication. He seemed very dejected. His sister was there. Oh how I pitied her.

12.

Today brother S. is a freeman again. I have been making several calls among the good people, among other places at a good old German doctor's. Was very kindly and warmly received.

Evening. A letter from B. which caused a hearty laugh. Another from ——— which caused the same kind of a *cry*. I would like to know some one's opinion on *sacrifices, some* one's, who is disinterested and could enlighten me. Dr. Turnbull was correct when he declared those of *feeling* to be greatest. Passed a restless night, and have found myself today questioning the Providence that led me here; and *why* I am thus afflicted. I cannot tell whether it is to punish me for not going to Oregon, or whether all my discouragements have been in consequence of my presumption in thinking that *I* could be of any use, or do any good here. Perhaps I have done *wrong* in daring to come *West*—and all this is because of my sin in this respect. Perhaps I am not a—Christian. We read that "the joy of the hypocrite is but for a moment." One thing *is* certain. I never felt so unhappy in my life. Earth seems dark and low. Miss Swift asked me just before we parted if I did not expect "to feel very *desolate* here," it would be so far from friends. But I never felt its meaning fully before. It seems that there is *no place* for me, and *no friend* to comfort me.——

Monday evening I received a kind letter from the dear, good Gov. Slade, approving my course in coming here, and leaving it to my own judgment to decide whether it is best for me to remain. I wish he could know *all* the circumstances. Oh my head aches dreadfully, and I feel scarcely able to move my pen— *Why did* I come west? and *what do* I live for?

[A page was torn out of the diary here and a new page pasted along the ragged edge.]

I am glad I have ascertained the truth, and I know the test I applied was a trying one, but I never shall regret having used it, for my happiness was too deeply concerned. I hope I may be aided in my duties and sustained by the grace of God, feeling that He will never deceive and His arm never fail. When the heart yearns for earthly sympathy, I'll seek consolation at the Great Fount of sympathy, and goodness. I will go forth smilingly and happily and let tho'ts of injustice and meanness disturb me no longer.

———

I wish I could see sister Eliza tonight. I never shall forget her love and tenderness. My mother, too, I often think of thee with tears, and wish I might lay my head upon thy bosom as in childhood and tell all my cares and sorrows —

16. Sabbath.
Messrs. Everley and Nash went out of town to attend a wedding. Very cold and much snow. I staid at home from church, feeling very unhappy.

Monday Eve'g.
Wrote a letter.

Tuesday.
Attended prayermeeting.

Wednesday.
Wet and rainy this morning. Went over to make my fire, and the wood was all wet and unchopped except a couple of sticks which lay under the stove. It was a serious matter whether to be discouraged or not, and as I puffed away to make the wet mass burn I found myself all at once crying like a child merely because the wood would not chop and dry *itself,* and the fire would not kindle of its own accord. I could not tell what I was going to do thro' the day, for I was resolved not to ask Mr. E. to chop any if I never had any more: and I have so frequently requested him to get some one to chop any wood, and he would then come and chop enough himself to last a day or two. And Judge McK. seems to think I can do it *myself,* I suppose, for he has not been near me but *once* to know whether I want assistance or not.

While I was thus ruminating over my troubles, the door opened and a lad of 13 or 14, one of my scholars, walked in, with an ax in his hand. He said he *"seen* last evening there was no wood, and he tho't he'd come early and chop some." "David," said I, "who *told* you to come?" "Nobody," said he; And he soon sundered sticks enough to last thro' the day, and promised to chop for me some time. [11]

Friday.
Could not conjecture how my fire came to be burning this morning, and concluded it must have been put into a magnetic sleep last night from which it had unaccountably awakened itself; but at the Bible Class this evening the mystery was solved, for Miss McClellan, who lives near the church said her brother made it. C. Myers, a young man of my school, was there early, and we were speaking of an old gentleman, one of the wealthiest of the place, who tho't that $2 was too much for the tuition of his children. I then told C. all the circumstances of my coming here, and how I had barely cleared my expenses for the past term, and I did not know as I should do as *well* the coming term, and how my fire, and wood, and all, troubled me, and he kindly offered to see to it in the future, and I think he would have done so before had he known of it all.

I seem to have been regarded as a sort of adventurer by the people here. No one knew any thing or cared a copper about, Gov. S. or the society, and I learned not long since, that it was the greatest mystery to the people how I

11. Arozina wrote her first letter to Nancy Swift that night and told her the story about the firewood and about her journey to Iowa, much of which is also covered in her diary. She said, "And it is really a serious matter with me whether to be discouraged or not. Sometimes I think I have been presumptuous in thinking *I* could do any good West, and *all* my trials are to check my enthusiasm and punish my presumption."

got here so suddenly, and where I came from. None except the McK[ay]'s
and Mr. E[verley] or S. knew that I was coming, and hence my difficulty in
gathering up a school. The question with regard to my religious principles
became a serious matter. Some, because I stopped at Judge McKay's, tho't I
must be a Baptist; and some, from the fact of my having bro't a letter of
introduction to Rev. Mr. Bird, concluded that I was a Presbyterian; while
others, since I occupied the Methodist church, and opened school with
prayer, inferred *therefore* I was certainly a Methodist. And one Sabbath, I was
not a little amused to receive a visit from old Mr. Hewett who had just heard
that I was a Roman Catholic!! and he came, expressly, as I afterwards was
told by him, to decide the momentous query. After a long string of
questions with regard to my belief, private devotions &c., &c. (perhaps
some one may have been eavesdropping and spied me *worshipping images* or
daguerreotypes!!!) he said that it had been ascertained that I was a *Yankee,*
and as that "cute" division of the human race are considered capable of
anything or everything, people had been much puzzled in their conjectures
concerning me. All this while I had been quietly pursuing the even tenor of
my way, innocently ignorant of the little excitement I had raised in this
delectable city. And tho' unable to perceive what right Mr. H. had to
question me thus, I still hesitated not to give him the reason of the hope that
is in me with meekness and fear. He was satisfied; and from that memorable
era my school increased until there were 32; from the child of five years, to
two or three young men, one maiden on the shady side of 30, or 40, and one
married woman; a variety that presented some curious contrasts.

This is one of the strangest looking *cities* I ever saw. The houses are mostly
of logs and have one, two, and rarely three, rooms. These rent at $5 per
month. There are a few framed houses of one story, which rent at $100 to
$160 per year. There are two taverns, and several stores where poor letter
paper can be obtained for $0'30 per quire, and 'calicoes' at '15 to '50 per
yard, &c., &c. There are about 20 lawyers, eight or ten doctors and three
ministers among the mixed population, and every body seems to be contented with saying that "Fort Des Moines *will be* a great and important place
sometime," when the railroad gets thro' to the Pacific—and—the North and
South poles meet.

Well it *is* a matter of interest, that, in this country, where not five years
since could be found five white families, and the whole surrounding land was
in the possession of the Indians, there is now a population of 5000, and this
little insignificant town numbers 500. Many of the first settlers lived some
time in the old log cabins left by the dragoons [U.S. Cavalry], and Mrs. S.
says she stayed three or four weeks in their *wagon.* Now, they are better
"fixed," in many respects, than any of their neighbors. The streets are
named, a la Cincinnati, from the river up, first, second, &c. and *one* bears

the very significant title of "Coon row."[12] But I do not care for streets, houses, nor people if the flowers will only spring up in their due season. I can scarcely wait till Spring comes, for I may find among them some familiar ones, which will seem like old friends.

March.

Our Singing School and Bible class furnish employment for the evenings of the week not occupied in any other way.

I have taken less interest in my school this winter than I ever felt before. I scarcely know *how* to reach the sympathies of the people here. And so many things have troubled me which I never tho't of before.

It is as I anticipated; ———— has discarded me *because I am so unfortunate as to have a prodigal brother.* Perhaps it is well, for this fact *might* have been a barrier to his usefulness in the ministry. But if *he,* who *professed* to love me so well, has turned from me, what am I to expect from those who feel *no* interest in me! Will not all the good and high-minded despise me? I feel just like making the experiment by telling some here of it. Sho'd *I* be the *only* sufferer, I'd not hesitate a moment. What strange beings we are. Now that I know R.'s true sentiments in this matter, and the more I reflect upon it, the more puzzled am I to decide whether he has done right or not. I will *not* decide, but let the future determine. "Judge not."

16.

We have had a half dozen of the pleasantest, sweetest days I ever saw. And the sun has seemed to rise smilingly every morning, and I have been happier than I have felt thro' the whole winter. Many long, dreary weeks have passed, which I would forever forget. *Now* I feel that I can go on calmly and

---

12. Arozina described Fort Des Moines to her brother in some more detail. "We have some of the most *sweeping* blasts here that you ever felt. The winds come all the way from the Rocky Mountains, and as there is nothing to break them *here we* have fresh *breezes* every day. This town is at the juncture of the Des Moines and Raccoon rivers. It is mostly a level prairie with a few swells or hills around it. We have a Court House of *brick,* and one church, a plain, framed building belonging to the Methodists. There are two taverns here, one of which has a most important little bell that rings together some fifty boarders. I cannot tell you how many dwellings there are, for I have not counted them; some are of logs, some of brick, some framed, and some are the remains of the old dragoon houses. . . . The people support two papers and there are several dry goods shops. I have been into but four of them. They keep 'calicoes' in plenty, one piece that I asked the price of was fifty cents per yard. Then there is a variety of fringes, gimps, tassals, &c., which are laid by at the East, brought *here* for sale.— Society is as various as the buildings are. There are people from nearly every state, and Dutch, Swedes, &c. . . . The great excitement here is about getting the Capitol located here. Whether they will succeed or not, I will not pretend to say." Arozina Perkins, to Barnabas Perkins, 2 January 1850 [1851].

Fort Des Moines became the capital in 1854 supplanting Iowa City. Within six years the population was 4000. See Henry Herndon Polk, "Old Fort Des Moines," *Annals of Iowa* 36 (1962): 425–36. Arozina's impressions appear in James S. Leonardo, "The Postal History of Des Moines, Iowa," *Postal History Journal* 21 (June 1977): 37–47 and 21 (October 1977): 27–37.

hopefully, again, yet with deep humility and praying for fervent trust. The Past has been a trial-time to my zeal—a temptation to turn me from my *duty*. And though I have been toiling without one expression of sympathy, or one earthly bosom in which to confide all my troubles—and tho' it be thus still, may I not despair. I would not dare to give expression (to any person here) to the enthusiasm which led me to the West, for I should only be chilled by looks of coldness and wonder. It seems hard to combat all the prejudices I find against Eastern innovations, and I deem it wiser, in many cases, to endure them; still pursuing my own course, however, as I choose.

March 22.

Yesterday was a cold, dismal, dreary day. The wind, rain, thunder and lightning vied for the supremacy without, and a serious cold rendered everything unpleasant within, and all combined, succeeded in preventing me from going to my school. And then, it was my Birthday too. I wonder if the coming year will be as stormy as the first day of it to me! On *Friday* too, it came, that chief of unlucky days! Shall I fall in with the superstitious belief, and think *this* is to be an *unlucky year*. No; I'll look on the bright side, as long as one side *appears* brighter than another, and hope that this, my first Birthday in the West, is but the first of many that will find me ready and willing to sacrifice all ease and pleasure if I may be the instrument of good. "Faint yet pursuing" I'll still press on.

From Fort Des Moines to the
Fairfield Female Seminary
March 31, 1851, to August 30, 1851

[*Fort Des Moines, Iowa, March 31, 1851.*]
Have received an invitation from Rev. L. G. Bell of Fairfield to come into his Seminary as a teacher, but have not decided the matter.

Have been making calls among my scholars—some of the families seem so miserably poor that I shall hardly have a heart to ask them for their children's tuition fees at the close of the term. Old Mr. Hewett is a curious sort of a genius. He has seemed to esteem me very highly since he questioned me so about my belief, and more so from the fact of my being a *Yankee.* Spent the evening at Mr. R.'s.

April 2.
Mrs. R., Sarah and Mr. Young spent the evening here.

4.
Mr. Nash, Mrs. Everley and myself walked down to Mr. Jones' and helped "stow away" a splendid supper. Was quite interested in hearing Mr. Burrard's remarks about California, Central America &c.——

5.
Saturday—an exercise at the wash tub and ironing table, with a few calls and a little reading.— Yesterday saw some Indians dressed in their own fashion red shawls &c. Believe I have seen most of the curiosities that I wished to, now, except it be *wolves.* I have seen none of these unless they wore *sheep's clothing.*

6.
Fancied I heard a church bell ringing this morning. How I would like to hear the dear, familiar sound again! But I "counted the cost" in leaving all Eastern privileges, and would not pine to possess them now, if I am in the right path—that of *Duty.* My dear Mother I scarcely allow myself to think of lest I should yearn to press my lip to her cheek—see my weakness even now— stop, my tears.

8.

Went out with a small party fishing. Had some sport and caught two large bass, one of which got away from me and slipped into the water again, greedily taking bait, hook and a bit of the line.

10.

A sore throat, and did not attend singing school tonight.

12.

A letter last evening from the First Baptist Church at New Haven to the little branch of Zion here. Why should I feel so sad at the idea of leaving only in name that dear, adopted church, when it is to unite with another circle of Christians? But many associations thronged sweetly yet sadly upon my memory and the warm drops of affection for that far off home of my heart flowed freely.—

13.

Bro. N[ash] preached a funeral sermon this morning from 2 La 12:22–23.

I have been very lonely this evening; read till my head ached, then put on my bonnet to go and visit a sick child, but it rained so that I tho't it best to stay in.

14.

Was invited to Mrs. Lyon's to tea.

16.

Misses Bonner and McSherry spent the evening.

19.

Was very domestic in the morning. P.M. made 12 calls and one visit, then came back and ironed. A letter this evening from the dear Miss Swift.

20.

Heard Bro. Bird in the morning; and Swan, P.M. Evening Bro. B. again.

22.

Spring is clothing the earth with green, and already a profusion of flowers are blooming by the waysides. Tonight I have gathered my first bouquet from the prairies of violets, wild phlox, spring beauties and the beautiful, liliaceous, delicate adder's tongue. Prayermeeting this evening at Mr. Berkley's.

23.

Went out shopping with Misses B. and McS. F.A. treated us to some maple sugar, and weighed us.

24.

The "Hook and Line Co" of Fort Des Moines as we have styled ourselves, met this evening, but very little luck attended us. We even crossed the river in a canoe and cast our lines on the other side, but to little better purpose. Became so completely fatigued with our sport that the bed will invite repose tonight, I think, at an early hour.

26.

My arms are so lame today with holding out inducements to the finny tribe the other day that they are really weak. Made a few calls.—

27.

Have been three times to church. Brother N. gave as faithful a discourse or lecture to Young men on Temperance as I ever heard.

28.

Was so tired this morning when I tho't of getting up that I could scarcely convince myself that it was *Monday* morning, for I usually get rested by this time. But I listened so hard yesterday, and we practiced singing so earnestly Saturday eve'g, that I have not yet recovered from the *exercise—*

29.

Was invited to Mr. R.'s last evening to tea. Misses Bonner and T. there, but Sarah was sick and we were obliged to make our own fun.

30.

Another day of trials. The wind would not permit us to keep the door shut at school, and I was obliged to station a lad there to *hold* it. I never felt wind push so as it does here. I have often experienced today's troubles.

This morning I was called to the door and received a letter from Misses Stevens at Albany, Ill. by the favor of a young man on his way to Oregon. Am truly glad they are so pleasantly situated.— Tonight went up to Judge McK.'s to see what he tho't about my decision to go to Fairfield. I have been so troubled to know what is duty that I felt that could I have the advice of some one it would seem pleasant, but he was very sparing of his. Perhaps it is because he is a lawyer, and has been accustomed to be paid for it. Came home, felt sad, but picked up a letter on the bureau with my name on the top of it, and, concluding it must be mine read it, of course. From my dear friends Mrs. P[otter] and her brother [Mr. Candee] at N. Haven. Laughed and cried by turns till I came to the end, then wound off with a most luxurious flow of tears. Does Mrs. P. think I take things "coolly"? I imagine she would think differently were she to read my heart.

May 1.

It was so cold this morning that the fire was more attractive than the anticipation of finding flowers; but, after breakfast I wrapped up the children in their shawls and went out. Had a fine time myself, as I always do with children, and coming home we called on Mr. Nash who has taken lodgings in a little log cabin on the river's bank. Today we have been very busy at school. This morning the scholars were perfectly delighted with trimming up for an *examination*. And this afternoon Mr. N. and several misses came in to witness the performances. We decorated the old church with the young-leaved willows, and the little ones gathered flowers to ornament the desk. I gave all the variety to the exercises I could think of and had hoped that *some* of the parents would be present. Mr. N. in this evening.

'Tis a difficult matter for me to decide about leaving here. When I look upon all this region as missionary ground, and consider the yet unformed state of society, and all the old and absurd notions entertained by some of the people who have been all their lives Westerners, &c., &c., I feel it is my duty to remain and throw in my mite towards the moulding of the mass into a pleasant and perfect form. I may be presumptuous to think that one so weak as I can accomplish anything here, and did I rely upon my own strength should not expect to do much. But I am just beginning to become acquainted with, and like the people; I have just weathered difficulties and even sufferings which I never before experienced, and to abandon the field now wo'd seem unwise, and, perhaps, wrong. And tho' I have received no compensation in a worldly shape, yet, I have the satisfaction of knowing that I have been striving for a higher reward than earth can give.

Should I remain I should be refusing a salary which would be greater in one session than all I could make *here* in two or three years at the present rate, and I sho'd be choosing toil, trials, privations, perhaps suffering and more than I can now imagine with the extremest poverty to which I have ever been reduced. All this would be unappreciated, perhaps my motives for so doing misconstrued; the act might be censured by those whose sole, pervading tho't is to make money, and I should be alone against a multitude. But there seems to be something in all this *inviting* to me. Providence has some mysterious purpose in sending me here, and shall I shrink from remaining if it be duty? No; if, upon making calls about and in seeking a boarding place, I find it advisable from the state of feelings exhibited, then I'll stay.

2.

Friday evening. Have been looking to find a stopping place, but no one thinks they have any room to spare or they are sick and unable to take a boarder. Pshaw! But, I'll try again. Called, too, at one place where they seemed very poor, and as I came away the unruly tears welled forth that *I* was so poor as to be obliged to charge them for tuition.

3. Saturday.

Have tried at almost every place I can think of, but cannot find a place to lay my head, except that one kindly offered to board me if I could be suited with what scant accommodations they could offer. They have no more nor less than one room containing two beds, and occupied by Mr. F., his wife, two children and a hired girl. This is rather more close than I, with all my boasted self-denial(?) can endure; and I question the propriety of a teacher's accepting such quarters, not to mention my unqualified horror of it. O, I am tired, weary—discouraged? not quite. But it seems that tho' all have treated me kindly, and expressed a wish for me to stay, today, still I may be obliged to go. I can go to the tavern for $2'50 per week, which *reduced* rate was offered me tonight, the usual price of board being $3, but the expense would be greater than prudence or any income would warrant me in paying, with small accommodations and a publicity I do not desire. If I should ever be so fortunate as to have a house of my own, what a pleasure will it afford me to gather in those who are wandering homeless, and strangers.

12. Monday.
Visited about last week some, and had the blues some; was disheartened and encouraged by turns. Spent one night at Judge McK.'s, and went with Miss B[onner] across the river into the country. That is a "right" western habitation of Mr. T.'s; or I should have used the plural number, for they cook in one cabin, eat in another, and entertain company in a third. But they are truly warm hearted people, and I enjoyed the visit much.

Saturday evening I received an answer from Mr. B[ell] of Fairfield, urging the necessity of my coming there immediately as the teachers which he wrote me he expected are not here, and, perhaps will not be, for some time. In a time of discouragement I had promised to go, but, upon reflection, I concluded it would be no inconvenience to him should I remain here, as he would have assistance enough; but now I must give up all ideas of remaining here altho' I have succeeded in finding a boarding place which I think will be quite a pleasant one if it were not so far from my school. I have just been making some goodbye calls, and have been trying, too, to collect a few debts. They promised to pay me this evening, but I fear will forget it. If they do not, I shall be obliged to get trusted for my passage to F[airfield] as I shall not have enough to take me there without it; and I must start early on the morrow.

Fairfield, Iowa, June 2 [1851].
Have been here since May 14, and it has rained every day but two or three. Mr. and Mrs. Bell met me very cordially and the teacher of the primary department Miss S. Weir, occupies the room with me, opening upon the porch above, a nice cosey little place and I have charge of all the advanced pupils who are so pleasant thus far that I have promised myself contentment, if not happiness this summer. Miss Weir has about 25, and I nearly the same number; and there are now six boarding scholars.

The buildings are pleasantly located, and where the grounds are covered with shrubbery, as they will be as soon as it can grow, it will be a delightful and healthful location. This is the first Seminary upon the plan of a Young

Ladies' boarding school as yet started in the state. It has been in operation only three sessions, but is quite popular, and thriving. Mr. B. is an old gentleman who has been very useful in the causes of education and church extension, and has undergone many privations and trials in his efforts for the West. He has only two children at home—Miss Mary, a curious, original (pleasant?) girl, and her sister Caroline, a sweet yet proud looking young lady. Her manners may, upon further acquaintance, prove to be merely the result of natural reserve. I like them all very much, and only fear they will not like me as well.[1]

Last night the sudden news of the death of her father came to Miss W[eir] and she, with her sister, one of the boarding scholars, has gone home. Oh, how I feel for her in her distress; but there lies a weight of agony upon *my* spirit that I must bear *alone*; worse, oh how *much* worse than the news of the departure of the dearest friend, were the contents of that letter to me. Oh, my brother! if you knew what anguish I have suffered on your account the past winter, how guarded would you have been to avoid a second fall! But it is not for *my own* sake that I deplore it, deeply as I feel the disgrace. Father in Heaven watch over and reclaim him! He never could have received my letter, or he would have been on his way to me, by this time instead of that horrid place again.[2] I fear that I may be blamed for accepting the responsible station I now occupy. Can it be that S.'s misconduct does not affect me? O may I be taught the way of duty, and nerves to perform it however onerous.

5.

Have been reading Systematic Beneficence, Nelson on Infidelity and Old and

1. The Reverend Lancelot Graham Bell, the minister of the Presbyterian Church of Fairfield, had the Fairfield Female Seminary built in 1848. It was a two-story brick building with fourteen rooms, divided into two divisions, a preparatory and higher department. Pupils boarded in the seminary building. The board, which included washing, was $35 for a session of twenty-one weeks. In the fall of 1851, there were four women teachers giving classes in arithmetic, algebra, chemistry, geography, rhetoric, grammar, physiology, geography of the heavens, intellectual philosophy, natural philosophy, first book of history, history of the United States, and vocal and instrumental music. Mr. Bell was succeeded as principal in the spring of 1852 by the Reverend Charles H. Gates, minister of the Congregational church. In 1852 the tuition for each of the two annual terms was $5 in the primary department and $8 in the academic department. Susan Fulton Welty, *A Fair Field* (Detroit: Harlo, 1968), pp. 153–54, supplied by Sarah Cartwright of the Iowa State Historical Department.

Arozina told her brother that when she arrived there were six boarding scholars under her care. She taught twenty-three young women and commented: "What strange leaps I have ever made thro' life. Think of my *hencoop schoolhouse* at Fairhaven and my transit thence into the Academy." Arozina Perkins to Barnabas Perkins, 20 May 1851.

2. About their brother Sullivan, Arozina wrote Barnabas: "I had a letter from Sullivan dated March 25. S. was then in Dayton, Ohio, and of course could not have got the long letter I directed to him at Covington, Ky. Oh Barney, what do you suppose will become of S. May we not hope that he will do better now! Let us pray that it may be so. Could you know all I have suffered on his account—but it is nothing if he will now reform. And he would do differently, I feel, could *he* know what I have sacrificed for him." Ibid.

New Theology and Tales of the Covenanter's by Pollok.[3] I shall have considerable leisure this summer, and it must be my strong endeavor to avoid selfish regrets and gloomy, wicked repinings. Suffering should sever the affections from earth, and fit the heart for high and holy duties. That this may be its effect upon me, and that I may be supported thro' it all by Infinite grace and strength, is my sincere and fervent prayer. There is *another* too, for whom I would implore more than this—even happiness on earth—and that enjoyment in the society of friends which *may* never more be granted me.[4]

[The last page of the diary was torn out.]

[The following letter, written nearly two months after the close of the diary, is the last letter from Arozina Perkins known to exist.]

Fairfield, Iowa, Aug. 30, 1851.

Miss Swift,

   My dear Madam,

Your kind letter last winter was truly welcome, and I thought then I could scarcely wait till summer before answering it, for I wished to assure you immediately how much I was encouraged by it. The summer has ebbed away and its close finds me not in the country of the "Sacs and Foxes," but more than a hundred miles to the south east. I have written to Gov. Slade, and given him my reasons for leaving there, the chief of which was a promise I made to Rev. Mr. Bell of this place to come here and teach for him. My word was given in a season of discouragement that I can never describe to you fully, and when spring opened, and my school prospects began to brighten, altho' sorry to leave, I felt under obligation to do so.

My second term at the Fort was more pleasant than the first, and at its close I had an examination which delighted the scholars, and drew in several visitors. I could have had quite a large school had I remained, for prejudices against the Yankee stranger had melted gradually away. But I should have

---

3. Arozina's efforts to sustain her faith and missionary spirit were supported by her readings. *Systematic Beneficence* (New York: American Tract Society) was a collection of essays encouraging Christians of different denominations to work together to increase the "moral power" of Christians. In his *Cause and Cure of Infidelity* (New York: American Tract Society, 1841), David Nelson described his work as a missionary. A popular writer of moral stories, Robert Pollok told of the sufferings of a Christian family who remained steadfast in their belief in *Tales of the Covenanters* published in several editions in Edinburgh.

4. Arozina wrote Barnabas about her feelings about ten days before the last entry in her diary: "I never was so completely low in spirits in my life as I have been for some time past. And I have striven to appear cheerful till it almost seems a vain effort. And I cannot comprehend how you could always feel so happy. Do write me something cheerful, for I scarcely care whether I live or die. I am *not* homesick, neither are my feelings the result of imaginary griefs. If I ever see you again perhaps I will tell you just the truth. Till I came West I never knew much of trouble, but I like here, and probably shall live and die here." She signed her letter "Zina." Arozina Perkins to Barnabas Perkins, 20 May 1851.

done little more than to clear my expenses, for I had scarcely done this thro' the winter, and it became necessary for me to change my boarding place, and tho' I was offered board at a tavern at the *reduced* price of $2'50 per week (a deduction of '50 or 1,00 having been made in my favor) I tho't it not advisable to incur any more than I knew I could actually meet. When I left there I intended to return in the fall, but the heavy rains during the early part of the season rendered it impossible for the church to be built this summer which I had depended upon as a *schoolhouse,* and I never shall think it my duty to occupy the comfortless house I did last winter thro' another cold season. Gov. Slade is very anxious that there should be a teacher sent to the Fort if I do not return, but the same difficulties that lie in the way of my return would be met by another, and perhaps still greater. I wrote to Rev. Mr. Nash about the matter as he requested, and Mr. N. said that he should not think it best to apply for a teacher at present, even if *I* should not return, and he tho't it would be as well for *me* to remain in my present situation thro' the winter.

I had a pleasant journey down here,[5] although you tho't I would not have the *courage* to attempt it, and the beautiful, rolling prairies, carpeted with Spring's softest green, were far more charming than when I first gazed upon them. In the *timber* (as westerners say) the earth was colored with wild flowers of every hue. Fairfield is a very interesting town contains about 1500 or 2000 inhabitants, and being several miles from any river, and in an open prairie, is a very healthy place. There are two brick churches and two brick school-houses, a University partly built, and several good convenient dwellings, of course. Somewhat different from the log cabins of coon-row at Fort Des Moines. Yet the society of the place is not much better than there, if indeed it is as good. The Female Seminary was started about three years ago by Mr. Bell, and for an experiment, in so new a region, has succeeded finely.

There are two departments and I have charge of the advanced scholars. There are some young ladies in school who would do credit to any similar institution at the East with proper training. I have classes in Algebra, Botany, Philosophy, Chemistry, Grammar, &c., &c. There is a music teacher with us now, giving lessons on the Piano. She has 11 scholars. Our examination will come off in about four weeks. They are usually holden at one of the churches. I am looking anxiously forward to the time, and hoping that the pupils will more than realize the expectations of their teachers. And I am weary too, and anticipate a season of *rest.* When this session closes it

5. About her trip to Fairfield, Arozina wrote Barnabas: "I had a delightful ride over the prairies. Oh, I wish you could see the country in the vicinity of Ft. Des M. and about Pella. I never saw more as beautiful, and so every one says that travels over it. Nothing in the eastern part of Iowa, that I have seen can compare with it. The town I left is improving rapidly. Strangers are coming in every day and we passed swarms of emigrant wagons going on." Ibid.

will have been 43 weeks that I have been teaching with only two weeks vacation during the time, and those two weeks were spent in toil about as laborious. But if I can be the means of accomplishing any good I am willing to wear my life out, if necessary.

Poor Miss Flint! You have heard, probably, that she is dead. I learned it incidentally. A gentleman called here a few evenings since and was casually remarking something about a classmate in Vermillion County, Ill. when I inquired if he had mentioned a member of our class last fall who is located there. He replied that he had written to him about her, and she is dead. He said he would bring over the letter, I want very much to know how she was and what her feelings were so far from home and friends. I never shall forget her sad countenance when she was so homesick on the way, and shall almost think that she had a presentiment that she should never return. She was a dear girl, and had effected much during the short time she was permitted to labor there. I had one long letter from her last winter and she seemed cheerful and happy, said that she had "just heard from her father and he was sorry he had ever consented to let her go away."

I received a letter from the Misses Stevens I think after I wrote you, by a young man on his way to Oregon and who had been their pupil. They are doing well and pleased with their situation. They had 100 scholars the first term and 90 the second, and had found several old acquaintances from Vt. I had the luck to meet one the other day, an old schoolmate from the sunny valley of that Green Mountain state, who is pastor of the Con. Church here. Miss Powers is contented and useful I infer from her letters. Miss Gillfillan is in Quincy with her brother. Miss Wheeler wrote to me last Spring, and Miss Wilson; both have seen some trials, but are striving to do good. I have not heard from any of those who went South for I have not written to them but intend to soon. Do you know where Miss Moore is? Please to inform me when you write of all that you have heard from as also of those who went to Oregon.[6]

Respectfully and affectionately yours,

Arozina Perkins

[side note] Not knowing where to direct, I think this will reach you from Northampton.

[side note] If Mrs. Grosvenor is in Hartford please to give her my love. I wrote to her last winter but have received no answer, perhaps she did not get my letter. I would like much to hear from her.

6. Augusta and Ursula Stevens in Albany, Illinois; Elvira Powers in Hillsboro, Illinois; Mary Wilson in Mooresville, Indiana; and Augusta Moore in La Salle, Illinois. J. M. Gilfillan was from Mifflinburg, Pennsylvania, where she was raised by family friends after her parents died. She had also been assigned to teach in Hillsboro, Illinois. Sarah Ellen Wheeler, who at seventeen was the youngest in Arozina's class, was from New Haven and wanted to support herself after her father's death. She went to La Grange, Tennessee.

Three Teachers Who Returned Home

Augusta E. Hubbell, Mary Augusta Roper, and Mary L. Chase

"B ut circumstances that I very much regret, have directed my footsteps homeward." The opening expression in the letter from Augusta E. Hubbell explaining her return from Tipton, Iowa, characterizes the following letters from two pioneer teachers who returned East because of experiences they could not cope with. The third teacher's letter represents the strength of the pull from home.

The three women whose letters are included in this section had similar backgrounds. Each of them was younger than the majority of the pioneer teachers and each came from families whose mother and father were both still living. They were daughters on family farms in the hill country of central Massachusetts and upper New York State. Two of the women mentioned that they were the eldest daughters and felt responsibility for their younger sisters. Mary Augusta Roper, from Templeton, Massachusetts, was only nineteen when she left for Michigan. She hoped "to exert a good influence over the minds of younger sisters, whose characters I feel I am forming." Augusta Hubbell, from North Bergen, Genesee County, New York, was also nineteen when she attended the institute at Hartford. "To pay my debts and support myself" were her goals. She believed the welfare of her sisters depended on her payment of the two hundred dollars she had borrowed for her education. Her younger brother, next to her in age, had recently died. Roper's older brothers had already left home.[1]

Mary Chase, who came from Delaware County, New York, at the western edge of the Catskill Mountains, was in her mid-twenties. She possessed the most teaching experience of the three women. In order to gain "the higher attainments," she explained in her biography, she taught for five years in public and select schools and was an assistant at Franklin Academy. She knew higher mathematics, but no languages; drawing, but no singing. Mary Chase came to Hartford to prepare for her position in Savanna, Illinois, directly from a term at Mount Holyoke Seminary. Augusta Hubbell graduated from Le Roy Seminary the year before she applied to teach in the West. She taught one summer in Auburn, New York, about seventy-five miles

---

1. Mary L. Chase, 1 April 1853; Augusta E. Hubbell, 1 April 1853; M. Augusta Roper, 16 April 1852; biography folder, NPEB Papers. U.S. Manuscript Census, 1850, Worcester County, MA, p. 284; Genesee County, New York, p. 59; *Vital Records of the Town of Templeton, Mass.*, Births, p. 57.

from her home. Although Mary Augusta Roper stated that she attended Mount Holyoke, alumnae records do not include her name. She did not mention the nature of her previous teaching experience.

The women revealed religious goals. Both Hubbell and Chase were members of the Presbyterian Church. Mary Chase had been a member for nine years and wanted "some part of the great missionary field." Roper looked forward to "being the feeble instrument in God's hand, of bringing, perhaps *one soul* to Him."

The future life of Augusta E. Hubbell after she returned to her home in western New York State is not known, but it appears unlikely that she sought another assignment in the West. Five months after her last letter Mary Augusta Roper, by then twenty-two, married Lyman J. Taft and moved to the city of Worcester, Massachusetts, where her husband operated a restaurant and fruit store in the center of town. She died in Worcester in 1909 at the age of seventy-seven, a widow, and had at least one son.[2] Mary Chase eventually returned to Illinois, as a minister's wife. Within months of her letter, she went home to marry the Reverend James Redfield Smith. They had two sons, William Scott Smith and J. H. Smith, the latter of whom named one of his three children for his mother. Mary Chase Smith died in Illinois in 1901 or 1902, a year and a half after the death of her husband.[3]

The teachers were caught up in the problems created by the competitive spirit that characterized the growing towns of the Old West. Mary Roper became involved in one of the most common divisive forces in frontier towns—sectarianism, the rivalry between religious sects and their splinter groups for control over the religious life and even the moral values of a community. School politics caused Augusta Hubbell's dismissal from her teaching position and forced Mary Chase to give up the public school for a select school. Each of the women writes at a moment of personal crisis in her life. Each expresses her feelings with frankness and honesty, giving us the opportunity to understand the issues each considered important in making her decision to leave her Western teaching position.

Augusta E. Hubbell from North Bergen, New York
Returning from Tipton, Iowa

North Bergen, N.Y., Nov. 19, 1853

My dear Miss Swift,

You will be sorry when informed that one teacher of the Thirteenth Class

---

2. Massachusetts Vital Statistics, Marriages, vol. 80, p. 274; Deaths, vol. 108, p. 2; *City Directory, Worcester, Mass., 1852–54. 1855–57, 1864.*

3. J. H. Smith, Collingwood East, B.C., Canada, to Sec. Alumnae Assoc., 26 October 1918; Mount Holyoke College archives.

A teacher and her class in Solon, Iowa, probably on examination day. Augusta Hubbell taught in a similar schoolhouse in Tipton, about twenty miles away, a few decades earlier. The teacher is Hattie Price Carr.

has already returned East. But circumstances that I very much regret, have directed my footsteps homeward. These circumstances were entirely beyond my control, for I would not willingly leave my field of labor before the expiration of two years at least.

I reached Muscatine the 11*th* of May, but did not succeed in obtaining a conveyance to Tipton until the 14*th,* and commenced school on Monday May 16.[4] I taught one quarter, and four weeks on the second, when I was taken quite ill and obliged to leave my school. My disease was the Billious and Intermittent Fever. I was confined to my room about three weeks and then found myself too weak to enter school.

Oh, Miss Swift, I cannot begin to tell you of all that I suffered during my short residence in Tipton.

4. Augusta Hubbell and Mary Chase traveled together. They took the train from Chicago to La Salle, but muddy roads prevented them from taking the stage to Savanna. They had to take a boat down the Illinois River to St. Louis and up the Mississippi to their destinations. H. N. Wellman, Montrose, Iowa, to Nancy Swift, 12 May 1853, letters folder, NPEB Papers.

I was warmly received by Mr. and Mrs. Goodrich, and anticipated finding a happy home with them, which I did for some time. They kept a public House, but it was in a retired part of Town, and near the school-room.

Mr. Bets who kept an other Hotel in the center of the Town, offered to board me much cheaper than the regular price, and the Directors wished me to go there. But I was told that some young men who boarded there, had persuaded Mr. Bets to make this offer, saying that they would make up the difference from their own pockets for the sake of my company. I felt very indignant and Mr. Goodrich knowing that I felt unpleasantly about going, said I might remain if I chose and he would board me as cheap as any one. Mr. G. was such a kind friend to me, but after a short illness, he was called home about the last of June. I was much disappointed in Mrs. G., and did not understand her coldness toward me, after I had been there a short time. Mr. G. was very fond of singing, and often requested me to join him in that exercise Sabbath afternoon in the Parlor. Mrs. G. could not sing, but was always present with us, besides others. But after his death I was surprised to hear that Mrs. G. was very much displeased with me on that account.

From the time of Mr. G.'s death my home was not a pleasant one, for I did not find what I expected in Mrs. G. a friend. She had a girl who reported many very false stories in regard to me, and Mrs. G. upheld her on this course. I always treated this girl perfectly civil, but seldom entered the kitchen, and did not make myself intimate with her, for she was very ignorant and vulgar. This did not please her, and she sometimes remarked in my presence that I was very different from Miss Fortner,[5] for she would come and kiss her every morning before she went to school &c., &c.— Though I gave her no reason she endeavored to injure me all that was in her power, and as she had many relatives in the place did succeed to some extent. Jealous eyes were continually watching me for evil and the tongue of slander was busy against me. I accepted invitations a number of times to ride out Saturday afternoons, but always returned before dark, and did not consider it improper. But when I found that so much talk arose from it, I gave it up, and lived very much retired. I am certain that I never passed the bounds of prudence in my intercourse with the gentlemen and it was a great source of consolation to me that my conscience was clear.

A week before I was taken sick, Mrs. Goodrich left Town and Mr. Shaw one of the Directors took possession, but I still boarded at the same house. The domestic who was my enemy, also remained, and she was a cousin of Mrs. Shaw's. During my sickness Mrs. S. nor the girls scarcely ever entered my room or paid me any sort of attention but would report that I was not sick, but had probably lost interest in my school and wanted a rest. If I had

5. Catharine A. Fortner from W. Dryden, New York, who taught in Tipton the year before Augusta Hubbell's arrival.

desired a vacation, I think I should not have sought it in the confinement of a small room, with a raging fever, during the warm days of September, with bitter medicine for my portion, instead of nourishing food. My physician's wife acted as nurse, and was very very kind to me—Mr. Shaw reported that I had sat up with a gentleman until midnight a number of times. This gentleman had called occasionally but I had never kept his company later than 9 o'clock.

One morning shortly after I found myself able to descend the stairs, two of the directors called to see me. They were Mr. Long and Mr. Hammond. They said that some complaints had been made, and as I was still unable to teach, they thought it best to employ another teacher in my place. I immediately asked the ground of complaint, and was told that all expressed great satisfaction with my school, and say that their scholars had never learned better but that some thought me imprudent. I told them that I thought it quite unjust to discuss a teacher on the ground of mere rumor, and they only sought to justify themselves by saying that they did not act with their own free will but to please some others.

[Side note] A certificate was brought me signed by the first gentleman in the place. I will enclose it to you. [end]

They afterwards denied this, that they dismissed me on that account, but stated various other reasons, but none of them sufficient. The next week, a friend who was a Lawyer called upon me and told me after some inquiry, that I was not legally dismissed, and advised me to enter school again the next day, after notifying the Directors, if, I felt possibly able to do it. I followed that advice, but my strength was not equal to the task and I taught but one day. This effort, together with the excitement and trouble, produced a relapse, and, I was again confined to my bed for a week, and another teacher was in my place. I accepted the invitation (as soon as I was able) of a very fine family to come and board with them until I should recover my health entirely. I was received as a daughter and sister, & began to improve, for they sought to divert my attention from my troubles, and I began to smile again, and feel more like myself. My parents were very anxious on my account when they knew of my sickness among strangers, and now wrote for me to come home as soon as I was able to travel. I reached home three weeks ago, and now my health is quite good.

I united with the Congregationalist Church in Tipton, and received a letter from the same before I left. The three [School] Directors were all Universalists and one of them intemperate, and I have known all of them to be guilty of falsehood. I hope they may be forgiven for the injury they have done me.

During my first quarter, the school numbered eighty different scholars, averaged sixty, but during the sickly season the scarlet fever raged among the children, and when I too was obliged to leave, it numbered only thirty scholars.

I was much disappointed in the character of my school. You know they wished a teacher of the higher English branches, but when I arrived a gentleman was employed to teach the higher Department, and my pupils were all small children. I taught over thirty children the alphabet. I was very sorry at first, and thought I could never endure it, but I soon became very much attached to the dear little ones, and they learned very rapidly. I was much interested in my school, and rejoiced in watching their improvement.

You will excuse me Miss Swift, for writing so lengthy, for I know I will have your sympathies. I received at the rate of $150 per year, and of course it was not enough to pay my heavy doctor Bill, and my expenses home. The Directors made me some trouble, by their long delay, and tried to detain me as long as possible by not settling with me, until the last moment. They did not send me the money due me for teaching until the morning I left Tipton. I had received but a portion of my compensation for my June quarter's work until that time.

Mr. Shaw was collector, and I have reason to believe that he was angry with me because I refused the attentions of his brotherinlaw.

I feel under obligation to the Board and would like to fulfill the same, if I could obtain a situation near home, that is, near in comparison with my former one, for Mother is quite unwilling that I should go so far again.

Should the Committee of selecting Teachers have an opportunity of finding me such a situation and should feel so inclined I should be happy to be informed. If there is anything improper in my communication will Miss Swift please excuse and believe me.

Your grateful friend,

Augusta E. Hubbell

Mary Augusta Roper of Templeton, Massachusetts about Teaching in Mill Point, Michigan

Mill Point Ottowa Co. Mich Oct 18 '52

Committee for selecting Teachers, Hartford, Ct.,

Ladies,

Since leaving Hartford last May, I have been actively engaged in the school of this place, which has been quite large averaging 40 scholars. No time has been left unoccupied, to be filled up with unavailing regrets, that home and friends are so far away, and I had been unconscious that time had flown so rapidly until the arrival of Miss Bell[6] at Grand Haven reminded me

6. Lucy P. Bell from Malone, New York, taught in Grand Haven from September 1852, to September 1854, when she expected to return home for a visit. Nancy Swift's assistant, Amanda Ferry, was the daughter of the Reverend William Montague Ferry, a missionary in Grand Haven who took an interest in Lucy Bell's school.

that another class had been collected and scattered over the broad west, and I had not written one word to you.

Lest the circumstances in which I have been placed excuse the delay, I have waited on one account to see the end of a difference of parties which would not be decided until the annual school meeting, which took place a few days since, but for you to understand the position in which I have been placed I must describe the place and people.

Mill Point is a village separated from Grand Haven entirely by water, containing about 400 inhabitants. A collection of foreigners mostly, who are employed in the steam mills which give the place its name. There are only four families in the place of intelligence. A few other families possess influence but are bad men. A few men in the place wished for a teacher from Gov. Slade's class to supply the place of Miss E. Chandler[7] (a lady sent out several years ago and who had taught in this place a year) who was going to leave on account of her health wishing a smaller school. The other party said "they had had a pious teacher long enough" and wished for a Universalist in principle. Mr. Smith was appointed school Director, and he with the advise of 2 other of the officers applied for a teacher, and I was sent here. At the same time a lady, destitute of religious principle was hired to teach the children of the dissatisfied ones. No effort was left untried to injure my school. I fortunately succeeded in gaining the affection and confidence of my scholars, so that all avenues to that were closed up.

Completely foiled in their attempts to break up the school in this, they resorted to another expedient which has alike failed. They cautiously circulated suspicions of my good character, and growing bold, finally asserted with barefaced boldness the most indecent stories. At first no attention was paid to it by my friends, but they finally met the Authors of the slander, and before they left them, received the acknowledgement that a miserable fellow—a personal enemy of Mr. Smith made such by Mr. S. on one occasion reproving him for profanity had been induced to commence the slander, to gratify his hatred of Mr. Smith. It caused a great excitement at the time, but did not interrupt my school, although I suffered severely at the time.

At the last school meeting a great effort was made to take from Mr. Smith the office of Director, had it been accomplished, I should not have continued the school but the cause of right and virtue triumphed, they failed to elect an officer consequently, my employers are still at the head of affairs. They assure me of their unbounded confidence and respect and will not hear on any account of my leaving unless it is so unpleasant that I should *greatly* prefer a location elsewhere. I am firmly attached to my scholars, and I think I can say that they are to me. Attempts have been made repeatedly upon members of

7. E. E. Chandler was sent out by the board in the fall of 1848.

my school, to induce them to find fault with school, and leave it for the other, but never have they in but one instance succeeded, and that was the case of two Dutch [German] boys of passionate tempers, who combined in their character the worst traits I ever met in children, their absence was an advantage rather than a loss to the school.

I open my school with prayer and I never have seen any disposition to levity during devotions. We have a large Sabbath School, with only three teachers, we have hitherto felt the want of books, but a large library is on its way hither from my native place, a donation from the church of which I am a member.

We have had no regular preaching but are now making an effort to raise money for the support of a minister, and I think shall succeed. The same opposition has been made to that movement as to all others of such a nature, but it has succeeded beyond our expectations. I think that eventually the cause of religion will triumph but there is a great amount of irreligion, skepticism if not infidelity now.

Miss Bell arrived safely and has commenced her school under favorable circumstances, but she has to fill the place of one of the most successful teachers the state affords, viz. Miss Mary White, her scholars were singularly attached to her always speaking of her with all the tenderness of a mother.[8]

Mill Point and Grand Haven are favored with the most beautiful natural scenery, the views from Lake Michigan's shores are very fine, sand hills of the purest white sand lying as steep as it is possible for sand to lie and in some instances covered with wild roses to the waters edge. Our sunsets on the Lake are magnificent in the extreme, and now in midsummer when the forests are robed in their varied hues the effect is fine.

Lake Michigan announces the approach of winter by his deep wild roar and it is a beautiful scene to see his snow crested breakers, dashing in fury and dying upon the shores.

I have heard from no member of the class of last spring, a wide correspondence of my own has prevented my writing to them and I have received no letters.

I shall ever retain the most grateful recollections of the kindness experienced at Hartford. I have found the facts learned by visiting schools there most important, enabling me to have a standard of school discipline in my own mind which if never reached, is a constant incentive to active exertion.

8. Mary A. White was the sister of Amanda White Ferry, wife of the Reverend Ferry, who lived with the Ferrys in Grand Haven. Hannah White, one of the superintendents of the National Board's institute, was also their sister.

With an humble wish that your society may receive Heaven's blessing I will close.

Respectfully yours,

Mary Augusta Roper

Mill Point, Ottawa Co. Michigan
June 10, 1853

Miss Swift,
  Dear Madam,

I received your kind letter of Dec., last, but words cannot express the support and consolation it afforded me in those hours of trial, and I now find myself surrounded by circumstances calling once more for your advice.

You expressed a wish that I might continue my school here for two years. I have found it impossible to do so. As the first year was drawing to a close, the time for which I was engaged at first because Mr. Smith was Director only for that time, the opposition had been so violent to every measure he had taken, he decided to make no farther effort, to hire a Teacher. This is founded, as I think I have written you before, on his decided opposition to the almost frightful immorality existing here.

My school before its close had become reduced in number to less than one half, its first size, still numbering the scholars of the most intelligent unprejudiced portion of the people, even those who joined in railing Mr. Smith would send their oldest daughters to me, and the smaller ones away. And as far as I know all the fault that has been found with me has been "that my scholars loved me" too much.

An old Irish woman whose dirty little ones cried to come back says, "Oh! she's no Teacher, she don't *lick* them at all, she ought'er at' em with the broomstick."

Perhaps it may be well to give a short account of my manner of conducting the school. I never used the rod unless when a scholar refused to obey me and I believe I can recall but three instances of the kind. A record was kept of the Attendance, Deportment, and Recitations of each scholar, the last numbering three grades Perfect, Good & Bad lessons so that each Scholar & Parent, if they chose, knew the true standing of all. The highest number received the prize.

At the close of the last term, I received a present of $30 from the people, and the satisfaction expressed by all whose opinion I valued. Mrs. Smith assured me she had never sent the children to a Teacher where she had been so gratified with their improvement.

I did not write you directly because I knew it would be your wish for me to engage again and I had received repeated intimation that I could engage in the Union School at Grand Rapids from my kind friends Dr. Shepards family of that place whose elegant home has been my own from the first. Several circumstances have prevented. The Principal has been succeeded by a gentleman from the east, bringing two assistants with him so that all Vacancies are filled, and at the close of the last term I felt completely worn out in mind and body and knew that I must have rest. The ague has taken away my strength so entirely that my friends tell me that it would not be possible for me to teach as the least fatigue brings it on. Under these circumstances it is my earnest wish to return home and regain my health and spirits in the peaceful quiet of home, its shade. But I await your advice.

I know my experience the past year has in a measure disheartened me but I feel that through its heavy trials an all sustaining arm has held me up. A victim of misrepresentation from the first and the basest calumny, it created a sensitiveness about entering society I never felt before, and I have remained with those few who knew me aright and scarcely know any others. I have tried indeed to live near to God and have ever realized the promise "ye shall not seek me in vain."

Miss Bell I do not meet often but always hear that she is happy. I saw Miss Chandler before she returned East, she said she had always regretted advising Mr. Smith to send for another Teacher, but she had no idea of the opposition she would meet with.

I thank little Helen for her affectionate remembrance,[9] and wish to be remembered to her. I cannot close without an apology for my letter, it has been written while a chill has been on me.

Respectfully Yours,

Mary A. Roper

[Side note] If it is convenient I would like to receive an answer soon.

Templeton [Mass.] July 22/54

Miss N. Swift,

Just one year has passed away since my arrival in my mountain home and I once more address you asking a word of advice in regard to my future.

---

9. Nancy Swift was the guardian of her niece Helen, who was orphaned at the age of six and present at the institute at Hartford. Many teachers sent affectionate greetings to her.

You will remember, perhaps, some of the circumstances of my return from Mill Point, my location in the spring of 1852. I shall never forget the depression of spirit I was suffering when I penned that last letter to you asking if it was not best for me to return—nor the salutary lesson of that years experience in which I learned that a life of nineteen years in New England had not fitted me for a position in which the "Wisdom of a serpent and the harmlessness of a dove" were certainly needed.

But my health is now reestablished and my desire to be active somewhere brings home the question, where I can best labor? In the stillness the quiet of my home I have reviewed that eventful year—brought home its trials; its stern teachings to my soul and strove to learn their source—their aim. With an humbled heart I have seen my shortcomings—been comforted with the pure motives with which I labored and realized with heartfelt joy the fullness of the promise "My grace is sufficient for thee." In view of it I can feel to shrink from no mental or physical suffering where Christ, duty, point the way in my future and if my trials are peculiar to a location or be the result of evil in my heart, may He but give me grace to endure them until their end is accomplished.

When the Circular for August appeared, I decided to ask your advice in regard to my return to the West considering the state of my health while there and all other circumstances. I have a friend in Petersburg O[hi]o— A teacher in the Collegiate Female Seminary of that place who will gladly find me a position in that place or state if I choose.

If it is convenient I should like an answer soon. My humble attainments you know— They are advanced only by *experience* and by an attention to instrumental music for a few months,

Respectfully yours,

Love to Helen.   Mary Augusta Roper

Mary L. Chase of Otego, New York,
Writing from Savanna, Illinois

Savanna, [Ill.] Aug. 27, 1853.

Dear Miss Swift

You charged us not to let the last month of Summer close. I find you unadvised in regard to our well being & well, or evil doing; though of the latter I presume you do not care to hear. The occasional "scar leaf" that flutters past on the chill breeze reminds me that the death hour of another year's loveliest season is near at hand, & if I would comply with your request it must be quickly done.

Were it not for this perhaps I should still postpone for months, & yet 'tis better to write now for you have a right to know all, & I want your advice, which I know you will kindly give.

On my arrival at Savanna I found but one schoolhouse & that occupied by a gentleman whose term was to continue six weeks. A school meeting was soon called to decide how to dispose of me & a vote was taken to request me to wait until the present Term expired & then take the public school. As this seemed to be the wish of the people & Mr. Emerson thought I could better gain the confidence & a better influence over the people, I consented to wait, meantime sewing for Mrs. Bowen with whom I board.

I entered the public school & taught four weeks with seventy young minds looking up to me for the bread of life as well as of knowledge. At the close of the fourth week a note was handed me from one of the Directors stating that there was some dissatisfaction respecting my method of conducting the school & the Directors therefore wished me to relinquish it. I immediately replied asking wherein I had offended, as I was willing to leave the school if I had not conducted it satisfactorily, but to this I have received no reply nor do I yet know what was my offence.

Mr. and Mrs. Bowen have been as a brother & sister to me; so much so that I often feel that I am not worthy of the confidence & regard they manifest in & for me. Mr. B. immediately after my dismissal procured the Methodist church as a schoolroom for me & the next week I opened a select school with thirty pupils; in this I have been engaged five weeks.

I asked Mr. Bowen in what I had displeased the people: he says, in nothing, nor have I lost their confidence. He says the matter lies thus: the present Directors were not in office nor were they at the school meeting when a vote was taken to apply for a teacher, nor were they specially consulted in regard to the matter—that they coming into power about the time of my arrival, felt that there was a good opportunity of exercising their "brief authority" & avenging themselves upon those who had presumed to apply for a teacher without asking their consent. Whether this is so I know not: it may be that there was some complaint but I tried to be faithful & do all I could: especially by word & act to lead my pupils' young hearts to our Father & Savior.

The people intend to build a new school house this coming Fall & sustain two schools during the winter; but as the term of office of the present Directors does not expire until October I doubt whether this will be accomplished, however I presume if I remain here through the winter I should be sustained in a Select school. Miss Swift, perhaps you would ask me how I kept my heart & lips during those petty trials. I felt it to be a punishment for my wayward acts & sinful unbelief of other days & I tried to look above the human instruments & receive the chastening from my Father's hand & I was kept, but not by my own strength, from succumming.

Dear Miss Swift have patience with me a few minutes & I will try to be brief; you know my scruples about coming here: you for a time allayed them but after

I left you they sprung up with double power & for weeks I was wretched in the extreme. At Albany—at Buffalo I longed to throw myself at Gov. Slade's feet to tell him all & beg him to let me go home, but feeling as I did, that it was ordered thus as a punishment for my past sins, I feared it would be still a greater sin to abandon the cause to which I had offered myself & so I came on. I have most deeply regretted that I did not go home from Hadley [Mount Holyoke Seminary] instead of offering myself to the Board, but regrets avail nothing, & I hope I am nearly done wasting time, strength & tears in idly bemoaning the past. I know & acknowledge that I deeply sinned a year ago in refusing to come to this western field at the bidding of Providence, but I hope my many sins are all forgiven: & I hope I may be the more earnest laborer for the sad & dark experiences of the past year.

Miss Swift you will partly realize how near despair I was, when I tell you that for long weeks my most earnest wish & the one most constantly present, was that Mr. S[mith] would discard and forget me. I wrote & told him so;—but so far from this he freely forgives all & urges an early union.

He says he cannot labor efficiently alone & begs me to lay aside my morbid sensitiveness in regard to the world's opinion & join him at the close of my present term. Now Miss Swift what shall I do? Will it be a betrayal of the trust your Board have reposed in me, if I comply with his wishes? I would rather stay here till Spring at least for I feel that I am but just beginning to work & there is very much to do: I know too that I am very unfit for a minister's wife & though Mr. Smith is my dearest earthly friend I would cheerfully give him up to one better fitted to make him happy, but Miss Swift I have suffered too much to dare again to refuse to enter the field for I am now convinced that God has bidden me go. If I leave here I shall not lay aside the teacher's office, but I should not probably have as many pupils, perhaps only a class of ten or fifteen.

Pardon me for consuming so much of your time & please reply very soon if only in few words.

Truly Yours,

Mary Chase

[on side of front] Don't think, Miss Swift, that in my bitter wretchedness I blamed you; I felt that God had ordered all & I blamed no one but myself. I have felt that you did wrong in overruling my scruples, but not purposely & I have not felt to blame you.

Yours M.L.C.

[side note] I will write to Gov. Slade but if he does not receive it you may if you think best give him this.

[front note] She rec'd while *here* a letter from an old friend asking her to join him in his work. She thought if she consented to entertain the idea, she must leave the class. I did not think so, but persuaded her to go & teach as long as she could. She shrinks from hearing it said that she married before the 2 years were out.

N[ancy] S[wift]

9

Professional Teachers on Their Own

Cynthia M. Bishop and Martha M. Rogers

Cynthia Bishop and Martha Rogers represent the women who already saw themselves as professional teachers, who possessed a strong sense of mission, and who exhibited a high degree of independence. Both were in their late twenties when they went West, and had been self-supporting for a number of years.

Cynthia Bishop left her home in Georgia, Vermont, when she was about twenty-two to work in the Lowell mills so she could earn money to pay for more education. She alternated working in the mills with going to school and some teaching. Her mother died when she was nine and some of her family had already gone to Ohio and Indiana.[1] Anxious to grow in her profession, Bishop was conscientious about applying the teaching methods she learned at Hartford. She also experimented with such techniques as a post-office box for students' questions, and won a prize for an essay on the construction of schoolhouses at a teachers' institute in South Bend, Indiana.[2]

Her letters are particularly significant because they deal with her personal and somewhat public conflict over the use of the Bible and prayers in the schools. As long as she taught in a select school in New Durham, Indiana, she met no opposition to her use of the Bible and prayers in the classroom. But when she decided to teach in the first public schools in Lafayette, Indiana, she found herself confronted with a dilemma. The superintendent and school board, hoping to attract Catholic children, opposed bringing the Bible into the new schools. Bishop insisted on making her own decision, saying, "I was determined never to *ask permission of man* to read the word of God." Instead of asking her superintendent for advice, she decided to explain her solution to him. Her resolution of the problem—to use precepts from the Bible without bringing the Bible itself into the school—is an example of the willingness of the pioneer teacher to adapt to new conditions in the West.

---

1. Cynthia M. Bishop, 1 April 1853, biography folder, NPEB Papers; U.S. Manuscript Census, 1850, Middlesex County, MA, p. 336. Bishop gives her birth date as 17 November 1826.

2. Maria L. Barrett, South Bend, Indiana, to Nancy Swift, 14 January 1854, letters folder, NPEB Papers.

Martha Rogers came from Champlain, New York, on the border of Quebec where her father, a farmer, had remarried and had a large new family. Little is known about her background except that she had taught "more or less for eight to ten years" when she applied to the National Popular Education Board. She could speak French and had taught among French-speaking people. She was a member of the Presbyterian Church in Champlain. Her letters cover the period when she was between twenty-eight and thirty-two years old.[3]

Her wry comments on Cassville, Missouri, a county seat and political center in a slave state, offer the reader a view of conflict in a frontier town that approaches the stereotype. Her spirit unwittingly fired up a political rally and she described a knifing on the public square with all the detail of a Western novel. Possessing a restless temperament, Martha Rogers taught in three places in the Ozarks during the period her letters cover. In each case, she used active teaching methods and held successful public examinations. She comments on the religious revival held in her area and was particularly gratified that one of her young women students was converted at the camp meeting.

Both Cynthia Bishop and Martha Rogers were dedicated to temperance. When a student used Bishop's school post-office box to ask why men got drunk, she used the question as a springboard for lessons on the dangers of alcohol. She attributed the poverty of a family in her school to the father's drinking. Martha Rogers laid the blame for a murder of a prominent lawyer in Cassville on drinking and also saw it as a major social problem.

The later life of neither Cynthia Bishop nor Martha Rogers is known, but it is easy to imagine them teaching for a long time in the West, probably moving frequently. Cynthia Bishop is listed as a teacher in Lafayette from 1853 to 1855. When the Indiana school law was declared unconstitutional in 1854, the city of Lafayette was forced to close the public schools and rent them to teachers who conducted them as private schools until they reopened as free schools in 1856. It is probable that Cynthia Bishop left Lafayette during the controversy, but both her family's location and her adaptiveness point to a future in the West. She resigned from the Lowell Baptist Church in January of 1855.[4]

Martha Rogers returned home for a visit and traveled back to Missouri with the class that left Hartford in the spring of 1853. She used her sister

3. Martha M. Rogers, Champlain, New York, 10 November 1849, applications folder, NPEB Papers; U.S. Manuscript Census, 1850, Clinton County, NY, p. 484; letter from Carlton C. Wu, pastor, First Presbyterian Church, Rouses Point, NY, 8 December 1981.

4. General R. P. De Hart, *Past and Present of Tippecanoe County, Indiana* (1909), vol. 1, p. 499; *Biographical Record and Portrait Album of Tippecanoe County* (1888), pp. 304–05, supplied by Sarah E. Cooke of the Tippecanoe County Historical Association, Lafayette, IN; note from First Baptist Church, Lowell, MA, December 1981.

teachers from the board as a support network by keeping up a wide correspondence with them, giving us the opportunity to follow the experiences of some other pioneer teachers. In the excitement of events in Cassville she wrote in a stream-of-consciousness style, omitting periods and paragraphs. It has been necessary to bring sentences and paragraphs to a close and to eliminate repetitious sections in order not to obscure her narrative. Her two letters from Cassville and the last two of her letters from Erie are included here. The events described in her three letters from Colonel Love's School in Wright County and her first letter from Erie are summarized. Some detail and repetitions have also been eliminated from Cynthia Bishop's letters.

Cynthia M. Bishop from Georgia, Vermont, and Lowell, Massachusetts, to New Durham and Lafayette, Indiana

New Durham, Laporte Co., Ind., July 23, 1853

My dear Miss Swift,

Considering the very kind interest you have taken in my welfare and usefulness I fear I have done wrong in not writing sooner; but trust you will excuse me.

I arrived at this place, Thurs., May 5th & was met by Miss Flynt, with whom I spent one week.[5] During this time I had the offer of two schools, one of which I could not refuse if I had tried. They were so importunate in their application. They had heard accidentally last fall from Miss Flynt that she expected a teacher friend from the East, & ever since had watched for my advent. I was amused by their confidence that they would have a good school if they obtained my services, though it made me fear lest I should, in the result, lower their estimate of eastern teachers. The principal actor in engaging me was the Hon. C. H. Cathcart, late a member of Congress. I board at his house which with its furniture & arrangements is that of a plain, respectable farmer. He sends four children to me—the oldest a girl of 15. I have two other girls of a similar age & the rest of my pupils are of all ages from five to thirteen.

I find them rather backwards on account of seldom or never having a well qualified teacher. It is only seven years since the first school was taught in the district & they have been taught only part of each year.

---

5. Elizabeth E. Flynt was from Tewksbury, Massachusetts, and went out to teach in New Durham in the spring of 1850, where she started the first school. She later joined Bishop in teaching in the first public schools in Lafayette.

I hope you will pardon my saying I was amused, but I really suppose I am the best qualified teacher they have had & I believe not a word of fault is found with me, at least I hear of none.

I do not know *how* to write about the school at present, so that you can, as it were, see it, but I shall have to put down my thoughts as they occur to me.

I open the school in the morning suggested by yourself, though I have practiced nearly the same before. I stated to Mr. Cathcart & Mr. Flood, the trustee, when they came after me, that I would use some religious means in school, & stated, briefly, my own sentiments. This I did with perfect frankness, & before I knew anything of the sentiments of these gentlemen, I found them perfectly willing I should do as I pleased, though it seems that neither of them usually attend public worship. I was glad when I found this to be the case, that I gave them my views at first.

None of the Cathcart family are professors, & I believe none of Mr. Flood's. There are several professors in the district, however, all of whom belong to the Methodists. Many of the children attend a Sabbath School, some three miles distant, & in order to give some Spiritual instruction to those who cannot go, I proposed to meet all who chose to come at six o'clock p.m. on each Sabbath, & I spend an hour in appropriate exercises. . . .

I believe you wished to hear about our daily labors in the school. Before commencing it, I called on every family accompanied by Mrs. Cathcart, & the people seemed pleased with the proceeding. I think the influence of it good.

I have not adopted your plan for the exercise *fully*, but I have a particular time for every class & in *much* the same order as you proposed. I have the children read first after prayers, & then hear two classes in Arithmetic before recess. After recess the little ones read again, & then the two largest classes, & then a half hour for writing closes the forenoon session.

I have an hour & a half intermission, then the little ones read, classes in Peter Parley's & Mitchell's Geography[6] recite, the older scholars spell, & we have a few minutes to devote to miscellaneous exercises, which have excited so much interest that they have been willing to *shorten* the recess as a means of *prolonging* them. This I do not do, except occasionally.

After recess little ones again, then Grammar, which my three largest girls study, then I give some assistance in Arithmetic, hear Tables & sing to close. One of the most important events which take place in school (i.e. in the estimation of the pupils) is the opening of our Post Office—a box in which

---

6. Peter Parley's tales and readers ranged from primers to story tours of the world. In his tales about Asia, he devotes several chapters to missionary Sarah Judson, who died in Burma. Peter Parly was the pen name of Samuel G. Goodrich. *DAB*, vol. 4, pp. 402–03; *The Tales of Peter Parley about Asia* (Philadelphia, 1836).

they drop written questions on any subject which interests their minds. The questions are various, & sometimes require preparation in order to answer them. They have sponge to wipe their slates with—& the question is deposited "where does it come from," &c. We are about to have a new schoolhouse built, & they ask (& I cannot tell them, though I *guess* the Puritans, at Plymouth) "who built the *first schoolhouse* in the New World?" And the last time I opened it, I found the query, "what do men get drunk for?" I told them I would talk about it sometime— I hardly knew what to say, lest I should not make as strong an impression as I wished in favor of temperance, so I have borrowed Miss Flynt's drawings of the drunkard's stomach, & shall show & speak about them next Monday.

What can I do to help this cause? Would that I knew, for the father of one of my large girls, who *has* pretended (it must have been pretence) to preach the gospel, sometimes loses the dignity of *man*, by the use of alcohol. If I could receive any light upon my duty to an interesting family in their circumstances, I should be glad. The man received five thousand dollars, it is said, with his wife, some eighteen years since, & with the advantages then offered here, might have been worth ten times that amount or more, yet they are now so poor that people wonder how they manage to appear respectably. It is thought that they could not if none but honest means were ever used. I say this trusting that it is not too much to *whisper* to you if I could, & ask you how I could save the children,—a son of fourteen, who will enter my school bye & bye, if I stay,—from dishonestly getting what is not his own—for it is said he will pilfer orchards—& perhaps other places—& it is believed is secretly *allowed* in it. The oldest girl is an interesting one. I want to see her qualified to teach, but I have some misgivings about the family. I have written freely, but it is to Miss Swift, so I know all will be as it should be.

Mr. Cathcart has sent & bought a ten dollar set of maps for the use of his children & the school; they are beautiful & the pupils are much pleased. The scholars noticed that the *largest* countries on each map were colored *yellow* & the query *why* was put in the P.O.

I think I have improved as a teacher in consequence of the instruction received at Hartford. I feel the need of more of the same high order, when, as I often do, I find it difficult to make my large girls *love* Grammar. They were put into it by unskillful teachers at nine and eleven years of age, & have *learned* it by rote enough to disgust them, & that is all the *good*, but not all the *evil* it has done. I think we are gaining slowly. . . .[7] I have governed the school without using the rod thus far, though I sometimes think it would do one or two rogues good, who *forget* quite too often what they admit to be *right*.

I do not know whether I had better remain here some time, or go into a larger school. I have only twenty scholars, but shall have more soon. I engaged

---

7. The paper on which the last part of this sentence appears seems to be wormeaten.

only for one term, but I believe they are intending to keep me as long as they can. They are able to pay me well, & I do not know as I shall be exacting, if I stay, in asking the $150 per year. I suppose I should have had that if you had given me a location. I like the country, & enjoy good health, though my eyes have been sore, & are quite weak now. It is almost mail time & my only chance to send this for three days.

Yours affectionately,

Miss Nancy Swift   Cynthia M. Bishop

Lafayette, Ind., May 16, 1854

My dear Miss Swift,

In much haste I snatch a moment to write you. I want a word of advice, & wish I had written a day or two sooner.—

The long-looked-for day for the opening of the public schools in this city is now near at hand; probably will be two weeks from yesterday, May 29. Myself & Miss Flynt are expecting to teach in the grammar schools.— We, as you know are Baptists, two or three others of the ten lady teachers engaged are Congregationalists or Presbyterians, & two more are members of the Methodist church. How many of these are impressed with a sense of obligation in regard to religious influences in school, I cannot say.— Other teachers are Universalist or—*nothingarian* perhaps; our Superintendent is a Pennsylvanian—was brought up a Quaker, his wife still says "thee & thou" & I have no evidence that he will *desire* even if he tolerates the use of the Bible & prayer in the schools. He *may* not oppose—the directors would not, probably, but the impression seems to be that in order not to exclude the Catholic children from the schools, it will be considered *not best to use the Bible at all there.* You know, my dear Miss S., that it must be a hard question for me to decide how I ought to act under these circumstances, especially as I am to conduct a grammar school in a quarter of the city where Catholics are most plenty. I think that if the superintendent & directors were all pious and prudent men, who felt the need of Christian influence in this city, that we could carry out our wishes without any serious trouble with either parents or children. But they (the directors) seem to fear to stand firm, &, as near as I can learn, the superintendent cares nothing about it.

I did not waver in my design to read the Bible at the opening of school until a day or two since, when I talked with one of the teachers, a Presbyterian, & one of the very *best* of the teachers elect, & she said she thought we could accomplish more good by giving way in *appearance*—not reading the Bible, &c., so as not to frighten the numerous foreign children away—but we could give oral & apparently accidental religious instruction in such times & ways as to excite no tempest.— If she, who is a resident of this city & a very pious, well-educated lady, thinks so, do you wonder I hesitate as to my duty?— Some say to me, Ask the superintendent if he will approve it, but if it is duty I dislike to ask *permission* of man—Another, the wife of a returned missionary tells me to open my school as I wish, making no allusion to the fact that I am *aware* of any difference of opinion in others, & as though considered it a matter of course.

Now, if I know my own heart at all, I wish to do what God would have me in this matter, that which, in the end, will result in the greatest good.—If you were within a short distance, so that I could visit you, it would be a *comfort* to go to your feet & sit down to be instructed.

If this letter reaches you in the time it ought, will you not sit down & answer it briefly, so that I may know your mind before Sun. May 28; & please write some suggestions how I had better *vary* or *carry out* my forms of proceeding, if I should have *commenced* before I receive it, either *with* or without my customary religious exercises, I *hope* I may get it *before* the schools *begin*.

The opening session will be very short, perhaps seven or eight weeks, & in Sept. the school year will commence.

We are in tolerable health of body, but do not, especially myself, enjoy that spiritual health so desirable in our station.

We have got to meet the superintendent within an hour, & spend most of the day in school exercises which is my reason for writing so hastily. I *must* put it in the next mail.

I will write again more deliberately soon so that the Committee can know how we are situated.

If you cannot consistently answer this—so be it, but offer one prayer that I may not make false steps. I will try to do my duty as far as I know it.

I shall teach the scholars the golden rule & many *other Bible precepts, whether I tell them* where I found *them or not. This I can* do at all events.

Yours with affectionate respect,

Miss N. Swift   Cynthia M. Bishop

Lafayette, Ind., Aug. 21, '54

Dear Miss Swift & Ladies of the Committee,

I will now, after some delay, report myself to you, but as I am spending my vacation at the sick & probably dying bed of an esteemed Christian friend, a clergyman, you will excuse the hasty & informal manner in which I write. Miss Swift will pardon my repetition in this letter, of what I may have communicated to her in a private note.

I came to this city last fall to take charge of a select school for girls, which had been established two or three years, intending if it pleased me & seemed best, to continue it. It was to remain during the winter term under the nominal control of its founder, & I was encouraged to think he would make some effort to assist me in finding rooms for it to occupy after that time, or such assistance as he might be able to render; but I found that it was of little use to look for aid from that quarter, & my compensation being very small, with much difficulty in governing, (which I find has ever attended private schools in this place), I at once concluded to enter the public schools where I could *depend* upon being supported in having order, &c. The Trustees told me the school houses which they were building would be finished in May, so I thought I would wait six or eight weeks for them. But the builders were so negligent my "tarrying time" was prolonged until June 27th, when the graded schools, the first of the kind in this city of 9,000 inhabitants, were opened, creating quite a pleasant interest among some of the citizens. The schoolrooms are ten in number, in three buildings, & into them are crowded from seventy to one hundred and four seats apiece. The houses are of brick & well built, but the rooms are not large enough for the seats put into them by one fifth.

The schools were suspended at the end of four weeks on account of very hot weather & the alarming prevalence of sickness, some cases of cholera, &c. We expect to open the fall session Sept. 4th. So you see I have had only one month's regular employment in five. If I had known that the houses would be so long in preparing I would have tried to find a *place* for a school to occupy, & taught. *Scholars* enough were ready for me, but a place a *decent* school-room was almost impossible to be found, therefore I hope I shall not be considered censurable.— I love the Society whose agents you are, & would fain help on its objects, & carry out its designs in my little sphere.

The schools are classed as primary, intermediate & grammar departments; one of the latter is under my charge. I had about forty pupils enter during the short session, but expect seventy five this fall, of ages ranging from ten to twenty, male & female, many of whom have never had a *good* school to attend before. *Do pray* that I may have grace & wisdom equal to this arduous responsibility. Is it not a great work to *begin* a *systematic* course in such a school? How *can* I succeed? The superintendent is not a religious man, & though he inculcates *good morals,* does not *wish* to have us use the Bible in school. He seems to fear that sectarian prejudices, of the Catholics princi- pally, may be aroused & the Trustees are about of the same opinion. A part of the latter are men who "care for none of these things" either way, & two of them are evangelical professors, but are so *timid* or something else that they fall in with the rest.— I was determined never to *ask permission of man* to read the word of *God,* so I spoke to the Supt. (Mr. Naylor from Penn.) just before the schools opened, & told him my views of duty & asked him if *it was his*

intention to use any means to prevent the *teachers from acting their own judgement &*
pleasure in this matter, saying that I inquired for the sake of knowing what to
depend upon; that my course had been & would be the same, in substance,
wherever I went; & that if the performance of what I deemed a sacred duty
was to be the means of trouble with those who employed me, I wished to
know it *then,* as there was other situations to be had & I must go where I
could act freely in the matter. I addressed him with perfect good nature, but
with decision, in presence of another teacher & he replied, "Miss Bishop I do
not wish you to leave, you may do as you think you ought to, *I* will make
you no trouble."

But in my school are *some* Catholics, & there are *many* in the neighborhood
who would attend if the priest would let them alone; so in view of all
circumstances, instead of taking the Bible directly into school, I wrote off
selections on the natural & moral attributes of God & our most prominent
social duties as well as the great duty to love & worship Diety, & read them,
offering a short extemporaneous prayer. I get the pupils to sing a verse or two
when I can, but they are backward in this as in every thing, & being an
inefficient singer myself, I find it hard to get along. Yet I am determined to
persevere & we shall soon do better. . . .

Last winter I did not feel that I had so good an opportunity to *do* as I now
have. I have not received a saucy word from my pupils in the public school
yet, not has any one *persisted* in disobeying. They have never been accustomed
to strict *order* & I did not "draw the reins" *very* tight as the weather was so
warm & they were not used to confinement, but we *hope* to improve this fall
so much that we should not be ashamed to have you visit us any day. I can
truly say that I never loved any school as I do this at present & I think most
of the pupils are well pleased with me. I have never spoken a cross word in
my new school room & hope & pray that I never may, yet I expect to be a
tolerable disciplinarian. "Who is sufficient for these things?" May I feel that
you all pray for me? If I fail it will do more than to injure *me.* My pupils will
suffer & many others.

I do not, cannot say that I enjoy religion personally—I have no pastor this
summer to counsel or encourage me in the little trials & vexations which
have continually beset me; it has been difficult to find comfortable rooms or
accommodations for myself, most of the time, without paying an extrava-
gant price; I have been dealt rather unfairly with & cut short for means; &
have given way to hard & repining feelings. But our church expect a pastor
soon, & if things brighten up I shall probably try to make myself contented
here, if the school prospers. I must say that I have been lonely & homesick
owing to the above circumstances, but hope is now in the ascendant. I think
if I were situated in a smaller place—a small village perhaps—that I should
enjoy *society* better than in a city of the peculiar character which this
possesses.

The Ladies of the Committee may be pleased with a word of explanation in relation to the last remark, therefore I will tell how the place appears to me. *Backward in intelligence,* as may be seen by the fact of its reaching the present size before building a public school house or supporting schools; *nothing to boast* of in *refinement—money,* which is the great object of pursuit, seeming to be the main passport into the "first circles," in which many persons move who are any thing but well-educated; & the continual coming & going of strangers rendering the newcomer an object of *cold criticism* to stated residents here, rather than of friendly interest. I do *not* love the *place,* but as I do love my *school,* I think I may become better pleased after a time.

My salary is $300 per annum, which I think *too low,* while board is higher here than in Chicago or Cincinnati, but I shall not accept so small a remuneration for so hard a place next year. The people, no doubt, really think it good wages.

I should be very happy to receive suggestions from any of the Committee, or of other intelligent Christians respecting my past or future course in relation to the *use* of *the Bible* & religious influence in school. If *truth* prevails I am content.

Yours affectionately,

Cynthia M. Bishop

Dear Miss Swift,

A word more to you. Miss Flynt remained here waiting until June 20th when the hot weather brought on some of her difficulties afresh, & she left for Glen Haven Water Cure[8] in N.Y. Dr. Jackson examined & prescribed for her & then she proceeded to her home in Maine for "home treatment." This is successful, as she soon began to "gain rapidly," as she expressed it some four weeks since. I have no later news from her, but expect it every day, & rather expect her back in two weeks to enter the schools. But she is to teach in the school which the Supt. mostly directs, &, of course, will not be allowed to use the Bible. She has had to govern *alone* so long that she wants to avoid the responsibility, partially on account of her health. Miss Maynard is about to leave for Mississippi.[9] She taught with the Supt. the four week session but does not like to remain, though all persons interested were well pleased with her as a teacher.

My health remains good, not a sick day in Indiana, i.e., not to be "laid

---

8. For a description of the water cures so popular with women in the nineteenth century, see Sklar, *Catharine Beecher,* pp. 206–09.

9. Laura Maynard taught in New Durham between 1853 and 1854. A native of Potsdam, New York who attended Mount Holyoke, Maynard went West with the spring class of 1852 to Bellemonte, St. Louis County, Missouri. She married Franklin Flint in 1859 and died in Denmark, Iowa, in 1908.

up." Rather gaining in flesh. Love to dear Miss Ferry & any other friends. Excuse haste as I am needed at the sick bed very often & must do some of my writing *piecemeal*.

Yours with much love

C. M. Bishop

Martha M. Rogers from Champlain, New York, to Cassville, Waldo, and Erie, Missouri

Cassville Barry Co. Mo. July 5th -50

Dear Miss Swift

Considering the length of time that letters occupy in going from here & also the change in my location, I have concluded to write. It may perhaps be too soon to tell definitely as to my *continuance* here—but not too soon to tell the past & present. . . .

At Buffalo we parted with our northern division the last day of Apr. amid tears, good byes & such things. Gov. Slade took thirteen of us to the boat about seven at night after having paid our fare to Cin[cinnati] & given us our allowance for the remainder of our route as he was to leave us that night & go on to Chicago with the others. And after much kind affectionate advice, not forgetting his voluminous motto "Modest pretentions & Great works," left us alone, as Mr. Maltby had taken boat the night before with Misses Plimpton & Washburn for Cleavland & would join us next day.[10]

The lake [Erie] was so rough that we did not stir till morning. It was still rough & short seas & the consequence was that every body were sick & all our company excepting Miss Ladd some more, some less. Misses Kilgore, Brooks, Taylor & myself were among the worst.[11] So we lay all day groaning. It was a clear bright *May Day*, but not very 'joyous' to us. Miss Kilgore laugh & cry by turns to say if she "had only know this she never would have been caught on that *dreadful* lake." Miss Brooks, & Miss Taylor—"O, if they

10. The Reverend Benjamin K. Maltby of Cleveland was an NPEB agent who escorted teachers across Ohio. Charlotte Plimpton of Hopkinton, Massachusetts, went to teach in a girls' school in western Pennsylvania and Mary Washburn from Burlington, Vermont, was going to teach in Henrietta, Ohio. *Third NPEB Report, 1850,* p. 17.

11. Abby D. Killgore of Topsham, Maine, was headed for Mooresville, Indiana, where she became the second wife of James S. Kelley, a successful merchant. Harriet N. Brooks of Dalton, New Hampshire, married Ranselaer Winchell in LaHarpe, Illinois, in a few years. Emilie Taylor not only joined Martha Rogers's class in 1850, but went out again in the fall of 1853 to Boonville, Missouri. She apparently went with her sister to Missouri the first time. She eventually returned to Hinsdale, New Hampshire, where in 1857 she married the Reverend Moses H. Wells. Mary Jane Ladd from Meredith, New Hampshire, married in the West. An alumna of Mount Holyoke, she married William T. Hatch within the year in Henry County, Indiana, and died in 1861 at the age of forty-six.

could only see home again they would never be seen on that lake" but poor I was too sick to even wish to get well. Indeed I had but one thought all day & that was "O how sick." We got to Cleavland about seven O'clock at night when Mr. Maltby came on board & began to doctor us with brandy & some of his spicy jokes which latter in connection with the Lake becoming less boisterous proved highly beneficial & the next morning with the exception of a light head & very empty stomach I was well but not so Misses Brooks & Taylor. They were sick two or three days after.

We got into Sandusky about 8' O'Clock in the morning & took the cars at five for Cin. At about seven we left the Wilkinsons at Belvue.[12] The Rev. Mr. Waldo was there to receive them. We than rode on till after eight before we got any breakfast & we were *right* hungry to be sure. It was ten O'Clock at night when we reached Cin. the night of the opening of Burnet House. The next day Mr. Maltby distributed us on three different boats. The four going to Ind. left at noon. Misses Brooks, Grosvenor, Ela Taylor & self took boat for St. Louis—And poor Miss June like the "Lone Star" to which she was hieing took boat all by herself.[13]

I would say here in explanation of our being out on the Sabbath—we found that we must be out one Sabbath either on this river [Ohio] or the Mo. And after looking it all over & considering how far some of us had yet to go Mr. Maltby concluded that it was best for us to go. Misses Brooks & Grosvenor were very reluctant to go & took care to remind us all along the route that we must bear Gov. Slade's displeasure for they were innocent to which we humbly acquiesced probably feeling that Gov. S. was too good a man to let his wrath continue after sundown, &, that it could not reach us so soon in this far off land. . . .

Our boat kept us *waiting* one day & after taking on a cargo of babies (twelve in all), they left about nine o'clock in the evening. The next morning about seven, we left Miss Ela. We had a pleasant time & got to St. Louis the next Wednesday about three P.M. I sent my letter up to Dr. Ballard & about an hour or so Mr. Emerson came & said he found there was no boat going up the Mo. that night & we must wait till next evening.[14] Misses

12. The Wilkinson sisters, who first went together to teach in Bellevue, Ohio, eventually went separate ways. They were in their early twenties and were probably the oldest daughters of a Brandon, Vermont, physician. Mary married Emerson Covel within the year and Caroline went on to teach in Tennessee.

13. No information is available about either Miss June or E. C. Grosvenor. Martha Rogers's letter is the only reference to Miss June, who appears to have gone to Marshall, Texas. E. C. Grosvenor did write a letter in the "Regeneration" folder of the NPEB Papers on 25 March 1850, but it contains no information other than her name. She was apparently assigned to teach in Iowa.

14. The Reverend Mr. Emerson of Springfield, Missouri, was part of Governor Slade's network. He had requested a teacher for Colonel Love's school from the board and apparently offered his home as a way station for teachers coming to Missouri.

Brooks & Grosvenor stepped off of our boat on to another just started for the upper Miss[issippi] so that they were not detained at all. We went to the City Hotel & next evening took boat for [because] Mr Emerson was going up the Miss. & would not be back till the next week so we came on alone. When we got into the Mo. we had a "right smart chance of snags, sawyers & sandbars" & we also had the pleasure of getting on the sandbars several times. We reached Jefferson about one P.M. Sat 11*th*. There parted with Miss Taylor who went to Boonville.

There I waited two days for the stage. Tuesday morning took the Stage at one in company with three gentlemen. . . . I was three days coming from Jeff City to Springfield rising at one in the morning & riding till seven & eight one night. I rode one day in company with a gentleman who was in the Stage last fall when Miss Sawyer came out & showed me the spot where they upset & he remarked that she was a woman of a strong mind for she made no fuss atall when they upset.[15] The last day of the trip was performed in a rough lumber wagon 45 miles & I was tired out when I got to Springfield.

Mrs. Emerson received me very kindly and did all She could to make me comfortable. Soon after tea she told me not to feel bad but that Col. Love had engaged a teacher for the summer session but that she doubted not that I could soon get a School & that I was very welcome to a home with them till I found a Situation. But it all could not quell the rising of tumultuous feeling in my heart so far from home & friends, the people all strangers & everything so strange & different from all that I had been accustomed to that my heart died within me & when I went to bed that night tired weary & sad, I felt that there were some very rugged paths in this journey of life that we are travelling. I arose next morning sick in body & mind & I finally had to give up & be sick three days.

But my case soon excited the sympathy of the people & all were ready to assist me in any way & gentlemen would call & offer to write wherever they were acquainted & showed me every attention. When I had been there a week Col. Love sent me word that he was sorry he had engaged a teacher since I had come & that he would feel under obligation to employ me in the fall. He pretended that it was because he had not heard from the East & thought that he would not get a teacher before fall. . . . But I suspected that was not the real objection & I got it out of his son in law [Mr. Lee]. Mr. Emerson became obnoxious to them last Feb. through a letter of his that was published in the Jan. No. of the "Home Missionary" not intended for publication. This came to Springfield just about the time of the Benton excitement & the cry was instantly raised that he [Emerson] was a Abolition-

15. Ann E. Sawyer from Franklin, New Hampshire, went out to teach in an academy operated by R. D. Smith in Pleasant Retreat, Polk County, Missouri, in the class immediately preceding Martha Rogers's. She was twenty years old and had recently attended Mount Holyoke Seminary for two years.

ist & of course ought not to be suffered to live.[16] So they stopped him from preaching & then they said he was distributing Abolition Tracts & then the old Col. [Love] got it into his head that he [Emerson] wanted to get Abolition teachers in the country to poison the minds of the young so he would have none of them. They might all go together for they were all alike.

I told Mr. Lee after he had told me this that he could tell Col. Love that the Society did not mean to send teachers here or anywhere else that did not *know enough* to mind their own *business* & that if he should want a teacher in the fall he had better send to the Society for one. Mr. Emerson laughed after the man was gone & said he thought the old gentleman would feel bad when he found what a "peert" teacher he had lost. . . .

Miss Sawyer's Mr. Smith came ten miles out of his way to see me & give me any assistance in his power & wrote to this place for me & offered me his home if I should not find a situation. He felt very bad because he said he feared the Society would perhaps refuse to send any more to be so located. . . . Mr. Emerson left S[pringfield] on Friday May 7th & I stayed till Monday to take the Wagon not stage for this place. . . . I found very kind friends in one of the two Pres[byterian] families in S. & stayed with them from Thursday to Monday May 10*th*. I left that morning at one & rode all day in the hot sun 55 miles to this place. It is on the Stage route & twelve miles from the Ark. line, and 100 to Van Buren Ark. The mail comes here three times a week.

And now after so long a story what shall I say? I wish you could *see* for I can not picture the place to you as it is. The Courthouse is a two-story frame house with a chimney at one end outside. . . . The Hotel is made of three log houses—one has two glass windows, the other one, & the kitchen none. . . . We have three stores here—one of which is a log building without any windows—one grocery—three Blacksmiths—two Doctors & two Lawyers. As to preaching we have none of any sort. There [are] two Cumberland Presbyterian preachers living in town but one has lost the confidence of the people by his mercantile & other speculations & the other has other appointments. He is a fine man & came last Sabbath to help me organize a Sabbath School. . . .[17]

16. Thomas Hart Benton (1782–1858), senator from Missouri since its entrance as a state in 1821, opposed the Compromise of 1850 because he believed it would give southern secessionists too many concessions. He was also opposed to Abolitionists and supported the gradual elimination of slavery. Because of his stand on the Compromise of 1850, he was defeated for reelection as a senator that same year. *DAB*, vol. 1, pp. 210–13.

17. The Cumberland Presbyterians waived traditional educational requirements for the ministry in order to meet the religious needs of the West more quickly and depended on camp meetings to produce converts. They tended to reject the traditional Presbyterian tenet of predestination. The Campbellites were also an offshoot of Presbyterianism, emphasizing the autonomy of each local church, and attempting to return the church to its more primitive roots. See Ahlstrom, *Religious History*, pp. 445, 447–49, 466, 844.

The log schoolhouse in Barry County, Missouri, was the last to be built in the county. The design remained unchanged from the time Martha Rogers taught in the same county forty years earlier.

And I must not forget the Schoolhouse which is a log house thirty-five by thirty with four windows & two doors, the south are boarded up & in the four windows of twelve panes each there are ten panes of glass. The cracks are filled with mud plaster & there is no "loft" & the shingles are very holey so that when it rains we take the books up & stand in one place till it begins to drop down & then we move to an other spot & then an other. . . .

For a week after I came here I thought I would have to quit because I could not find a spot to put myself till I hit upon this place. . . . I have the best room in town. It's lathed & one coat of plaster put on about as well as I could put it on I should think. There is a fireplace in it two windows with curtains a closet on one side of the chimney & shelves on the other for books. The lower one being broader serves for wash stand & toilet stand. There is a door that opens on to a piazza 70 feet long & it faces the court house, grocery & one of the stores.

I commenced School Monday the 7th of May with sixteen scholars. At the end of the week I had twenty two & the next Monday I had twenty five & this week I have twenty-nine & they say that more are coming. But the difficulty now is a schoolhouse. Some want to build one but the majority are so inert that they come for nothing & I am now telling them that I will stay if they build such a House as I want but in that thing I will not Stay. . . .

There is no congenial society in this place, not one. The doctor with school board is intelligent but a Cambelite. The lawyers are *smart* but one is the greatest drunkard out. . . . There is a vast vast field for usefulness & I only hope & pray that I may make myself acceptable to them & so be useful to them. There is great need of female culture here. I have young ladies 22, 19, 18 & so on that can hardly read & some whose parents cannot read. . . .

I shall probably have my trials here for I expect that wherever I may go I shall certainly be very lonely—but still I think could I have chosen, I could not have selected a place more in need of one of your teachers & I only wish there was one here better qualified for the work. I have not yet visited much as I have written about twelve letters—none of the length of this one & much shorter. They go altogether on horseback here as there is not a buggy in town. I have not received a letter since I came to Mo. & I suppose it will [be] August before I get one. My dear Miss S. I should like to hear from you & know what you think of my acts. I endeavored to do as well as I could. As to the books I have sold about three dolls worth. There is no paper currency in this state and coppers but as soon as I can get some paper I will send you the five dolls.

Affectionately Yours

M. M. Rogers

Cassville, Sept. 18th -50

My dear Miss Swift

Precious, very precious is the sympathy of christian friends though they be afar off. Your letter of remembrance & sympathy was to my perplexed feelings what oil is to the troubled waters. I thanked God for it & took courage: but I will explain. I told you I think the condition of the Schoolhouse here & that I could not stay unless they built an other & in the Spring they talked as if they would.

A few weeks after I came here I received two letters from Col. Love offering me his school in the fall & all that I could make from it. Well I thought I would be in no hurry to answer him; this was a good location better than his for a permanent School & it was a dark region & if I could be useful here I would use these letters to stimulate the people to exertion for a permanent School. If I could not make a permanency here then I would go there as the next best thing I could do. When I showed the letters here some said they would give $50, others $25 towards the erection of a new house & I must not leave &c. But from their general liberality I did not put much faith in all their says and thought I would wait & see what they would *do*. . . .

The school averaged 24 all the quarter; only six boys the oldest 13 had never seen a school. [He] did not know a letter when he commenced. I had some tall girls with corresponding (southern) tempers but it has been the pleasantest & most easily governed school that I ever had. The only punishment inflicted during the three months was slightly pinching a little fellows ear for laughing. They were never tardy always respectful, & always obeyed cheerfully. They were happy in school & loved to come & I attribute my success to the reading of the scriptures & prayers at the opening of the school mornings. . . .

I have also gained the respect & confidence of the people generally & the warm esteem of the religious part of the Community. The married ladies all come to hear my instructions to their children on the Sabbath & I would not mind if they would not bring their nursing babies. They are very dear little things in the nursery—but in the S[abbath] S[chool] O how annoying to old maids! Mr. [Charles] Beecher did not tell us what to do in such a case. I would like to ask him. [18]

About three weeks before the close of the school I told the people that they must tell me decidedly what they would do for I must let Col. Love know. So three persons—one a Cumberland Presbyterian "Parson" another an elder & the third a Campbellite went round to ask assistance, about a house, & could raise *nothing*—as I anticipated but they came to me & said if I would stay—they would pledge themselves to make the house comfortable for me this winter & they thought by next spring there could be a new one built. I asked if there were objections to me. They said none to me nor to my teaching. It was only the fear of expense but they could not give me up. This place would never be any thing till there was a good permanent school besides they wanted me in the S.S. & it is a fact that there is not a female in this place competant to teach in the S.S. & but two men & they wanted my influence in the community. The Parson said since God had sent me to them they ought to keep me & they would do what they could to make my stay comfortable. . . .

That Saturday the Whigs who are weak in this country assembled from all parts & had an illumination or feu de joie—and when they began to light up the courthouse, the Dr.'s wife [Mrs. Means] came along and says Miss Rogers let's illuminate the house for sport. I said yes, & I put three lights in my window & the other lady boarder put three in hers & Mrs. M[eans] lighted up her part of the house. [19] These ladies husbands are Whigs & their

18. The Reverend Charles Beecher, Catharine Beecher's youngest brother, addressed Martha Rogers's class at Hartford.

19. The household Martha Rogers lived in consisted of A. H. Burton, whose occupation was listed as "speculator," his wife, and four children; James Means, a physician, and his wife, who was Burton's daughter; and a single male lawyer and a single male merchant. U.S. Manuscript Census, 1850, Barry County, MO, p. 230.

parents are Bentonites but they side with their husbands so that we were all Whigs here. Just then Mrs. M's father "Parson" Burton & his wife came in—who are Benton—& went to blowing out the lights. I saw them coming so locked my door & put the key in my pocket so when they got to me they tried to raise the window. I held it & kept my lights burning. This was all observed from the courthouse & applauded but I did not know it. The Parson said laughing "You can never leave Cassville after this, the Whigs will never let you go. A Whigwoman is such a rare thing here that they will keep you as a curiosity" &c. & so he joked me.

We then went & stood under the windows to hear the speeches. Then the resolutions & proceedings of the meeting, & you may fancy my consternation when I heard it resolved "to fire three salutes for that lady who illuminated her window." They did, shouting at each fire "for Miss Rogers for illuminating her window." It raised a great excitement among them & one man said he would come and throw mud in the cracks of the school ten days before he would let me go, & he would sign one scholar if he sent none. An other said that was worth a "thousand dollars." And Monday morning they got out an article and all the Whigs signed or promised to send children or [had] no children. It was not confined to the Whigs of course & the prospect before Wednesday was fair for as large a school as the summer session.[20]

But I thought I would wait till after Examination before I made any new decisions. I made no extra preparation for examination. Tuesday & Wednesday morning was spent in reviewing & the parents & others were asked to come in the afternoon. There was a very good attendance (babies included). The girls were very much dressed—some of them in comical taste to be sure but that we will remedy in time. They all appeared unembarrassed & easy. They sang three songs "Try try again" "Sparkling & bright" "Up the Hills on a bright sunny morn" for the close. This is something new here & takes well. At the close I told them we had no writing to exhibit as we had no desks to write on. I had tried to do what I could with slates. I then said I would be glad to have every one present offer an opinion & make any suggestions on any thing. My friend the "Parson" then rose & complimented both teacher & pupils & spoke of the inconvenience of the house and called upon all present to unite in making the House comfortable & keeping me among them &c. Then brought our exercises to a close. It was five O'Clock & I was so exhausted that I feared I could not get through. I closed the 4th of Sept. to commence again the 1st of Oct for five months. . . .

My dear Miss Swift I am ashamed to trespass upon your time with such long letters, & yet I do not know how I could make you understand my

20. The Whigs did defeat Benton in 1850. However, the Whig party Martha Rogers knew in New York did not support slavery. In Missouri in 1850, the Whigs were strong only because they united against Benton, a Democrat, and his opposition to the Compromise of 1850.

position otherwise. . . . As to the moral conditions of the people—there has been preaching twice in this place since I came here. . . . There is a grocery just across the square & there every day the sound of revelry, debach, & cursing is heard—& I have more than one scholar whose father is a sot. Rev. Mr. Cook of Auburn sends me the "Youth's Temperance Advocate" which I distribute very gladly.

A shocking circumstance took place here the 30th of Aug. Some four weeks before that, a Lawyer named Smythe, who got drunk every day & always carried knives & pistols fell out with a neighbor of his & brother drunkard both being drunk at the time. S. fired a pistol at the other [B.] but the cap burst. He [Smythe] then struck at him with it. The other's wife got between them & wrenched it from him. He [Smythe] then got his knife and wounded the other [B.] in five or six places. B. got on his horse & rode up here a mile & a half to have his wounds sewed when he swore that he would kill S.

He [B.] had kept sober since that till the 30th Aug. when he had been drinking some; but was not intoxicated. That morning S. was seen riding into town with a bowie knife unsheathed in his hand. About 3 in the afternoon B. was sitting in front of one of the stores, when S. rode up very drunk & offered his hand to the merchant first. He refused & went inside. S. then offered his left hand to B. who put his hand in his [own] hand & said "no, you tried to kill me & I'll not shake hands with you."

On this S. brought over his right hand & aimed a pistol just between his eyes. Again the cap burst & B. escaped but on the instant he [B.] drew a knife twelve inches long & three wide & thrust it through him [Smythe]. The first thrust cut through both lungs & would have been enough but he [B.] dug at him till he had inflicted eleven wounds each of which would have been mortal. It was in the square where all saw it. S. never uttered a word after he was hit but the last words heard from him were curses upon B. He slid from his horse & lay there. He groaned heavily two or three times but no one went near him till a brother lawyer came up—urged them to come & help take him some where for he was a human being. They then took him to the Doctor's office. The tailor made his shroud, all the women refusing to do it & but two men were willing to touch him any way. B. was tried that night & acquitted on the plea of self defence, it being the third time that S. had tried to shoot him.

I was horrified & could not sleep that night atall and I wondered that people did not exterminate that grocery at once. The next day his butchered, bloated body was taken to its last resting place, his wife & three children riding in the same wagon. This is a picture of Cassville. S. was a man of superior talents & education & the only thoroughly educated man in the place. He had formerly been a class leader & Methodist exhorter. He was also a "Son of Temperance" some two years ago. B. is also a man of good education & sense & would be a fine man but for this demon rum. He has not drunk since & says he will not. May God help him keep his resolution.

I have read Mary Carrow's School to my scholars with very good effect & also some of the stories [in] the book which Mrs. Sigourney gave me. [21] They all love to have me read to them & I [am] trying to excite curiosity & a desire to read themselves but the parents are no readers, have no books nor papers—& there is not a woman in this town who is a fluent easy reader & there are more than one who cannot read atall. I have thought that I would like to have a few books for a sort of circulating Library to excite a desire & taste for reading—such as "Miss Ellis's works," "Charlotte Elisabeth Tales for the People" & "Temperance Tales." [22] I think such would be read & would create a taste for reading. I intend to write to Mr. Myers for a S.S. Library. I would have done so before only that I was so unsettled all summer not knowing if I should stay. What I next want is one of Winchester's Charts; and Canvas & posters for working worsted with. I could sell all such things if I had them, for the parents are very desirous that their daughters should learn needlework. I could not obtain the materials & therefore could not teach it. I would like very much to have this coming session a class in Physiology & one in United States History, but cannot obtain the books. A box directed to me to the care of J. & W. McDowell St. Louis would be forwarded to me as they have a brother here selling goods & he sends wagons there every two or three months, but the freight is four cents a pound from there here so that it would cost more from St. L. here than all the rest of the road.

You say "mention any little personal comfort you may need." If I had a pound of Spermatici candles & a rocking chair I should feel quite comfortable—as it is I think I shall live but they have nothing but the most inferior kind of tallow candles, which are sometimes green, & sometimes black, & so debilitated by the heat that they cannot stand alone when put in candlesticks—so that like the Coffee they have to be laid by to rest. I have dispensed with lights all summer but can not any longer. I have been accomodated all summer with a table a foot square—so since vacation I have had one of larger dimensions—made a rough pine table without paint or anything for which I had to pay $2.50. I got the cheapest thing I could find for a cover for which I gave $1.50—making just $4 so that is the way with

---

21. Lydia Sigourney, a well-known Hartford author, wrote poems and stories with strong moral themes. She was president of the Female Beneficent Society and met with several classes of teachers before they went West. *NAW*, vol. 3, pp. 288–90; *Hartford Directory, 1850*, p. 198.

22. A collection of these books is in the Connecticut Historical Society. Sarah (Stickney) Ellis wrote such works as *First Impressions; or, Hints to Those Who Would Make Home Happy* (New York: D. Appleton & Co., 1846). The Charlotte Elizabeth Tales were written by Charlotte Elizabeth Tonna and published by the American Tract Society. Like the Temperance Tales, published in Boston by Ford & Damrell, they were little paperback tracts teaching morals in story form.

everything. I am allowed two chairs—those straight backed kitchen chairs —(they have no others in this place) which feel hard enough when I come home tired & exhausted as I used in the hot weather, hardly able to hold my head up & then I would have given any thing for an arm chair to hold me up, for I was often as drooping as the candles.

It is the Season of Camp meetings now. There was one two weeks since some 30 miles from this where two of my pupils went & one a young lady of 18 who has been a very rude, dancing, trifling girl, returned home rejoicing in a new found Saviour. I have not seen her since but they say she is a bright christian & that her very countenance is changed. Last week there was one some 8 miles from here where four more of my pupils came out bright—the daughter of the Parson with whom I board, two daughters of the elder I before mentioned, & the fact that a bright whole souled girl is cousin of the first young lady mentioned, has a deist father, careless mother, & a wicked sister who was so enraged at her when she returned that she cursed her & abused her cruelly. She is but 13 & will require much grace & encouragement to be able to endure the persecutions of such a home. I was not well enough to attend those meetings & I can not tell you how I felt when I heard that my pupils were the only converts at those meetings. . . .

Miss Sawyer & I have opened a correspondence which I hope will prove as profitable to me as it is pleasant. Her school numbers between 60 & 70 this session & Mr. Smith has charge of the male department. He is a dear good man I often wish I had such an ally here. With the exception of Misses Taylor & June, I have not heard from one of our stars. I have received a letter from Miss T. & Miss June sent me word by one of the gentlemen who went to Texas from here that she had sent me a letter the week before they got there but I have not received it. The account you gave of those teachers heard from was so characteristic of each that I could not help smiling when reading it. We all anticipated difficulties for Sister Lord for she was always full of them even in Hartford. Miss Arnold's combativeness was rather too large not to excite opposition. Miss Warner would doubtless be as easy with her pupils as she was with her *hair*. And Miss Carpenter has such a truely Christianly amiable disposition that she will be pleasantly situated any where. . . .[23]

My compensation for the past quarter was seventy dolls. Paid for board & washing for eleven weeks—eighteen dolls fifty cts. I have on the list 32 different scholars—but the average attendance was twenty four & they pay

23. Susan A. Lord, who was living in Boston when she applied to the board, first taught in Wisconsin. In the spring of 1852, she was one of three teachers who went to San Francisco, where she taught at the Benicia Young Ladies Seminary before marrying a judge. Mary S. Arnold from Monmouth, Maine, was teaching in St. Charles, Illinois. Fanny A. Warner, who came from Sunderland, Massachusetts, taught in Aztalan, Wisconsin, until her marriage in 1851 to Alonzo M. Morrison, a lumber dealer in various parts of Wisconsin. S. Augusta Carpenter, who was only nineteen when she went West, returned to her native Greenfield, Massachusetts, sometime before 1854, when she married James Averill.

only for the actual attendance of each pupil. Was not able to teach writing the last quarter as there were no desks & I deducted something in my charges lest they should say I had not taught all I agreed to but I shall do so no more.

An other class will have been assembled in H[artford] & scattered before this reaches you. The Oregon class will also be on the boisterous Ocean[24]— busy & anxious hearts those would wish & hope that none would meet with such rebuffs as I did but I dare not for though it was trying to the flesh, yet if God could & would be best glorified in it it was all *right,* & I thank him that it is as well with me as it is. I shall look with some solitude to know if you censure the course which I took with regard to my breach of promise to Col. Love. Be not too severe for my inclination was to go, feeling that I would have more personal comfort & better society.

Throwing myself upon your mercy for sending such a long & illly written letter I will close with my many thanks for your dear letter, & may God spare you long to be a comfort to your friends & us, poor isolated ones so far away from home & friends is the prayer of M. M. Rogers.

Teaching in Wright and Camden Counties, Missouri: April, 1851, to August, 1852

A few months after the preceding letter, Martha Rogers did leave Cassville to teach in Colonel Love's select school east of Springfield, Missouri, near Waldo in Wright County.[25] Although thirty-eight pupils registered, the attendance averaged twenty-four. "The pupils made very good progress," she wrote, "considering the irregular attendance & astonished & delighted their parents & friends at examination." At the end of her third session nearly a year later, she planned to give her school "a little fête in the shape of a 'Christmas tree' on Christmas day." She described the supper put on by Mrs. Love on the day of the recent examination. "A table was spread under a rough bower which we have erected in the Schoolyard & bread & butter, cold fowls, & cakes in any quantities were dealt out bountifully to the Scholars first & then to all who would partake," she wrote. "It was a *great* Examination & a great feast out here & was much talked of, & by many thought that it ought to be published in the 'Springfield Advertiser.'"

Rogers was particularly encouraged by the arrival of a Presbyterian minister who preached in her schoolroom every other week. She encouraged the Loves to keep the Sabbath. "Mrs. Love says that she never had so few *Sunday visitors* since she came to the State as she has had since I came here &

24. Arozina Perkins was in the fall class Martha Rogers mentioned, but the group for Oregon did not leave until the spring.

25. The letters omitted are from Hazelwood, Missouri, 4 April 1851; Waldo P. O. Wright County, Missouri, 1 December 1851, 10 March 1852; Erie, Camden County, 26 August 1852.

playfully says that I keep them away," she wrote Nancy Swift. "They have also stopped cooking on the Sabbath & have a cold dinner. There were many remarks made about it at first—that I dictated the family & made them do it &c. But the Col. & his wife only laughed at it & said I might take all the credit of it, they had not the least objection."

Her position in "Love Ridge School" continued for only a year and a half. The death of Colonel Love, a month after the Christmas fête, caused the school to close at the end of the spring term. In July 1852, she began a new position in Erie, Camden County, north of Springfield. She had decided to start teaching immediately because the number of pupils in her last session had been small after Mrs. Love decided not to take in boarders. "I felt I must teach all the time to make up losses," she said, "but it is a losing concern all the time as to the money part." When she wrote Nancy Swift to tell her of the new position, she was suffering from an attack of "Billious fever," probably malaria, and taking quinine. Despite her sickness, she was again encouraged. "I have improved myself in the *article* of *Society* very much— with the exception of my kind friends in Springfield they are the most refined people I have met in the S.W."

Martha Rogers continued her correspondence with her sister teachers. She mentioned the marriage of Sarah Ballard and noted that Ann Sawyer, who was home for a visit, planned to return West. "There is much to do out here," she wrote, "& such teachers as she is are much needed. Miss Sawyer has done much for Education in South West Missouri. She broke down strong prejudices & established a school which stands high in point of thoroughness & discipline."[26] Her only request from Nancy Swift was "some sort of *short hand* or *steam* process whereby could make scholars learn every thing in *three months* if they did not attend half the time at *that*."

Martha Rogers's health improved after a trip back East in the spring of 1853. Her final two letters follow; the first describes her return to Missouri.

Erie, Camden Co. Mo. June 18th -53

Dear Miss Swift,

Will you accept many thanks for your very kind letter which reached me the day I left home. I did not expect you to write while you were in Hartford, for I do not forget the piles of letters which came to you almost daily while *we* were there, & I can therefore appreciate your kindness—also in remembering me in the distribution of the books which you sent us.

---

26. Ann Sawyer did return to the West in 1853. She went to Michigan, where she helped start the first state school for dependent children. She married John Chandler in Coldwater, Michigan, in 1859, and had one son, the Reverend E. S. Chandler of Amboy, Illinois. She died at his home in 1899. Ann Sawyer Chandler, Beatrice, Nebraska, to Mrs. Blanchard, 23 July 1886; Ann Sawyer Chandler, obituary, Mount Holyoke College Alumnae Records.

You can well imagine how happy Miss Wilkinson & I were to meet at Albany, so unexpectedly too & we were inseparable after we met at the Delavan House, & remained there till Monday—so did not see any of the Class but Miss Rix who came to Mo. She called Sat. evening with Gov. Slade. How glad I was to meet that good man again, so like a father. Monday morning after we got en route for Buffalo, Gov. brought Miss Adams & introduced her; then she gave me the parcel which you sent me. Miss Wilkinson was sitting by me & looked very hard at the books and then said in her quick hoping way—you remember it I suppose, "Well now Miss Swift is *partial* to send you so many books & not send me any." I replied laughing—if Miss Swift had not sent them to me, I would divide with you, but I can not. It was not long however before Gov. brought up an other lady & introduced her to Miss W. She then handed her a parcel from you also. When she opened it & I saw the *tracts* with the books, I laughed at her & said "O yes Miss Swift *is* 'partial' but to *whom*!? I will write & tell her"—which I have as you see.[27]

My journey this time was pleasanter than the first. We had our good *father* with us to Cincinnati & Miss W. to the mouth of the Tenn. And when we got to St. Louis I found a party from this place, my pupils some of them & concluded to wait for them. So I bade goodbye to our young ladies & spent a week in St. Louis & came up on the same boat that they did.

The Capt. said they all went up to Boonville in company with the Indian agent who resides at Neosho, so that Miss Adams had an escort all the way & the others took Stages.[28] I reached here the 21st of May. People seemed very glad to see me. The following week I got myself & schoolroom ready & *visited* some. This last you know is very important out here. I commenced school the 30th for three months. I have 30. Just now I am sailing in smooth waters—school is pleasant—my rest last winter & journey this spring home improved my health very much & I have much better spirits than when I left.

We reorganized our S. School last Sabbath. I was anxious to do so; but thought it best to wait till solicited & they have all seemed very urgent. It consists mostly of young people. All my teachers (four) are young men & none of them pious. And as I can find no gentleman to superintend, the Office rests with me. The duty of praying in our school has been very plain to me all the time, but the question whether a woman should pray in such a

27. There were two Mary Adamses in the thirteenth class leaving Albany in the spring of 1853. Martha Rogers meant Mary E. Adams, who went to Neosho, Missouri, to teach. The only information on Miss Rix is in Martha Rogers's letter and Mary E. Adams's letter talking about how two sisters named Rix parted, one to go with her to Neosho. Caroline Wilkinson also enjoyed meeting Martha Rogers, and told Nancy Swift that they decided that "Missouri and Tennessee are almost *twin sisters.*"

28. Mary E. Adams married an Indian trader, Alexander Warfield, within a year. It is probable that he is the man described here as escorting her to Neosho. Mary E. Adams was only twenty and from Bangor, Maine. She had studied at Mount Holyoke. She died in Nashville, Tennessee, in 1903.

public place was not so easily answered in my own mind & I have compromised the matter by reading a form of prayer suitable for the S. School. Do you not think it the most prudent & feminine course for me to take in a place so public where men of all ages & creeds come merely to be amused & pass away the time? This is my greatest cross at present but if God will make this school a blessing to these young people & to the community my trials will be very insignificant indeed.

Please excuse my long letters for you are well aware by this time that I do not know how to be brief.

With much love I remain
Respectfully Yours

M. M. Rogers

Erie Aug. 24th 1853

Dear Miss Swift

Your last kind letter has been received some time, but I thought I would wait till the close of school. Our examination was held on Thursday & Friday. I had large classes in Botany, Philosophy, Physiology &c. The Scholars did very well but the people did not attend till the last afternoon when they knew the Compositions & speaking were to come off. I regretted that but am glad to get them in at any rate. I believe all my employers are satisfied—at all events they let me have my own way about everything—& if there were places for boarders I would have a large school next session I think.

I feel a little anxious to realize something in the money line more—as it proved a losing concern all the time before & my friends were very unwilling that I should return as they thought I could make more at home with less labor and more "creature comforts." All which was true—but I am willing to labor here for small salaries even only that I think I should follow the counsels of those who have the right to advise & direct. I would have been glad to correspond with all the young ladies who came out with me & asked them to do so but I have not heard from any of them directly or indirectly. I am sorry for I would like much to hear from them.

I would like much to learn the difficulty with Miss Wait farther than the fact of her having married Mr. Smith's brother which of itself I can not consider so great an offense & I can not think that Mr. S. did right to come here & talk as he did, all being strangers. Still he may be able to justify himself in doing so.[29]

29. Martha Rogers is referring to R. D. Smith, who operated the academy in Pleasant Retreat where Ann Sawyer first taught. Fidelia Wait, from Hatfield, Massachusetts, joined Ann Sawyer there and apparently married R. D. Smith's brother. Ann E. Sawyer, Andover, New Hampshire, to Nancy Swift, 18 April 1853, letters folder, NPEB Papers.

The Springfield people are not at all suited in Schools yet—although most every family has a school & some of my friends talk of sending their children here if they can get them boarded—but I think they will send for a teacher from the present class. The mail which brought your letter brought one from Miss Wilkinson. She told me all she had passed through but said she was now very happy—& had also engaged in a S. School—the responsibility of which devolves mostly on herself, & there I can sympathize for I know all about that. I send this to Hartford. Please present my respects to the Class & tell them not to be afraid or discouraged at trials for they *must come* but there is a reward beyond.

Please give my love to Gov. Slade and say that my school has averaged 35 all this Session & my health has been better far than for a year before I went home—

Very affectely Yours

M. M. Rogers

~~~~~~~~~~~~~~~~~~~~ *10* ~~~~~~~~~~~~~~~~~~~~

From Pioneer Teacher to Pioneer Settler:
The Mississippi Valley

Mary A. Hitchcock and Sarah Ballard Thurston

"And besides it seems to be just the place for me," wrote Mary Hitchcock soon after she started to teach in the new settlement of Princeton, Cass County, in west central Illinois.[1] She was not happy with her first western assignment in a select girls' school in Beardstown, a rapidly growing center on the Illinois River. But like many of the pioneer teachers who became pioneer settlers, Mary Hitchcock had already decided to stay in the West. It was a matter of finding the right place. Although at twenty-two she was younger than most of the teachers who chose to make new homes in the West, her ties to a particular place in the East were not strong. Before she was ten, her family moved from Fort Covington, New York, on the Canadian border, to Bangor, Maine, and back to Ticonderoga at the tip of Lake George. She returned to the area north of the Adirondacks to attend the academy at Malone. During her first spring in Illinois, she looked forward to a visit from her father and two brothers-in-law, who were thinking about following her initiative in moving West.

Mary Hitchcock's spirit of adventure was evident in the first reason she gave for wanting to teach in the West—"to see more of the country"; Sarah Ballard's chief goal was the increased opportunity to support herself. By the time she joined the class at Hartford in the spring of 1850, Ballard was thirty-two. She was a resident of Worcester, Massachusetts, but had recently taught for seven seasons in Vermont. Of the West she said she hoped to find "a wider field for usefulness there, than here." She also looked forward to a life dedicated "to the Service of God."[2] When she encountered problems in

1. Although Princeton, about ten miles east of Beardstown, was a thriving small town at mid-century, the railroad passed it by and the town was vacated in 1875. William H. Perrin, *History of Cass County, Illinois* (Chicago: 1882), pp. 158–59; reference supplied by Marjorie Taylor, Cass County Historical Society.
2. Mary A. Hitchcock, 2 September 1852, biography folder; Sarah A. Ballard, Worcester, Massachusetts, 7 February 1850, application folder, NPEB Papers.

195

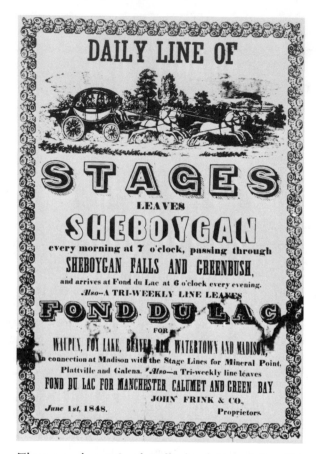

DAILY LINE OF

STAGES

LEAVES

SHEBOYGAN

every morning at 7 o'clock, passing through
SHEBOYGAN FALLS AND GREENBUSH,
and arrives at Fond du Lac at 6 o'clock every evening.
Also—A TRI-WEEKLY LINE LEAVES

FOND DU LAC

FOR

WAUPUN, FOX LAKE, BEAVER DAM, WATERTOWN AND MADISON,
In connection at Madison with the Stage Lines for Mineral Point,
Plattville and Galena. *Also*—a Tri-weekly line leaves
FOND DU LAC FOR MANCHESTER, CALUMET AND GREEN BAY.

JOHN FRINK & CO.,

June 1st, 1848.   Proprietors.

*The stagecoach route Sarah Ballard probably took from She-
boygan on her way to her first school in Rosendale, Wisconsin.*

Rosendale, Wisconsin, particularly with the question of boarding around,
she worked them out. Her large school, with students ranging in age from
three to twenty-three, interested her from the beginning, and she demonstrated to her new community that a woman could control the school. She
participated in professional activities outside her own town by attending
common school conventions and preparing local women to teach.

Mary Hitchcock also looked to the West for opportunity. Many others
followed her occupation of common schoolteacher, she said, concluding, "I
thought it would be much better could places more needy be supplied." She
would not go West over the disapproval of family and friends, she added,
had she "not thought duty was involved." She was supported by some
friends, however, because three other members of her class at Hartford in the

fall of 1852 had also studied at Malone Academy. In Princeton, she looked forward to a visit from her Malone classmate Judith Daggett.[3]

Both Mary Hitchcock and Sarah Ballard soon married. Not quite five months after Mary Hitchcock wrote that she found it much easier "'governing by love' in Princeton than in B.," she married William B. Montgomery of the most prominent family in Princeton. She continued to teach, at least for a while.[4]

Two years after she reached Wisconsin, Sarah Ballard married Charles Edwin Thurston, a member of a family who came from New York state. They settled in a new area in the Wisconsin Dells at Grand Marsh. She continued to teach and they made plans to build an addition to their house so she could have a permanent school. It is probable that Sarah Thurston died in 1855. In that year, a husband of a teacher in Wisconsin wrote the National Board about his wife's death, saying, "She acquired a large acquaintance in this community, and exerted an influence always in the right direction. She was a faithful Sabbath School teacher and an exemplary Christian. Our little church has lost one of its best and faithful members." Charles Thurston eventually left for the Sandwich Islands (Hawaii) and died in California in 1867.[5]

Mary A. Hitchcock from Ticonderoga, New York, to Beardstown and Princeton, Illinois

Beardstown, Nov. 27th 52

Dear Miss Swift—

I have for some time past, been hoping I could find time to address you, but school has prevented me.

3. Lucy P. Bell taught in Grand Haven, Michigan, from 1852 to 1854; Judith Daggett taught in a family school in Mount Pulaski, Illinois, nearly seventy-five miles from Mary Hitchcock; and Cemantha Currier taught in Sabula, Iowa. Cemantha Currier married in Iowa just a month before Mary Hitchcock's wedding.

4. Although Mary Hitchcock Montgomery and her husband are not listed in the 1860 census for Princeton, the Montgomery family is shown as the largest property holder in dollar value. The town's population in 1860 was only 320. U.S. Manuscript Census, 1860, Cass County, Illinois, p. 160; Mary A. Hitchcock to William B. Montgomery, 30 August 1853, Cass County, Illinois, Marriages, #512.

Jane Doty, who was in Mary Hitchcock's class at Hartford, wrote Nancy Swift, "I received a letter from Mrs. Montgomery (formerly Mary Hitchcock) which suprised me somewhat, but I suppose she thought there could be no harm in getting married providing she continued to teach." J. A. Doty, Henderson, Kentucky, to Nancy Swift, 24 October 1853, letters folder, NPEB Papers.

5. Brown Thurston, *Thurston Genealogies* (Portland, ME: 1892), pp. 450–51, reference supplied by John Holzhueter of the State Historical Society of Wisconsin; *Ninth NPEB Report*, 1856, p. 5. Although no Adams County records exist for this period, Sarah Thurston's father-in-law, Peter Thurston, is listed in the 1860 census as the only Thurston family living in Grand Marsh. He is listed with his son Albert, a teacher, and his daughter and her husband. U.S. Manuscript Census, 1860, Adams County, WI, p. 88.

The marriage certificate of Mary A. Hitchcock and William B. Montgomery in Cass County, Illinois, 30 August 1853.

It is with much pleasure that I think of the time spent in Hartford, and of your kindness to me, which I shall never forget.

I presume you have heard an account of our journey, which was very pleasant, except that some of the young ladies were quite unwell. I received a letter from Miss Doty a short time since, and she said that when she seperated from her company at Cincinatti (I think) Miss Perkins was so indisposed, that she made a remark to her, that she was afraid she never should live to reach her place of destination. She had worried about her ever since, as she had not heard a word from them after that.

We were favored with the company of Gov. S. until we left La Salle, and I can tell you, Miss Swift, that it was a trial when he left us.[6] He was so *perfectly kind.* It seemed like bidding home "Good Bye" again. May the blessing of Heaven attend him, as I believe it has.

I reached Beardstown, Thursday, Oct. 7th about one o'clock in the morning. I have found Mr. Dummer's family a very pleasant one indeed. He is a lawyer, one of the first in the state, but not a member of the church though he attends the Congregational meeting very regularly. His wife is a member of the Methodist church, and an excellent woman.

I began my school the next Monday after my arrival, had 21 scholars the first day.

My number has increased or might have done in all to 35, but one young lady died of the Typhoid Fever and three others, I was obliged to turn away, as 30 was as large a number as I could manage alone. One new scholar came yesterday, and as she was from the country and her Father was one of the first in engaging a boarding place for her, (her mother having been sick) I could not very well refuse her.

---

6. Lisette Perkins recovered as soon as she reached her teaching position in Mooresville, Indiana. Jane Doty, recently a student at the Castleton, Vermont, Seminary, taught music at a female seminary in Henderson, Kentucky. At Chicago Mary Hitchcock and six other teachers took a canal boat for La Salle, where, after stopping for the Sabbath, they took a boat down the Illinois River. See Julia S. Ware, Lexington, Missouri, to Nancy Swift, 14 November 1852, letters folder, NPEB Papers.

I have classes in History of the United States, Ancient History, Philosophy, Astronomy, Geography, Arithmetic, Grammar, Reading, Composition, Drawing, & Spelling & Writing.

I have also 2 in Latin, but as they do not come very steady, they do not learn in it, enough to speak of. I did not advertise to teach Latin, but as they had studied a little and were anxious to continue it, I told them they might, though I was not much in favor of it. So you see that I have something to do.

Now Miss Swift I would like a little advice though I know it is asking a good deal, as your time is so much occupied.

The truth is, I have a pleasant school, by making a *great effort*. I find that I am obliged to be on my guard every moment in order to succeed with some young ladies I have.

They are about fifteen or sixteen, and have been away to boarding school, where I think they have acquired habits, not the most pleasing. Besides which they are accustomed to being *indulged* in every thing and it comes very *hard*, if I cross them in the least, as they seem to think their ways are better than any others.

Even their parents concluded, that being away from home, and, away from their counsels, was ruining them, and for that reason it was that they applied to the board for a teacher.

So you can see by this, that I need a great deal of *wisdom*, to know in what way I can best influence them. I know *you* will feel for me Miss Swift though I realise that *One* alone can bring about what is necessary for the prosperity of the school, and the advancement of His Kingdom. Sometimes I have been so tried that it has seemed as though the darkness was too great to pass away. I remember one night in particular and all at once things seem to grow brighter & that beautiful passage came to mind.

"When thou passest through the waters they shall not overflow thee, and through the deep, it shall not cover thee." Then I thought I would have more confidence in future, but sometimes, it is almost impossible. O, if I had more religion I could rise above it all, but I forget that my being is in the hands of God.

One other thing has taught me a lesson. Perhaps you remember when I was in Hartford I was troubled much with the tooth-ache, and I told you that I did not know what I should do when in school. But I have not suffered one day yet, sufficiently to unfit me for my daily duties. And I have come to the conclusion, that if God has sent me to labor for Him, He will provide the means.

One very unpleasant habit those young Misses have, is that of talking aloud in the place of whispering; and as it all appears to be accidental I can not use very severe means, to break it up.

I never had that to try me before. When school commenced they would leave their seats, whisper, or talk aloud without liberty, but I believe I have broken up all but the last; now if you will tell me, what you *should do* in such a case, I shall be thankful.

M. A. Hitchcock

I staid in Mr. Dummer's family until I found one, but as they had but one spare room, of course could not urge them though on many accounts should have prefered it to this. I pay $2'00 per week for board, and hire my washing done.

I saw Miss Helen Cotton a short time after I came, which was very pleasant to me though she only called.[7] She is 20 miles from me, but thinks she shall not stay there another year, as Dr. Chandler is responsible for her pay, and is not willing to be after this.

I have no assistant yet, but as the people appear anxious I should have, so as to take all who wish to send, I think I shall: perhaps not until Spring.

Now Miss Swift, I do not wish you to think that I have tried to magnify my trials, for the sake of receiving a letter from you. I am sure that was not my intention, but as I thought you a very safe adviser, I really would be much gratified to hear from you.

I think Miss Swift that no one member of the class, unless it is Miss Hooker,[8] has a more responsible situation where there is more expected of her, than myself, but if I am blinded, I would thank you to tell me, just as you used to do.

If you see any thing where I miss it please tell me & I will try to take it kindly.

I was thinking, perhaps you would say that I do not love my scholars well enough but I really do feel much attached to them all, and my prayer is that my influence over them may be instrumental in winning them to Christ.

We have a very interesting Sabbath School, connected with the Congregational society.

The superintendant is also the leader of the choir of which I am a member.

We have a very pleasant little brick meeting house, finished neatly, and carpeted aisles.

Mr. Temple, born in Smyrna [Turkey], being the son of a missionary, preaches here, and is liked very well. I think he is settled.

The Sabbath School is held in the Lecture Room where I am teaching, and overhead is a hall for "The Odd Fellows," "Sons of Temperance," "Masons," &c.

---

7. Helen Cotton came out to Chandlerville, Illinois, the year before. She married John Goodell, a local farmer in 1853 and died in 1863. The community remembers her as laying "the real foundation of public school work" in Chandlerville. Josephine Craven Chandler, "Dr. Charles Chandler; His Place in the American Scene," *Journal of the Illinois State Historical Society* 24 (October 1931): 512–13; reference supplied by Marjorie Taylor, Cass County Historical Society.

8. Martha Hooker took charge of a large select school for girls in Geneseo, Henry County, Illinois.

There is also a Methodist Church besides Methodist, Lutheran & Congregational, belonging to the Germans.

The place is incorporated, and is growing fast. The people are very kind and do not appear to be envious in their dispositions. I am now boarding at Mr. Clendenin's a good place, but I should think half a mile from the school-house. I had to take a great deal of trouble to find a boarding place at all, and finally did not obtain one, until Dr. Turpin (one of the trustees of the building) assisted me.

[Side note] My love, and a kiss for Helen. How often did you wish me to write to the committee in Hartford? My memory is rather treacherous.

[Front note] I have now taught 7 months and the night before Christmas will probably close my first term. I am thinking of having an examination then, in hopes it will encourage them. I do hope I shall succeed in my school as the parents are very anxious as well as myself. I do not teach music though I might, if I had time, as there are a number of beginners would be glad to have me teach them. They have a very good German music teacher, but she was married a few days since, and intends leaving in the Spring. My friends do not feel quite as unreconciled to my absence as they did while in Hartford.

Yours, in much love,

Mary A. Hitchcock

Beardstown, March 7th 1853

My dear Miss Swift—

In great haste I sit down to direct a few lines to you on the subject of school. I hardly know how to commence, or come to the point, without giving a full explanation. I wish for another situation as teacher, and have for a month or two past been looking out for such an one, as would suit me but as yet have not succeeded. This term will close in three weeks, after which, I have concluded best to leave, for various reasons.

First, I am satisfied that there was a prejudice against the Eastern teachers when I came, and I think it has been increased, I do not know for what reason, unless my youth has something to do with it.

There were several young ladies the first day, whom I spoke of to you in my last letter, and though I did not like to believe it, I could not help seeing a disrespectful manner toward me, at that time, a disposition to obey, *only* as far as my rules agreed with theirs. I tried winning them over by love as was recommended at Hartford but before long, in conversation with Mr. Dummer on the subject, he said "that it was a rule that would not work in the West; that the Western & Eastern children were different in their dispositions, that what would suit in one place, would not in the other," & that severity had to be called in operation. Well, Miss Swift, you remember when I wrote you before the complaint I made of their talking loud, & leaving seats without permission, well this I believe I have succeeded in breaking up, but in doing it, some have become displeased and left the school, and since that, have been exerting their influence over the remaining ones, so as to make me all the trouble in their power.

Well, Miss Swift, I hope it will be easier for my successor than it has been for me, but no earthly friend knows the anxiety I have had on account of it. I find no fault with the smaller girls, or the young ladies from the country, as they do not seem wilfully to wish to disobey, but it is time to go to school, and I must leave.

Now Miss S. perhaps you will understand me, and I presume you will think, that part of the failure at least is in me, indeed I am inclined to think so myself, but you know it is very difficult teaching, unless one can be sustained by the parents. I do not think I am, and after deliberating and praying over the matter, have finally concluded best to write to another situation. I have learned some lessons by experience, and think I could do better another time. One lesson is, that when I receive a *very* cordial reception to begin with, I may fear lest it will not last.

Well, it is noon, a beautiful day in Spring, and as warm as April days are, where we live at home. I am in the school-room writing to a friend I *trust,* for to tell the truth, Miss S. I have learned to be rather suspicious of friends in the West. I fear you will think me to blame but I know that this is not my natural disposition, and however much may be the prejudice against me, I came here rather prepossessed in favor of Beardstown.

Those that are the best acquainted with me *seem* to like me, and I am generally treated well to my face. I think I have the affections of most of my scholars, or all who now attend, and perhaps, in time, this prejudice might be overcome, but I am satisfied that it would take a long time, and that a western teacher would be much better fitted for the place.

To show you that I am not wrong in my opinion, I will mention a little circumstance.

Last month, I called at a house where they had sent a daughter to school last term but through some misunderstanding, she left. I never had seen her mother, but had told her Father all the circumstances. I ventured to speak of my pay for her tuition, as I was going to leave or expected so to do before long. This excited the woman, and she replied that I came here, and thought I could impose upon the girls, just as I pleased, that they were all agreed in this, and I had done her daughter a great injury, &c. &c.

She said if she thought I had earned it, she would be willing to pay it, but &c.

I undertook to explain the circumstances to her but she did not wish to hear it at all. I persisted, however, and when I finished she acknowledged that I had done right, and said she never had seen me before but she had heard so much, that she did not care about it. She appeared very much changed, invited me to visit her, &c.

Well, I have consulted some influential persons about leaving, & though I have been advised by one person to stay, and it will all come right in the end, yet I conclude, all things considered that it is not best.

One reason for my not staying is this. there seems to be a lack of interest in education of any kind, and now a summer is coming on. I find that it is not customary to send to school or to have schools continued through the warmest weather, and as some six or eight of the girls are from the country, it is doubtful, or improbable, that I could have a full school. Besides, they have just commenced the public school and there are two other females teaching on their own responsibility. Well, as I said, my term closes in three weeks, and if I could have a situation somewhere not far off I should like it. should prefer going to Wisconsin, Iowa, *Michigan,* or some state east of this, to going much further South, and feel very anxious to be in a healthy location. Miss Swift, I should prefer not teaching a select school this time, as I think people would feel much more interest in some other school. I have a pleasant boarding place, and find the family very friendly. My health also is very good at present. have had no toothache to speak of.

I am acquainted with Mrs. Billings. find her a very intelligent & agreeable lady. She lives near the school-room, and I feel quite at home in their family.

I presume you have heard that Miss H. Cotton was married about a fortnight ago, I have not seen her but once since I came here but I understand she has married very well.[9]

I expect a cousin of mine, will join this spring class. she is quite an intimate friend of mine please give my love to her & my respect to Miss Ferry, and the ladies of the committee, also to Helen. I would very much like to join you at Hartford and shall always remember the time spent there with pleasure.

Yours &c.

M. A. Hitchcock

Beardstown, March 22 '53

My dear Miss Swift—

I suppose that by this time you have received a letter from me asking for another situation as teacher.

I think I wrote that I had taken measures to locate myself, and that if I succeeded in doing so, I would inform you.

Last Saturday I received a letter from a gentleman whom I had seen once, saying "That he had been informed that I thought of teaching in the country,

9. See note 7 of this chapter.

and was anxious to hire me in Princeton, (a small place, about 20 miles from Beardstown) that he wished I would not engage anywhere, until he could see, or hear from me."

Saturday night, after we had retired, one of the neighbors tapped on the window, and said that he had been to Princeton, and this same gentleman, Mr. Bergen had sent word by him to me, and seemed very anxious about it. Yesterday I received a letter from another man, with reference to it, and last evening Mr. Bergen came to see me about it, so I have reason to think they care something about it.

It has been through the influence of a gentleman whose daughter has attended both terms of my school, and for that reason I think I must have been, in some degree, mistaken with regard to the opinion people have had of my teaching.

I have agreed to go to Princeton, and have the promise of 30 pupils: for the common branches I am to have $2'50 per quarter and although it is a public school, there are several young ladies, that have attended the female seminaries in Jacksonville, who are wishing to attend, and for them, he thought it best to ask $3'50. There will be some small boys, but on the whole, I think I shall enjoy myself very well. It is not much of a village, but I think there are two meeting-houses, and I am to board in Mr. Bergen's family, who is a very pious man, a member of the Presbyterian church. He says that they will take the responsibility of paying me 150 dollars, and as much more as I can collect, which, all things considered will suit me better than being in B., where I have to pay $60 per year for rent & fuel, and $2'00 per week for board, washing not included.

Besides I am in the way of my duty, I trust, because I have asked for direction from above, and felt to leave it in the hands of a Higher Power. I hope I may be useful in the Sabbath-school, and other places, for I cannot feel reconciled to exerting no influence, though I believe my efforts have not been entirely unavailing in Beardstown.

I remember your kind advice, and that the place for the teacher was in her school, that if she teaches with an eye single to the glory of God, she does a great deal. Yes dear Miss S. I believe I shall always be benefited for the labor that you bestowed upon us, and I hope that at best it may tell for the good of souls, and the promotion of Christ's kingdom. It is noon and I must leave this, to enter upon my school-duties.

Wednesday morning. I have a few moments, now, before school time, which I may spend in the school-room writing. This term of my school will close next Friday, and after a weeks vacation, I am to commence in Princeton.

My health has been very good since I came here, have not had a spell of the tooth-ache to last 24 hours since I landed in B. I am expecting a visit from Miss Daggett before long, and better than that, from my Father, and two brothers-in-law whom I expect about the *1st* of May. They are thinking of coming West to settle, if the country suits them, especially one of them a physician is, and always has been, wishing to come to the West.

When you write, in future, direct Princeton P.O. Jersey Prairie, Cass Co. *Ill.* The mail does not go there but once a week, and I expect it will be something of a privation for me, as here it comes three times or every other day. When I wrote you last, I refered to a cousin of mine, but I have since received a letter from her, saying that her friends were very unwilling that she should join the Board, and she had given up the idea, for the present.

I have not time to write more, for I am in a great hurry now-a-days, it being the last of school, and expecting to leave B some time next week: besides, I have a letter to write home before to-morrow's mail, and it is now noon.

Miss Swift, do you think that Gov. Slade will come to B. this Spring? I should be very happy to see him, and would make arrangements to come to B. if I knew the time.

In much love,

M. A. Hitchcock.

[Side notes on each page in order]

Next Saturday will be my twenty-third birthday, and I do not feel much older, than at 17: for one reason, it seems as though I made but a very little progress.

My love to Miss Ferry and Helen.

We have had two days school, without a fire, but to-day the wind blows very unpleasantly, and we may expect the equinoctial storm, before we again have settled weather.

I feel quite lonely for many of the parents in the country have sent for their daughters to come home, so that now I think there are only eighteen. They seem well satisfied.

Miss Swift, I am sorry to have caused you anxiety, about my school, as I know I must have done, and would have avoided it if I could, but school was so nearly out, and I so little acquainted in the West, that I feared I should be obliged to call on you at last. I think you need give yourself no further uneasiness about the matter.

Princeton, Apr. 13, 1852 [1853]

My dear Miss Swift,

It is with feelings of pleasure that I again seat myself to write a few lines to a dear friend.

It is morning and nearly school time, but I knew you would feel anxious to hear that I was pleased with my new home. I am, though denied some of

The Liberty School in Hancock Township, Illinois, about fifty miles northwest of Mary Hitchcock's school in Cass County, Illinois, shows the continuity of the one-room country schoolhouse for nearly a hundred years. The teacher is Maggie Forney.

the priviledges of Beardstown, yet I find warmer, and less suspicious friends (unless I am deceived) than in the city. I suppose it is not to be expected where people have so much to think of, besides B. is a very growing place, and it requires much effort to keep up with the times, so that they would naturally be somewhat selfish. It is all over now, and not worth mentioning, I believe I had some warm friends among my pupils, and I doubt not, some others.

A fortnight ago Mr. Bergen came after me to B. and I returned with him the same day, Monday. Last week I commenced school in P. with a goodly number of pupils, and now have had thirty-seven in all. They are of both sexes, but all seem well disposed and anxious to learn; some walk a distance of two miles to school, and come very steady, but I suppose that some will stay out, when it is warmer, and they will be needed to help their parents, who are generally farmers.

Yesterday it was very rainy, so much so, that Mr. B. said he did not know as I had better go: I went, and had nearly thirty scholars some of whom lived a distance of two miles of course I was pleased to see so many smiling faces waiting for me, as it showed what an interest they felt. One could not help pitying them, to see them so backward, and yet so eager to learn, because they have had so little advantage of schools. The truth is, teachers are so very hard to be obtained, especially *qualified* ones, and for that reason there are but few schools wherein to educate teachers, so that if parents feel very anxious about education they must send their children to Jacksonville or some other high school, and as the expense and inconvenience are so great, they cannot afford it long. I have received several compliments telling how well they liked my school, so that I feel encouraged, through the assistance of Higher Power, to persevere. My prayer is, that I may not be left to lean upon my own strength, which I feel that I am too liable to do, especially if I am prospered.

My boarding place is in Mr. Bergen's family, but a few steps from the school-house, and as I have so many pupils, commence at half past eight in the morning, and with an hour's intermission generally teach till five.

I cannot *hurry* through, for I find them so lacking in being thorough in the *fundamental rules* of Arithmetic &c., that it takes time to make it clearly understood. At the close of every morning and afternoon we sing which they seem much interested in, as well as, are very quiet during the devotional exercises.

I like the place for several reasons, one as it is more moral and *religious* than Western places in general, and besides it seems to be just the place for me. We have preaching once a day nearly every Sabbath in my school-room— Sabbath-school at half past nine in the morning, which, with the Bible class, is very interesting—prayer meeting Wednesday evening in which the Methodists and Presbyterians appear well united, and which adds much to its interest, and we have monthly concerts once a month. But it is time to go to school.

Thursday morning

Yesterday I had three new pupils in addition to all my former ones, making forty in all. I like it as well as any school I have ever been engaged in, find them much more ambitious, and easily controlled than the children of B. so that it is not as hard on the whole, though I am obliged to be very busy. I have not had occasion, as yet, to use corporeal punishment since I came West excepting once, and then not with a stick, or ferule. Think it will be much easier "governing by love" in Princeton than in B, as yet, I have seen no disposition to disobey, worth speaking of, and I feel richly repaid by their smiling faces. I have heard that Miss V. Smith, a young lady of my acquaintance, is with the class of Hartford, please give my love to her: it would be very pleasant for me should she be located near me. [10] Expect Miss

10. Virginia Smith, who also attended the academy at Malone in addition to the State Normal School at Albany, went out to teach in Sterling, Iowa, in the spring of 1853. She married in Illinois two years later.

Daggett to visit me in May also my *Father,* & two brothers-in-law, as one of them wishes to live in the West. He is a physician, and the people of Princeton would like to have him settle here, which perhaps he will. It is a beautiful, *rich* country, but quite small, more so as one or two men own most of the land, and are unwilling to sell, even for building spots.

I have the tooth-ache today, so I hope you will excuse what is wrong in my letter. have had but a very little of it, as yet. The society here I like, though there is not much of it, and as yet, have not regretted coming West. should enjoy it much, could I enjoy the benefit of Hartford instructions this Spring. When I commenced this, I was intending to enclose about $20'00 towards my expenses, but I think it best to wait until I can collect all of my pay in Beardstown, when I hope to send the full amount.

[Front note] Miss Daggett wrote that she had received a very good letter from you, to comfort her, in her loneliness; we are depending much upon our visit. Love to friends, yourself & Helen included.

M. A. Hitchcock

Sarah Ballard from Worcester, Massachusetts, to Rosendale and Grand Marsh, Wisconsin

Rosendale [Wisc.], Aug 23 1851.

My Dear Miss Swift,

You doubtless will be happy to learn that I am still at Rosendale, and engaged in teaching. The *cloud* that was hovering over me, when I wrote to you last summer, has passed; and I am now enjoying summer days. I wrote you last summer, (I believe) that there were some dissatisfied because I had refused to board round. The dissatisfaction became so great, that I thought it best to try and board in most of the families; accordingly after teaching three months, I commenced boarding round in the district. But I found it very unpleasant, especially during the winter and spring terms, for one week I would board where I would have a comfortable room; the next week my room would be so open that the snow would blow in, and sometimes I would find it on my bed, and also in it. A part of the places where I boarded I had flannel sheets to sleep in; and the other cotton. But the most unpleasant part was being obliged to walk through the snow and water. I suffered much from colds, and a cough, which alarmed me some. When they had their school meeting to see in regard to employing me the second year; I told them that I could not stay unless they would give me a permanent boarding place near the school house. Therefore they granted it; but said they would be happy to have me board with some of the parents that lived in and near the village; if I was willing to do so.

I have prospered very well in my school since I wrote you last summer; had sixty-six scholars last winter from the age of three, to twenty-three. Have had very little trouble in governing my school; although it was thought by some that a female could not govern the school in the winter. The scholars have made good progress in their studies; and the parents say that their children have never learned so fast before. The school improves finely in singing which pleases the parents much; I have a few young ladies in school which are very good singers. I have a class of young ladies in Botany which is quite interesting, for we have such a variety of wild flowers here, that our botanical excursions are delightful. There are four young ladies which have been under my instruction, that are now engaged in teaching. There have been several Common School Conventions held in this part of the State; I have attended two of them; it was estimated that there were five thousand people present at the last one. There is to be a Teacher's Institute held here in Oct. also a C. S. C.

Our sabbath school is quite interesting; but we have had so many rainy sabbaths, that has not been so fully attended as it was last year. We hold female prayer meeting once a week. Mr. Bridgeman still preaches here, but probably will not much longer.

I received a letter from Miss Rogers last spring, she was prospering well in her school; appeared to be happy and contented. I also received one from Miss Plimpton in June; she was then engaged in teaching a select school had fifty pupils. She has had many trials, but I hope that she will be more prosperous in the future. Miss Warner returned to Mass. last Spring; expected to married in Oct. She will then come to Wis.[11] I should be happy to receive a letter from you if you can find time to write.

Sarah A. Ballard

Grand Marsh [Wisc.], Oct. 30, 1852

My Dear Miss Swift,

You will see by the date of this that I have left Rosendale. I remained there two years. Then left the school in charge of a pious teacher from Michigan. Some of the parents expressed a desire to send to the Board for a teacher; also expressed many regrets that I could not remain with them longer.

I was married in June to a pious man— But still I feel a deep interest in the education of the rising generations, and am now engaged in teaching.

11. All three teachers were in Sarah Ballard's class at Hartford. Letters from Martha M. Rogers are also included in this collection. Charlotte Plimpton, who taught in a school for girls in Lawrence County, Pennsylvania, was thinking of moving to a nearby district school because she was having trouble with the director of her school. Fanny Warner brought Alonzo Morrison, listed as "a trader," from Fort Atkinson, Wisconsin, back to Massachusetts for her marriage in October 1851.

The people in this place tried two teachers the first of last summer, but they were not either of them qualified to teach. I have taught eleven weeks; have a pleasant school—my school numbers 25 from the ages of 3 to 22. I conduct the exercises of the school, similar to what I did at Rosendale; but I do not find the scholars so far advanced in their studies as I did there. The scholars are much pleased with having the exercises changed on Wednesday P.M. Have also been much interested in hearing Mary Carrow read, and Childs Book on the Soul. [12] I do not have any opposition here in regard to having the scriptures read in school, and of having devotions. The scholars all kneel with me during devotional exercises; and most of them commit one verse of scripture to memory, each day; which they repeat in morning. They have improved finely in singing since I commenced my school, there were but few that were willing to engage in the exercise at first, but now all do it with pleasure.

This place has recently been settled; we had a sabbath school here last summer for the first time; most of the children have attended it; my husband has superintended it.

I have a pleasant home, situated on a beautiful Prairie in Adams County. And I am happy to say to you, that I have a small but pleasant frame house, situated about 25 rods from the road; and surrounded with shade trees. If you should ever come to Wis. we should be happy to receive a visit from you. We anticipate of building an addition to our house, so that I can have a permanent school in our own dwelling; I love to teach; for I feel that I am more useful than I could be to live a more retired life. The duties of the school room, and my domestic duties keep me very busy. In haste, Yours affectionately,

Sarah A. Thurston

---

12. Both *Mary Carrow* and *The Childs' Book on the Soul* by Thomas Gallaudet taught morals and religion in story form.

From Pioneer Teacher to Pioneer Settler: Oregon Territory

Mary Almira Gray McLench, with Elizabeth Millar Wilson, Sarah Smith Kline, Elizabeth Lincoln Skinner, and Margaret Wands Gaines

Mary Almira Gray McLench, whose reminiscence reveals the futures of the five women who traveled to the Oregon frontier via the Isthmus of Panama in the spring of 1851, does not discuss any of the women's reasons for choosing to teach so far from home. Arozina Perkins's struggle with her decision of whether or not to join the group bound for Oregon gives us some insight into the gravity of that decision; she finally let her mother's refusal make it for her. Because Elizabeth Miller and Sarah Smith were the only two women at Hartford who chose Oregon, Governor Slade was forced to recruit especially for the Territory during the winter of 1851.

For Mary Gray, the offer to go to Oregon came at the right time in her life. She celebrated her critical birthday, her twenty-fifth, the September before Slade offered her the opportunity to travel to Oregon at the expense of the National Board. The eldest daughter in a family who farmed in the Green Mountains of southern Vermont, Mary Gray was teaching in Grafton. Perhaps because her younger brother, Oscar, had decided not to become a farmer, her parents had decided to sell the farm and move into the nearby village of Townshend. A month before Mary Gray sailed for Oregon, an aunt and uncle started West on the overland route and arrived weeks after she opened her second term of classes. Mary Gray did not expect to stay in Oregon, but she did not visit Vermont again until 1877, on a twenty-fifth wedding anniversary trip.[1]

The Oregon Historical Society (OHS) has granted permission for the publication of the reminiscence of Mary Almira Gray McLench, included in the OHS manuscripts collection as Mss. 206, McLench Family Papers. The McLench Reminiscence was also published in the journal of the Ladd & Bush Bank, Salem, Oregon, which has also given permission for its publication "Early Day Teachers," *Ladd & Bush Quarterly* 3 (January 1916): 2–10.

1. "Miscellaneous Notes," McLench Reminiscence, Mss. 206, OHS, p. 12; U.S. Manuscript Census, 1850, Windham County, VT, p. 15.

Mary Gray McLench at the age of seventy-two with her grandson, Lester Watson, aged four. Written on the back of the photograph in her handwriting is a quotation from Lester: "Me Hold Grandma."

Elizabeth Miller of South Argyle, New York, in the northern Hudson River Valley, and Sarah Smith of Lima, in western New York, were prime candidates for Oregon. Elizabeth's father, the Reverend James P. Miller, was a Presbyterian minister whose longing for the West began in his boyhood through reading about the Lewis and Clark Expedition. When he was offered the chance to establish a mission station in Oregon, he was anxious to accept. Elizabeth, who was only twenty and a recent graduate of the State Normal School at Albany, reveals a strong identification with her father in her biography written at the institute at Hartford. She was the eldest of four children. Slade's offer to pay her way to Oregon and guarantee her a teaching position fulfilled her strongest wish. She had hoped to travel with her whole family on the *Empire City,* but there was only room for her brother Frank, besides herself. Since Governor Slade insisted that she could not wait and must travel with the other teachers, Elizabeth and Frank arrived in Oregon six weeks ahead of their parents.[2]

Sarah Smith, who was thirty when she left the East, possessed a strong sense of religious mission. A student and assistant teacher at Genesee Wesleyan Seminary, Sarah had matured in the section of western New York noted for its religious enthusiasms. The preceptress of the seminary and her friends not only encouraged her "to heed the call from the West" but were willing to assist her financially if the National Board accepted her for Oregon. She had wanted to go to Oregon for years, and, if she could "be instrumental in doing good" there, she said, "my desire would be to wear out and die among them." Little is known about the early lives of the two other women who joined the group, but Elizabeth H. Lincoln, who was thirty-four, was from Portland, Maine, and Margaret B. Wands from Albany, New York.[3]

When the women arrived in Oregon, the population of the entire Territory, which also included Washington and Idaho, was about fourteen thousand. Portland's population was too small to be counted and the largest town, Oregon City, where the teachers first stayed, numbered under seven hundred, with twice as many men as women.[4] Much of what can be learned about the lives in Oregon of the teachers comes from Mary McLench's reminiscence. Each of them settled into a teaching position and eventually married, three within a year. Only Margaret Wands, who had become the

2. Although Elizabeth Miller's name ends with an "er" in her application and biography in the NPEB papers, it is spelled "ar" in material about her dating from her marriage. Her older half-brother, the son of her father's first wife, had recently died. Information about Elizabeth Wilson was supplied by her granddaughter, Elizabeth W. Buehler, of Portland, Oregon, and her great-granddaughter, Janet W. James, of Cambridge, Massachusetts. See also Elizabeth Miller, September 1850, biography folder; 10 August 1850, application folder, NPEB Papers; Elizabeth M. Wilson, "From New York to Oregon via the Isthus of Panama, in 1851," *Oregon Historical Society Proceedings* (1900): 101–03; U.S. Manuscript Census, 1850, Washington County, NY, p. 153. There are collections of Elizabeth M. Wilson papers in the Archives of Pacific University and the Schlesinger Library, Radcliffe College.

3. Sarah Smith, Lima, New York, 13 July 1850, Maria H. Hibbard, Lima, New York, 12 July 1850, application folder, NPEB Papers.

4. *Seventh Census of the United States, 1850* (Washington, D.C.: 1853), p. 988.

second wife of Governor John P. Gaines, returned to the East, soon after his death in 1858.[5] The four other women were known throughout their lives as the pioneer teachers who had been sent out from the East by Governor Slade and the National Board of Popular Education. The essential facts of their shared story were told again and again as they reached legendary pioneer status.

After teaching five terms, Mary Gray married Benjamin McLench, who was the brother of Elizabeth McLench Thurston, the widow of the congressman who died on their journey. The McLenches built a cabin on land they acquired through the Oregon Donation Land Act in the Willamette River Valley. Within seven years they had developed an extensive farm and built a large gothic farmhouse. Three of their four children lived to maturity. Mary was a full partner with her husband and could remember prices received for their farm's produce over the years. "The highest price received for wheat sold from our farm was $4 per bushel," she stated. She remembered apples selling for $15 a bushel, onions for $3, and potatoes for $4. Their best price for butter was fifty cents a pound. "Bees once commanded from $100.00 to $150.00 per swarm," she said; "ours later were $40.00 a swarm."[6]

Sarah Smith taught with Elizabeth Lincoln in the Clackamas County Female Seminary in Oregon City for a year before marrying Alanson Beers, a Methodist missionary. He died a year later, leaving her with six stepchildren. In two years Sarah married a second widower with children, John L. Kline. Elizabeth Lincoln taught in the first school in Astoria, where she met her husband, Alonzo Skinner, who later became a justice of the Oregon Supreme Court. She continued to teach and assisted her husband in the public school. Elizabeth Miller taught at Tualatin Academy, the predecessor of Pacific University. She married an attorney, Joseph G. Wilson, in 1854, in the same year her father died in a steamboat explosion.[7]

Elizabeth Millar Wilson began a second career at the age of forty-three when the sudden death of her husband left her a widow with four children.

5. Governor John P. Gaines (1795–1858) was the territorial governor of Oregon from 1850 to 1853. His first wife was thrown from a carriage in 1851 and killed. Margaret Wands married him on 25 November 1852. He retired to his farm in Marion County before his death on 4 January 1858. *National Cyclopedia*, vol. 8; p. 3; Vital Statistics file, OHS. References from the Oregon Historical Society were supplied by Steven Hallberg.

6. Benjamin F. McLench (1825–1892) came from Maine the year after the teachers arrived in Oregon. After 1850, the Donation Land Act provided 160 acres of land. Information about the McLench family was supplied by a great-granddaughter, Gertrude Hobbs of Salem, Oregon. See also "Miscellaneous Notes," McLench reminiscence, p. 14; Herbert O. Lang, ed., *History of the Willamette Valley* (Portland, OR: 1885), pp. 719–20.

7. John L. Kline (1814–1898) came from Tennessee and Alonzo Skinner (1814–1876) came from Ohio in 1845. "Miscellaneous Notes," McLench reminiscence, pp. 10–11, 14–15; Alfred A. Cleveland, "Educational History of Astoria," *Oregon Historical Quarterly* 4 (1903): 25–26; Wilson, "From New York to Oregon," p. 104; Vital Statistics file, OHS.

They were traveling to Washington, D.C., where he was going to serve his first term as congressman from Oregon, when he died. Within the year, in 1874—and amid controversy, because she was the first woman to receive a presidential appointment—Elizabeth Wilson was name postmistress of The Dalles by President Grant. Located on the Columbia River seventy-five miles upstream from Portland, The Dalles was the central distributing point for mail designated for eastern Washington and Idaho. During a flood in 1880, Elizabeth Wilson removed the post office to her own church, the Congregational church, for safekeeping. She held her position for twelve years and died in her eighties, outliving all the other pioneer women teachers.[8]

The clarity of Mary Gray McLench's memories of her journey to Oregon, an event happening fifty years before, points up the intensity of the experience. Sailing on the *Empire City* out of New York harbor, crossing the Isthmus of Panama, sailing up the West Coast of Mexico to San Francisco on the *California* and thence to Oregon on the *Columbia* was a true rite of passage. It turned women who were pioneer teachers into pioneer settlers on the Oregon frontier.

Notes of Mrs. Mary Almira Gray McLench, Relating to Her Trip to Oregon Early in 1851, Prepared for Her Daughter, Mrs. Mary McLench Watson, Fair Grounds, Oregon.

March 1, 1901

For a number of years prior to my starting to Oregon there had been teachers' agencies, by means of which societies teachers had been secured for places needing them, especially in the West and South. Perhaps a few dollars were paid by the applicant—I know it was in my case—and I think also by those desiring a teacher.

Early in the winter of 1850–51, I was applied to by H. L. Wayland, then principal of the seminary in Townshend, Vt., whom I had met but once, as I was then teaching in Grafton, Vt. His letter was accompanied by one he had received from ex-Governor William Slade, of Vermont, an agent of the Society called The National Board of Popular Education. There was also considerable printed matter relating to the work of this Society. Gov. Slade wrote that another teacher was wanted to go to Oregon to accompany the four already secured, and all were to accompany and be under the care of

8. Joseph G. Wilson died in 1873 at Marietta College, Ohio, where, as a prominent alumnus, he had come to give the commencement address. Originally from New Hampshire, he arrived in Oregon in 1852. Elizabeth Wilson's son, Fred W. Wilson (1872–1955), who graduated from Whitman College and Johns Hopkins University, became a circuit court judge at The Dalles. Elizabeth Wilson died in 1913, Mary Gray McLench in 1907, Sarah Smith Kline in 1872, and Elizabeth Lincoln Skinner in 1894. "Elizabeth Wilson," in William H. McNeal, *History of Wasco County, Oregon* (The Dalles: ca. 1953), p. 30; U.S. Manuscript Census, 1880, Wasco County, OR, p. 244B; Vital Statistics, OHS.

Hon. Samuel R. Thurston, then delegate to Congress from Oregon Territory, who would return to his Pacific home as soon as Congress adjourned early in March.[9]

After due consideration I finally decided to go, my Grafton school was shortened one week, and I had a week at home, during which time our family moved to the village, father having sold the farm. Fifty years have passed since then, and many things are dim in memory's vision.

We left home March 10th, 1851, early on Monday morning, my brother Oscar going with me, and we stopped the first night at the Massasoit House, Springfield, Mass. Tuesday night found us at the Delavan House, New York [Albany], as directed, and the next day we met ex-Gov. Slade, Samuel R. Thurston, and my sister teachers, Miss Lincoln, from Maine, Miss Wands, Miss Smith and Miss Millar, the last three from different parts of the State of New York. Our expenses were all paid after our arrival in New York city, excepting for such shopping as we needed. Our fare was $350.00 each, but whether this included the cost of crossing the Isthmus I do not know, but suppose it did. A new saddle was provided for each lady, which it was understood that we were to keep for future use. These were taken from New York, with a bottle of claret, for the company, as the water at the Isthmus was unhealthy. Oscar remained with me and went with me on board the *Empire City*, Capt. Wilson, commander, and we sailed, or perhaps I should say steamed out of New York harbor Thursday afternoon, March 13th, and arrived off the Isthmus on Saturday, the 22nd, at dusk, when our vessel anchored, which was signified by the firing of rockets and responded to by the other side. We did not encounter any storm or wind of any consequence except off Cape Hatteras, where it is always rough, until we entered the Caribbean sea where we had rough weather for two days.

The next day the passengers were landed in small boats, about twelve or fifteen at a time. Several boats were employed, as there were about fifteen hundred passengers to disembark (so Mr. Chadwick said).[10] After walking down the steps on the side of the vessel to the place where the small boats approached at the nearest point, each one was told to "jump into that man's arms." If one did not, the boat would recede. It did not seem possible to do so, but it was the only way. One lady, going to San Francisco, waited a little too long and took a plunge into the ocean from which she was recovered. The sea was rough and sometimes it seemed as if the waves would enter the boat.

I cannot remember the name of the little town, perhaps it was Chagres, where our trunks had to be examined by the custom house inspectors. Maybe it was

9. Samuel R. Thurston (1816–1851), a lawyer from Maine, was the first elected delegate to Congress from the Oregon Territory. *History of the Bench and Bar of Oregon* (Portland, OR: 1910), pp. 278–79.

10. Stephen F. Chadwick (1825–1895) from Massachusetts became secretary of state and an acting governor. It appears that Mary McLench and Chadwick disagreed over their memory of the numbers on board the *Empire City*. Vital Statistics, OHS.

Gatun. I know we stayed there one night, but it seems to me that it was a little distance up the Chagres river, but I may be mistaken. A broken-winded little steamboat propelled two bateaux or flat boats, with awnings, as far as the river was large enough, after which the motive power was natives, with poles, after being transferred into smaller boats. We spent one night in our boats near a little town where, a month before, a number of travelers were killed by the boatmen in order that they might rob a large and strong box which they supposed was filled with gold, but which, in reality, was a carpenter's tool chest. This night the men of our company stood guard two hours at a time. Mr. Thurston was very weary and nearly sick, and got a hammock on shore. Tuesday noon we reached Gorgona, which is about sixty miles from the mouth of the Chagres river—perhaps the crookedest river in America.

At Gatun the "North American Hotel" had a ground or earth floor, thatched or tile roof (both were in use), no chairs, cot beds or beds on the floor, and just as many men and women as the room would hold, perhaps twenty or more. At Gorgona I remember a light, airy room, occupied by ladies, and not crowded; but I spent the whole afternoon in bed with a raging sick headache.

On Wednesday morning, as early as possible, preparations were begun for the day's trip over the mountains on muleback to Panama, twenty-seven miles distant. The baggage, also, had to be transported in the same way, i.e., on pack mules. Perhaps the Babel of sounds may be imagined! Peons shouting to their animals and to each other, in Spanish, English, and perhaps some other languages. But at last the different cavalcades had started. It was well for me that there were a few miles of comparatively level road at the outset, otherwise I could never have retained my seat on my mule.[11] Being totally unused to horseback riding, it seemed as if I should fall off at every step. Many times the trail looked so dangerous I felt very much afraid; but what could I do but go on? I could not stop my mule. The animal did not seem vicious, but only wanted to take the lead, and would do so if there was a chance to get ahead, which was the case on several different occasions. It was impossible for me to hold the beast, as I had no bridle—only a rope around the nose. Miss Millar was thrown, but not until after the mountains were crossed. Her mule ran away, and two went in pursuit. My mule would not be left behind, so I had to go, too, and kept up with the foremost. Upon catching up with the runaway mule I dismounted for the first time, and out of sight of the rest of the party kept guard over the three mules while the two men, one of whom was Mr. Thurston, took the runaway animal back to the scene of the accident. Miss Millar was but slightly hurt, and soon we were on our way again, and without further

11. The women were seated on sidesaddles. Wilson, "From New York to Oregon," p. 107.

mishap arrived at Panama about sunset, just before the closing of the city gates.

The railroad across the Isthmus was being built. The *Empire City* brought down about one hundred workmen under charge of a captain; and in different places we could follow the line of the railroad by the gangs of men at work a little distance away.

The streets of Panama were roughly paved with cobblestones, as were the roads for some distance back. The houses were sombre-looking, dark, and built of brick, I think—I know the floors were. Through the day the doors stood open for the admission of light and air. There were no glass windows —but a small sliding panel in the door.

Three or four boarding-houses were being built, of modern construction —light, pleasant and airy, and in a much pleasanter part of the city. The next day after our arrival we devoted to getting rested—indeed, I think all of us were incapacitated for any exertion or exercise. We found it very pleasant to walk about the place, but we could only do so early in the morning or just before sunset, on account of the heat. In that torrid zone the twilight was short. There were pleasant lanes shaded by orange trees in fruit. The oranges looked better than they tasted. There were plenty of good ones, but they did not grow by the highway. On the beach were several old cannon, partially buried in the sand, one of which was said to be the largest gun in America. (But that was fifty years ago.)

There was one Protestant meeting house for religious service in the place, and an Episcopalian chaplain preached. Several of our number attended, myself among them.

The drinking water was too warm to be good. It was brought to the city every morning in kegs on mules, from springs in the neighboring mountains, each animal carrying two. No fresher water could be obtained during the hot sweltering day.

The sign, "King of Clubs," was prominent just below our balcony; and in other places, also, similar signs seemed no more improper than signs of merchandise for sale.

Panama was quite different from any place I ever saw—indeed, it was a foreign country—a different nationality—but contained much of interest.

We remained in this place a little less than a week, and anticipated another visit to this ancient town on our way back to "the States" after a few years. (But this never came to pass.)

The second of April found us again on our way on the old steamer, *California,* Capt. Budd, commander. The harbor of Panama contained many small boats, and by stepping from one to another a dozen times or more, we at length reached one in which we were to be conveyed to our ship, which was anchored some miles away. For several days the heat was tropical, and probably affected us more on account of our speedy transition from a cold to a warm climate. My warm travelling dress, which I had expected to wear the whole distance, was discarded several days for the coolest and thinnest fabrics that it was possible to secure.

Mr. Thurston had complained of feeling ill at Panama, and while there took minute doses of quinine two or three times a day. (This was the first time I ever saw this drug, but from my knowledge of it since, it is my opinion that the quantity taken was not sufficient to have much effect in eradicating disease.)

Mr. Thurston seemed to grow worse speedily and lost much of his accustomed cheerfulness. We little thought, however, how dark a cloud was so soon to overshadow us. On Thursday night Mr. Thurston went to his stateroom sick, and some young men in his care watched over him. Sunday morning he was assisted to the captain's stateroom on deck, which the latter had kindly offered for the sick man's use, it being more commodious and airy. The disease—(Isthmus or Panama fever, I suppose)—was making rapid progress. Most of the time Mr. Thurston was conscious except during the last few hours. His death occurred early—not later than one o'clock—Wednesday morning, April 9th. Had he not been a public man, burial would have taken place at sea; but as it was, enshrouded or covered with the Stars and Stripes, our Country's flag, he was taken along on our course till Thursday morning, about nine o'clock, when our ship anchored near Acapulco. A coffin had been prepared on shipboard and he was laid to rest in the cemetery of that place.

All the men bound for Oregon attended the burial, and many others; but as it was a mile or more away, it was deemed hazardous for the ladies to go. So we spent the day at the hotel, with short rambles on the beach, while the ship took on coal.

Mr. Nelson, who was going to Oregon as chief justice, and Mr. Preston, who had the appointment of surveyor-general, showed us many kindnesses, which we thoroughly appreciated—but they were strangers to Oregon.[12] We often missed the thoughtful care and interest of Mr. Thurston, and sadly thought of the grief of his family when they should become apprised of their bereavement.

After leaving the Isthmus our course was southerly for several hours, in order to strike a certain ocean current, and sometimes we were near the shores of South America.

12. Judge Thomas Nelson (1819–1907) from Poughkeepsie was the federally appointed chief justice for Oregon. John B. Preston, (??–1865) who traveled with his wife, her sister, Miss Hyde, and the Prestons' daughter, Kate, was a federally appointed surveyor-general for Oregon. Margaret Wands married Governor Gaines in Preston's house. Also en route to Oregon was Zenas F. Moody (1832–1917), from Massachusetts, a future governor of Oregon. Vital Statistics, OHS; Wilson, "From New York to Oregon," p. 104.

After leaving Acapulco, the stopping places up the coast were San Blas, made memorable by one of Longfellow's poems—perhaps the last—"The Bell of San Blas," Mazatlan and San Diego. I do not remember any others and we did not go ashore at all these places. As we approached the Gulf of California the weather suddenly turned cold, and in two days from the time that the heat was so prostrating, we were clad in our warmest garments, with winter wraps, and yet shivered with cold.

Our ship was expected to stop at Monterey, but the engines were disabled; and being fearful that at any hour it might become necessary to hoist sails, we kept on our way, and anchored off San Francisco on Tuesday, April 23d. There was no wharf there, and small boats took the passengers ashore after experiencing considerable delay.

Here, too, everything looked strange—all sorts of people and houses, and many were living in tents down next to the water front. Also many families were living in flatboats, with cloth covers. Shops, likewise, were fitted up in the same unpretentious manner. Our hotel was probably as good as the place afforded, as Senator and Mrs. Gwin,[13] Gen. Preston's family, Judge Nelson and others, were among the number who stopped there; but certainly it did not come up to modern requirements except in price. The table, extending the length of the dining room, perhaps thirty feet, was good, and the viands delicious. Perhaps it was in honor of some sort of a dress occasion. I only remember that Mrs. Gwin, who sat opposite me at supper, appeared costumed in black silk, with a large white lace cape and light kid gloves, ribbons, jewelry, etc. At night the teachers and Miss Hyde occupied one large, unfinished room, on the door of which was posted a printed notice of prices. I only remember that board was $5.00 per day; lodging, $3.00 per night. When in San Francisco again in 1877 I could not find any place which looked like the site of this hotel. I know that it was near the plaza, and when another lady and myself went out with some one to direct our way to do a little shopping one morning, we took the middle of a wagon road down a little hill. I think there were rough sidewalks in some places.

We remained in San Francisco at this time a little less than one day, and the afternoon found the "Oregon Company" on board the staunch little steamship, *Columbia,* Capt. LeRoy, master, who was a much more genial man than Capt. Budd. There was an unusually large number of ladies among the passengers for Oregon, the number being nine, if I remember correctly, including Kate Preston, then ten years old. I do not know how many men there were, but certainly several times the former number.

The change from the cumbrous old *California,* crowded with passengers to its utmost limit, seemed delightful. I think Mr. Chadwick was wrong in

13. William McKendree Gwin (1805–1885) was the U.S. senator from California from 1850 to 1861. *DAB,* vol. 8, p. 64.

The steamer Lot Whitcomb, *which carried the Oregon teachers up the Columbia River from Astoria to Portland.*

claiming fifteen hundred passengers for the *Empire City*. My recollection is that that was the number on the *California*, on the trip from Panama to San Francisco.

Without accident or incident worthy of mention, we arrived at the mouth of the Columbia river early on Monday morning, April 28th, and securing a pilot, for which I could not see any need, as the sea was smooth as glass—only a little whitening of the water over the bar which we had heard was so formidable, we soon were anchored in the channel of the river off Astoria. We were then taken in small boats to a point where there was a huge fallen fir tree upon which we landed, and then climbing over its roots, we jumped down into Astoria. Whether that was the only way of access, or the better way, I am unable to state, but judge it was the better way for pedestrians. It seemed a wild, new place, with only a small sprinkling of houses scattered among trees and huge stumps. It seemed as if there was but little chance for Astoria's expansion to any great dimensions. The only house we entered that I remember was that of Gen. Adair's—a pleasant home.[14] Here we saw the chief of the Clatsop tribe of Indians and his squaw. My preconceived ideas of the "noble red man" received a stunning blow.

14. General John Adair (1808–1888) was the first collector of customs for Oregon. Vital Statistics, OHS.

Our stay in Astoria was short, and soon we were on our way up the noble Columbia river. The next morning April 29th, we arrived at Vancouver, and went ashore to see the place, the soldiers, barracks, etc. I remember, among other things, seeing apple trees in bloom. After a short ramble, which we greatly appreciated, we went aboard our vessel and steamed towards Portland.[15] I had the misfortune to get a cinder in my eye which I could not remove. It was exceedingly painful and I sought my stateroom and soon fell asleep. When I awoke the steamer was at anchor, and every thing was still. My eye was well. I went out on deck and found the members of our company returning from a visit on shore. They had not missed me for awhile, but soon discovering that I was not with them, returned to find out what had happened to me, and then I went ashore with them. In landing we had to step from skiff to skiff, as there was no wharf. Among other places, we visited the *Oregonian* office. Fifty years ago there was very little prospect that Portland would ever attain its present prestige. It now contains more than 90,000 population. Big fir stumps were plentiful in the principal streets, and occasional trees as well. The primeval forest was in close proximity. We dined somewhere in Portland, but where I do not know.

About the middle of the afternoon we went on board a flatboat covered with an awning, and started for Oregon City, then promising to be the future metropolis of Oregon, being rowed by Indians. "But the best laid plans of mice and men aft gang aglee." When at the foot of Clackamas rapids, the boat ran aground. After a few ineffectual attempts to get it afloat, the craft was made fast to a tree on the shore. It was now getting dusk. The crew kindled a fire and began preparations for their supper, while the passengers were in the dark and supperless, notwithstanding that they could see lights in the houses at Oregon City. Gen. Preston unrolled two mattresses he had purchased in San Francisco, and arranged them for the ladies of the company so that they might get all the rest they could. Early in the morning baskets of provisions were sent down, and thus refreshed, we walked through a stumpy bushy pasture to Oregon City, which seemed to be much pleasanter and much more of a place than Portland. Rev. Mr. Atkinson, to whose care the teachers were assigned, met us and took us to his home.[16]

We had an uncomfortable night and were weary and worn. This was April 30th. Friends of Mr. Thurston soon called, making many inquiries. Mrs. Thurston had been apprised of her husband's death the evening before. In the

15. According to Elizabeth Millar Wilson, the teachers took the new steamer, *Lot Whitcomb,* from Astoria to Portland. Wilson, "From New York to Oregon," p. 109.

16. The Reverend George H. Atkinson (1819–1889), from Newburyport, Massachusetts, had requested teachers to start the Seminary in Oregon City to which Sarah Smith and Elizabeth Lincoln were assigned. *Fifth NPEB Report,* 1852, pp. 6–7; Vital Statistics, OHS.

Oregon City, the destination of the pioneer teachers, shown in 1857, six years after the teachers first arrived.

afternoon several ladies called and the teachers were invited to different homes till they should get rested and take up their work. Miss Lincoln went to Mr. Hatch's; Miss Millar and Miss Smith to J. Quinn Thornton's; Miss Wands went to Green Point, a little out of the city, I do not remember with whom. I was invited to go to Rev. Ezra Fisher's, then living on the bluff, overlooking the city. He and his daughter Lucy were teaching a school in town, and they were to come for me next day.[17] Meanwhile Rev. Mr. Atkinson had been to see Mrs. Thurston and brought a request from her that the teachers should all call on her the next day, and that one should remain with her until she should commence her school. It was finally decided that I must be that one. Accordingly, the next day, May 1st, escorted by Mr. Atkinson, we crossed the Willamette river and wended our way to the little brown house on the hillside—the home of the stricken family.[18]

Here I remained three weeks or more, till a few days prior to beginning my school on Tualatin plains, fifteen miles distant. Miss Millar went to Forest Grove, the seat of Pacific University of today; Miss Lincoln and Miss

17. Peter Holt Hatch (1810–1898), an educator, became Oregon's state librarian; Jesse Quinn Thornton (1810–1888) was an attorney and judge of the Provisional Supreme Court; and the Reverend Ezra Fischer (1800–1874) was a Baptist missionary and teacher. Vital Statistics, OHS.

18. Elizabeth McLench Thurston was appointed preceptress in 1853 of the Oregon Institute, now Willamette University, at Salem. She remarried two years later. Benjamin McLench removed Samuel Thurston's remains from Acapulco to Salem in 1853. "Miscellaneous Notes," McLench reminiscence, p. 13.

Smith to Oregon City; Miss Wands went to Durham's, later called Oswego. In later years they all married and "Settled down" in Oregon. Miss Smith became the wife of Alanson Beers, and stepmother to six children. After his death she married a Mr. Kline, of Albany, I think, and the number of her step children increased in equal ratio. She became a widow the second time and died at the home of one of her daughters about twenty-five years ago.

Miss Wands became the second wife of Gov. John P. Gaines, whose large family of children by the first wife returned to their Kentucky home, with the exception of two grown sons, who remained in Oregon. Gov. Gaines died within a few years, and not many years afterwards Mrs. Gaines with one little daughter, returned to her friends in New York. Since then I know nothing in regard to her.

Miss Lincoln married Judge Alonzo A. Skinner. He died many years ago, and she lived to an advanced age in Eugene, and died five or six years since.

Miss Millar married Joseph G. Wilson, and accompanied him to Washington after he was elected a member of Congress from Oregon. Before taking his seat they visited his old college town, Marietta, Ohio, where he became seriously ill and died suddenly. Mrs. Wilson returned to The Dalles and is still living there. She has three married daughters and one son, and lost three or four children in infancy. She was Postmistress at The Dalles for a number of years.

(The sweet-faced old lady from whom I secured the foregoing narrative, Mrs. Benjamin F. McLench, formerly Miss Mary Almira Gray, was so taken up with reminiscences concerning others, that she scarcely thought of her own. She was married to Mr. McLench in 1852, and it was his sister who was the wife of Mr. Thurston.

G[eorge] H. H[imes][19])

19. George H. Himes was a long-time officer of the Oregon Pioneer Association and the Oregon Historical Society, who recorded the McLench reminiscence. He presented it with some additions from a second interview to Mary McLench's daughter, Mary Watson, of Fair Grounds, Oregon, just before her mother's death in 1907.

APPENDIX

~~~~~~~~~~~~~~~~~~ A ~~~~~~~~~~~~~~~~~~

National Popular Education Board Materials Available[1]

Teachers writing letters from the West	136	
Biographies or applications for teachers who wrote letters		104
Teachers' names without letters	110	
Teachers' biographies or applications without letters		63
Total whole names[2]	246	
Total biographies or applications		167
Total number of letters, including one diary and three reminiscences		244

1. The basic collection is in The Connecticut Historical Society. Other sources included in this count are the McLench reminiscence, Oregon Historical Society; Wilson, "From New York to Oregon"; Bishop, *Floral Home*; letters to Calvin Fletcher from Delphia A. Dean, Abigail Kies, Annie Perry, and Mary J. Wilson, Fletcher Papers, Indiana Historical Society; letters from Elisabeth Hill and Rebecca B. Veazie, American Missionary Association Papers, Amistad Research Center, New Orleans, Louisiana; letter from Ann Sawyer Chandler, Mount Holyoke College Archives.

2. Teachers who were known by last names only were dropped from the study; twenty-two whole names remain with no information other than name. A few names not included in the original National Board Papers or annual reports came from the Fletcher Diary and Bishop, *Floral Home*.

APPENDIX

~~~~~~~~~~~~~~~~~~~~~~~~~ B ~~~~~~~~~~~~~~~~~~~~~~~~~

Profile of Pioneer Women Teachers

Table B.1. Home States (N = 203)

	Number of Teachers	Percentage of Total
Vermont	59	29
New York	50	25
Massachusetts	40	20
Maine	17	8
Connecticut	14	7
New Hampshire	14	7
Pennsylvania, Ohio, Michigan	9	4

Table B.2. Pioneer States (N = 204)

	Number of Teachers	Percentage of Total
Indiana	65	32
Illinois	38	19
Missouri	27	13
Wisconsin/Minnesota	18	9
Iowa/Kansas/Nebraska[1]	14	7
Ohio/Western Pennsylvania	12	6
Kentucky/Tennessee/Arkansas	11	5
Michigan	7	3.5
Oregon/California	7	3.5
Alabama/Georgia/North Carolina	5	2

1. Nebraska includes Lucy and Sarah in the letter from Lucy ———, Bluff City, Nebraska, to Miss Ferry, 18 August 1854, cited at the end of Part 1.

Table B.3. Composition of Families (N = 135)

	Number of Teachers	Percentage of Total
Family losses: (includes 3 widows)	48	35.5
Older professionals on their own	48	35.5
Both parents still living	39	29

Table B.4. Birth Order (N = 85)

	Number of Teachers	Percentage of Total
Oldest daughter	45	53
Youngest daughter	16	19
Other rank	24	28

Table B.5. Teachers' Ages at Hartford (N = 156)

Under 25 years	79	50.5
25 years or over	77	49.5

Table B.6. Teachers' Previous Education (N = 128)

Attended academy or seminary	80	63
Attended normal school or Mt. Holyoke	35	27
Attended district school only	13	10

Table B.7. Teachers' Previous Teaching Experience (N = 145)

Experienced: 3 to 6 years	62	43
Professional: over 6 years	33	23
Beginning	50	34

Table C.1. Teachers' Futures[1] Compared with Mt. Holyoke Alumnae in Group and NPEB Totals

	Current Study Teachers (N = 97)		Mt. Holyoke Alumnae[2] Teachers (N = 24)		NPEB Total[3] Teachers (N = 460)	
	Number	Percent	Number	Percent	Number	Percent
Settled in West:	66	68	17	71	336	73
Married	50		12			
Married, died soon	5		2			
Total married	55	83	14	82	142	42
Unmarried	6		2			
Unmarried, died soon	5		1			
Total unmarried	11	17	3	18	194	58
Returned East:	31	32	7	29	124	27
Married	21	68	3	43		
Unmarried	6		3			
Unmarried, died soon	4		1			
Total unmarried	10	32	4	57		

1. A teacher was classed as staying in the West if she took a step toward settling: marriage, teaching more than ten years in the West or South, or death in the West. A teacher was classed as staying in the East if she married at home and no evidence was available that she returned West, resumed a career in the East, or died in the East. Whole careers are available for sixty teachers. The number of futures known represents 39.4 percent of the total whole names.

2. *Mount Holyoke Directory* and Mount Holyoke College archival material with the assistance of Elaine Trehub, College History Librarian.

3. *Eleventh NPEB Report,* 1858: 6–7. In the board's final report, Governor Slade's actual total was 481, including twenty-one teachers who died, but he did not state where. His grand total was 590 and included the 109 teachers from the Ladies' Society for the Promotion of Education at the West in Boston, from whom he had received only three letters.

Table C.2. Influence of Past on Teachers' Futures, Comparison between Teachers Settling in West and Teachers Returning East[1]

	All Teachers		Settling in West		Returning East	
	Number	Percent	Number	Percent	Number	Percent
Family Composition	(N = 135)		(N = 45)		(N = 25)	
Family loss	48	35.5	14	31	6	24
Older pro-fessional	48	35.5	21	47	7	28
Total:	96	71	35	78	13	52
Both parents	39	29	10	22	12	48
Age at Hartford	(N = 156)		(N = 51)		(N = 30)	
Under 25	79	50.5	22	43	21	70
25 or over	77	49.5	29	57	9	30
Teaching Experience	(N = 145)		(N = 46)		(N = 28)	
Experienced	62	43	26	56	10	36
Professional	33	23	11	24	5	18
Total:	95	66	37	80	15	54
Beginning	50	34	9	20	13	46

1 The influence of birth order was not significantly different between the two groups.

APPENDIX D

Lives of the Pioneer Women Teachers

Alum.	Alumni Records
Amistad	American Missionary Association Archives, Amistad Research Center, New Orleans, Louisiana
Arch.	Archives
Athen.	Atheneum
Cen.	U.S. Manuscript Census (unless state census is indicated)
Fletcher D.	*Diary of Calvin Fletcher*
His.	Historical Society collections, followed by place
NPEB	National Popular Education Board Papers: Admin. (Administration file), A (Application file), B (Biography file), L (Letters file), R (Regeneration file). L followed by a name identifies the letter writer as different from the subject.
NE His. Gen.	New England Historical Genealogical Society's collection of family histories
PL	Public Library, followed by town, city, or county name
VR	Vital Records, preceded by state, county, or town name

Lives of the Pioneer Women Teachers

Teacher[1]	Home Town[2] Birth Year	Academy or Seminary	Places Taught for NPEB, Dates	Sources: Early	Married	Later Life	Death Place & Year	Sources: Future
Ellen A. Abbott	Worcester, VT, 1828	Worcester Acad. Montpelier Acad.	Greenville, KY 1853	NPEB: B,L VT VR				
Mary E. Adams	Bangor, ME, 1830	Mt. Holyoke Sem.	Neosho, MO 1853	NPEB: B,L ME VR Cen. 1850	Alexander Warfield Neosho, MO, trader		Nashville, TN, 1903	Alum.: M.H.
Mary S. Adams	Hartford, PA	Mt. Holyoke Sem.	Calhoun, MO 1853–54	NPEB: B,L	Asa C. Martin, 1854		Clinton, MO, 1855	Alum.: M.H.
Augusta C. Allen	Mt. Holly, VT, 1829	Castleton Sem.	Osage Beach, MO 1852–54	NPEB: B,L Cen. 1850				
Emily Allen	Norfolk, CT, 1825		Indianapolis, IN 1848	NPEB: A Fletcher D:IV:179	Jacob Coffman 1850		Indianapolis, 1853	His.: IN
Martha I. Andrews	Hopkinton, NY, 1828		Mobile, AL 1850	NFEB: A	Reuben Freeman, Mobile, sea captain, 1852	Lived Fergus Falls, MN, 2 children; widowed 1901	after 1902	His.: St.Law. Cy., NY
Mary S. Arnold	Monmouth, ME, 1825		St. Charles, IL 1850	NPEB: A,L,R				

1. Twenty-two pioneer teachers of whom no more is known than their whole names have been excluded from this table. At Hartford in 1848, each wrote a letter on the subject of "Regeneration" and gave no personal information. Their names are Julia Bierce, M. A. Haraford, Ella M. Herrick, Isabelle J. Jinne (1849), E. H. Langdon, Elisa S. Littlefield, H. E. Ruggles, Elizabeth G. Shattuck, Mary Silsbee, Caroline D. Smith, Minerva Terwin, Philena Whitmore, and Maria M. Woodbury.

Each of the eleven National Board annual reports contained lists of teachers who had refunded part of their expenses. They were usually listed as Miss without their first names. Seventy-eight of the 130 teachers listed are known from other sources and included in Appendix D. Whole names given for which no information has been found are: Lucy Allen, N. A. Chamberlain, C. H. Drake, L. M. Lane, Laura Newton (Mrs. Cross) in Wisconsin, R. A. Rix in Indiana, Henrietta Starkweather in Arkansas, J. E. Swain, and J. B. Wilder in Indiana. Miss St. John (Mrs. Amidon) is the only incomplete name included because her married name, home town, and later residence were confirmed by an additional source.

2. Home Town refers to either the place where the pioneer teacher always lived and may have been born or to the place where the teacher was living when she applied to the National Board. Both places are listed if they differ. Unless vital records were available, the birth year was calculated from the teacher's age when she entered the institute at Hartford.

Teacher	Home Town Birth Year	Academy or Seminary	Places Taught for NPEB, Dates	Sources: Early	Marriage	Later Life	Death Place & Year	Sources: Future
Maria Atwater	Orange, CT (?), 1820 (?)		Perry, AR 1854–55	NPEB: L Cen. 1850				
Elisabeth Bachelder	Plainfield, VT, 1824		Mooresville, IN 1851–52	NPEB: B,L VT VR				
Elisabeth Backus (also Electa)	Franklin, CT, 1810		St. Anthony (now Minneapolis) MN 1849–52	NPEB: L Town VR	single	Taught Chocktaw people in OK, 1853–54; in Bolton, CT, 1859		His.: MN Amistad
Sarah A. Ballard	Worcester, MA, 1818		Rosendale, Grand Marsh, WI 1850–55	NPEB: L,R	Charles E. Thurston, Grand Marsh, 1852		Grand Marsh, WI, 1855 (?)	His.: WI (Thurston fam. his.) NPEB: 9th Report:5
Maria L. Barrett	Belchertown, MA	Franklin Acad. Ct. Lit. Inst.	South Bend, IN 1853–54	NPEB: B,L				
Julia E. Bassett	Montpelier, VT, 1827	Castleton Sem.	Paris, IL 1850	NPEB: B VT VR				
Lucinda L. Beach	Homer, NY, 1833	Cortland Acad.	Columbus, OH 1852–53	NPEB: B,L		home in 1855		NY Cen. 1855
Maria A. Beach	VT, 1829	Castleton Sem.	Henderson, KY 1854	NPEB: L Cen. 1850				
Louisa J. Bean	Candia, NH 1821	N.H. Conf. Sem., Northfield	Wyoming, WI 1852–53	NPEB: B,L Cen. 1850				
Lucy P. Bell	Weybridge, VT	Malone Acad., NY	Grand Haven, MI 1852–54	NPEB: B,L				
Lucy A. Bicknell	Windsor, MA, 1828 Lorain Cty., OH	Oberlin	Geneva, IL 1853 Waterloo, IA 1854–57	NPEB: B,L Alum.: Ober.	Rev. Charles Oldfield, 1857	lived Cedar Springs, MI	after 1908	Alum.: Ober.
E. Ellen Birge	New Haven, VT, 1830		Batavia, IL 1852	NPEB: B,L Cen. 1850				

Teacher	Home Town Birth Year	Academy or Seminary	Places Taught for NPEB, Dates	Sources: Early	Married	Later Life	Death Place & Year	Sources: Future
Cynthia M. Bishop	Georgia, VT, 1826	Bakersfield, VT H.S. (Lowell Mills)	New Durham, Lafayette, IN 1853–54	NPEB: B,L Cen. 1850				
Harriet Bishop	Panton, VT, 1817	Ft. Edward Inst., NY	St. Paul, MN 1847–50	NPEB: 7th Report: 35–37	John McCauley 1857, div. 1867	author, reformer	St. Paul, 1883	His.: MN Bishop, *Floral Home*
Emily C. Bowers	Brooklyn, NY (born NE)		IN 1849	NPEB: A,R				
Martha Boynton	Carlisle, MA, 1828 Lowell, MA	New Hampton Sem., NH (Lowell Mills)	Wyoming Valley, WI 1851	NPEB: B,L Cen. 1850 Town VR	Hezekiah W. Howe of Boston, 1858, mason		Dorchester, MA, 1907	MA VR NE His. Gen. (Boynton fam. his.)
Mary W. Bradstreet	Gardiner, ME, 1810		1851	NPEB: B Town VR	single		Gardiner, ME, 1858	Town VR
Mary R. Brainerd			Boonville, MO 1852	NPEB: L				
Evelina Bray	Marblehead, MA, 1814	Ipswich Fem. Sem.	IN 1847	Town VR Fletcher D: II: 389	Rev. William Downey, d. 1889		W. Newbury, 1895	Athen.: Minneapolis
Mary J. Bronson	New Haven, CT, 1817		Johnson Creek, Albany, IL 1849–52	NPEB: A,L	Ariel Crosby, Albany, 1851 (widowed before 1845)	daughter by first marriage		Cty. VR NPEB: L (Crosby)
Harriet N. Brooks	Dalton, NH 1821		La Hape, IL 1850	NPEB: A,L, R Town VR	Ranselaer W chell, Hancock Cty.			Cty. VR
Phila A. Brooks	Keene, NH, 1825		Howard, IL 1851	NPEB: B,L				
Martha C. Brown	Blandford, MA Whatley, MA, 1830		Portage Prairie, IN 1852–54	NPEB: B,L	Henry Brown Whatley, '57			MA VR

Teacher	Home Town Birth Year	Academy or Seminary	Places Taught for NPEB, Dates	Sources: Early	Marriage	Later Life	Death Place & Year	Sources: Future
Betsey C. Brownell	Weybridge, VT		Mooresville, IN 1852	NPEB: B,L				
Rebecca P. Burr	Haddam, CT, 1825		Evansville, IN 1851–53	NPEB: B,L Cen. 1850				
S. Augusta Carpenter	Greenfield, MA, 1831	W. Newton Norm. Mt. Holyoke Sem.	1850	NPEB: A,R Town VR	Rev. James Averill, Greenfield, 1854	daughter, Mary, Mt. Holyoke '84	Greenfield, 1877	MA VR Alum.: M.H. Alum.: Framingham
Jane E. Chamberlain	Peacham, VT, 1832	Mt. Holyoke Sem.	Wolcottville, IN, Kenosha, WI, 1852–57	NPEB: *11th Report*: 21 MA VR	single	missionary to Turkey 10 years	Cambridge, MA, 1914	Alum.: M.H. MA VR
E. E. Chandler			Mill Point, MI 1848–49	NPEB: L (Roper), R				
Amy L. Chapman	Palmyra, NY	Rochester Fem. Acad.	Sharonville, OH 1853–54 AR before 1861	NPEB: B,L Cen. 1850	single	taught freedmen, N.C., 1865–75[3]	buried Palmyra, 1880	His. Wayne Cty. NY
Louisa M. Chase	Harvard, MA, 1823		Naperville, IL 1847–48	Town VR	single		Naperville, 1848	NPEB: *2nd Report*: 8
Mary L. Chase	Otego, NY	Delaware Lit. Inst. Mt. Holyoke Sem.	Savanna, IL 1853	NPEB: B,L	Rev. James Redfield Smith, 1853	lived Pleasant Valley, IL, 2 sons	1901 or 1902	Alum.: M.H.
Ann M. Child	Derby, VT, 1834	Mt. Holyoke Sem.	Lexington & Seymour, IN 1852–56	NPEB: L Cen. 1850	Rev. Charles T. White, 1856	missionary in Madras, India, 1856–69	Cambridge City, IN, 1877	Alum.: M.H.
Octavia E. Chipman	Tinmouth, VT, 1827	Castleton Sem.	1851	NPEB: A,B				

3. The names of the pioneer teachers who later taught the freedmen were supplied by Ronald Butchart from his study of teachers of the freedmen. They are Amy Chapman, Elisabeth Hill, Sarah Parker, and Rebecca Veazie.

Teacher	Home Town Birth Year	Academy or Seminary	Places Taught for NPEB, Dates	Sources: Early	Marriage	Later Life	Death Place & Year	Sources: Future
Rebecca L. Clark	Concord, MA, 1830		Tipton, IA & Delavan, WI 1852–54	NPEB: B,L Town VR Cen. 1850	single	home in 1854; KS with brother in 1860s; home		NPEB: L PL: Concord Interview: G. Clark[4] NPEB: 9b Report: 24
Mary J. Coburn	Haverhill, MA, 1825		IL 1852–55	NPEB: A	Grout in IL			
Eunice Cole	Marshfield, VT, 1823		Vevay, IN 1854	NPEB: L Cer. 1850 VT VR				
Sarah A. Comstock	Saybrook, CT		Pomeroy, OH 1853	NPEB: B,L	Rev. George Moore, Andover, MA, 1855	to CA after marriage		State Lib.: CT (Comstock fam. his.)
Helen E. Cotton	Malone, NY, 1832		Chandlerville, IL 1852–55	NPEB: B,L Cen. 1850	John H. Goodell, Chandlerville, 1855, farmer		Chandlerville, 1863	Cty. VR His.: Cass Cty.
Aurilla Cross	Swanzey, NH	Gouverneur Wes. Sem., NY	Strawtown, IN 1852–53	NPEB: B,L				
Cemantha M. Currier	Chateaugay, NY, 1826	Malone Acad.	Sabula, IA 1852	NPEB: A,B, L	Julius A. Lewis, Jackson Cty., IA, 1853			Cty. VR
Elizabeth Cutler	Shrewsbury, MA, 1818		1849	NPEB: A,R				
Judith C. Daggett	Malone, NY 1814	Malone Acad.	Mt. Pulaski, IL 1852–53	NPEB: B,L Cen. 1850 His.: Franklin Cty., NY				
Myra Jane Davis	Danville, VT	Phillips Acad., Danville	Wautoma, WI 1852–53	NPEB: B,L				

4. Interview with Gladys Clark, grandniece of Rebecca Clark, in Concord, Massachusetts, 18 November 1982.

Teacher	Home Town Birth Year	Academy or Seminary	Places Taught for NPEB, Dates	Sources: Early	Marriage	Later Life	Death Place & Year	Sources: Future
Jane Dayton	Granville, NY, 1825		Vermillion Cty. IN 1848–50	Fletcher D: IV, 36		home Sept. 1850		Cen. 1850
Delphia A. Dean	Bakersfield, VT		Pendleton, Shawnee Mound IN 1847–54	Fletcher D: III, 387; IV, 11; V, 191				
Elena DePuy	Clay, NY		Elk Mills, MO 1852	NPEB: B,L				
Ruth Cushing Dill	Plymouth, MA Brooklyn, NY	Mt. Holyoke Sem.	Mt. Vernon, IN 1853–54	NPEB: B,L	James Browe		Belleville, NJ, 1886	Alum.: M.H.
Eloisa C. Dorsey	Pittsfield, NH	Wolfeborough Acad.	MO 1853–54	NPEB: B, 8th Report: 30				
Jane A. Dory	Castleton, VT, 1832	Castleton Sem.	Hebbardsville, Henderson, KY 1852–54	NPEB: L Cen. 1850				
Caroline E. Doughty	Orwell, VT, 1826	Troy Conf. Acad., Poultney, VT	Mooresville, IN 1850–54	NPEB: Admin., A,B	Amos Thornburg, Mooresville, 1854	3 sons	Mooresville, 1876	Cty. VR PL: Morgan Cty.
Mahala St. J. Drake			Camanche, IA 1854	NPEB: L				
Sarah J. Dudley	Chelmsford, MA, 1830		Dodgeville, WI 1851–52	NPEB: B,L Town VR				
Maria Dunn			Mt. Hawkins, IL 1852	NPEB: Admin., L				
Martha C. Eddy	Auburn, MA, 1817		Sugar Creek, Reedsburg, WI 1852–53	NPEB: B,L Town VR				
Emeline P. Eells	Cornwall, VT, 1829	Castleton Sem.	IN, 1853 Quincy, IL 1854–56	NPEB: B,L (F. Gleason) Cen. 1850	Judge Joseph C. Thompson, Quincy, 1856	2 or 3 children	after 1880	PL: Quincy NE His. Gen. (Eells fam. his.)

Teacher	Home Town / Birth Year	Academy or Seminary	Places Taught for NPEB, Dates	Sources: Early	Marriage	Later Life	Death Place & Year	Sources: Future
Jane L. Eggleston	Torrington, CT, 1831	Westfield, MA, Norm.	Neosho, MO 1853–54	NPEB: B,L Arch: Westfield				
Roxanna Ellsworth	E. Windsor, VT, 1816	Wesleyan Acad., Wilbraham, MA	Portland Mills, Montezuma, IN 1852–54	NPEB: B,L				
Rebecca W. Emerson	S. Danvers, MA, 1827		Franklin, IN 1850	NPEB: A, Admin.				
Frances R. Farrand	Colchester, VT	Burlington Fem. Sem.	Berlin Crossroads, OH 1853	NPEB: B,L Arch: U. VT	John C. Neal Jackson City, OH, 185?			Cry. VR
Emma P. Farrar	Malone, NY	Malone Acad. Burlington Fem. Sem.	Du Quoin, Liberty, Spring Hill, IL 1853–54	NPEB: B,L Arch: U. VT				
Mary E. Field	Greensboro, VT, 1828	Phillips Acad., Danville	Carthage, MO 1853–54	NPEB: B,L VT VR	John C. Ellsworth, Greensboro, 1857			VT VR
Joanna Fisher	Chester, VT, 1827	Chester Acad. Mt. Holyoke Sem.	Noblesville, IN 1851	NPEB: B,L Cen 1850	Rev. George H. White, 185?	missionary in Turkey; minister's wife in Chester, Grinnell, IA; son a minister	Grinnell, IA, 1904	Alum.: M.H. Arch.: Grinnell Col.
Susan Fisher	Chester, VT, 1828	Chester Acad.	Noblesville, IN 1851	NPEB: B,L	Shaw, Noblesville, 185?			NPEB: L,L (Hammond)
Annie Flint	N. Anson, ME, 1830	Gorham Fem. Sem.	Georgetown, IL 1850–51	NPEB: A,B	single		Georgetown, 1851	NPEB: L (A. Perkins)

Teacher	Home Town Birth Year	Academy or Seminary	Places Taught for NPEB, Dates	Sources: Early	Marriage	Later Life	Death Place & Year	Sources: Future
Elizabeth E. Flynt	Tewksbury, MA, 1828		New Durham, IN 1850–52 Lafayette, IN 1854	NPEB: A,L,R; L (Bishop)				
Ann R. Forbes	Canaan, CT; Warren Cty., NY	Albany Normal	Avon, MO 1853–54	NPEB: B,L				
Catharine A. Fortner	W. Dryden, NY, 1824	Cortland Acad. Oneida Conf. Sem.	Tipton, IA 1851–52	NPEB: A,B,L				
L. Emeline Francis	W. Hartford, CT	Mt. Holyoke Sem.	KS, 1855	NPEB: 11th Report: 21	James Wilson, Leavenworth, KS 1856			Alum.: M.H.
Maria Freeman	New Salem, MA	Wesleyan Sem., Wilbraham	Huntington, IN 1852–53	NPEB: B,L				
Sarah S. Getchell	Hallowell, ME, 1825		1849	NPEB: A,R Town VR				
J. M. Gilfillan	Mifflinburg, PA, 1828	Cedar Hill Sem., Mt. Joy, PA	Hillsboro, IL 1850	NPEB: Admin., B				
Ann Gleason	Enfield, CT		Hamburg, IN 1853	NPEB: B,L				
Femira Gleason			Marion, IN 1854	NPEB: L				
Agnes S. Goulding	Phillipston, MA, 1830	Mt. Holyoke Sem.	Evansville, IN 1851–53	NPEB: B,L Town VR Cen. 1850	single	worked with women's re-form schools, MA	Springfield, MA, 1907	Alum.: M.H. MA VR
Mary A. Gray	Townshend, VT, 1825	Leland & Gray Sem.	Tualatin, OR 1851–52	Cen. 1850 His.: OR	Benjamin F. McLench, 1852	farmed in OR, 4 children	Salem, 1907	His.: OR
Augusta M. Greves	Skaneateles, NY, 1825	Mt. Holyoke Sem.	Dodgeville, WI 1852	NPEB: B,L	Joel McCollum, 1858	lived Mar-shall, MI	Marshall, 1896	Alum.: M.H.

Teacher	Home Town Birth Year	Academy or Seminary	Places Taught for NPEB, Dates	Sources: Early	Marriage	Later Life	Death Place & Year	Sources: Future
Mary E. Griggs	Cazenovia, NY	Cazenovia Sem.	Bolivar, MO 185?	NPEB: B,L				
Susan Griggs	Fayston, VT, 1826		Wilmington, NC 1850	NPEB: Admin., A Cen. 1850	single	teaching Kendalville, IN, 1882		His.: VT (Brigham File)
E. C. Grosvenor			Tuscarora, IA 1850	NPEB: Admin., R				
Asenath M. Hammond	Eliot, ME, 1830		Millersville, IN 1851–53	NPEB: A,B,L Cen. 1850				
Jane E. Hammond	Westport, NY 1828	Essex Cty. Acad.	IA (?) 1849	NPEB: A,L (Joslyn), R		family settled in Camanche, IA after 1846		His.: Essex Cty., NY
Martha A. Harris			IL 1848–51	NPEB: R, 11th Report: 6	Rev. Rhea	missionary to Persia	Persia, 1856 (57?)	NPEB: 11th Report: 6
Nancy L. Harris	Westminster, VT, 1830	Cortland Acad.	Charleston, Paris, IL 1851–52	NPE3: B,L Cen. 1850	James M. Mill?, Edgar Cty. IL, 1852			Cty. VR
Emily J. Haseltine	Chester, NH		TN 1849–52	NPEB: L				
Sarah Hibbard			IL		single		Illinois, 1851	NPEB: 7th Report: 7
Elisabeth Hill	Scituate, MA		Lexington, MO 1852 Belleville, IL 1853	NPEB: B,L	single	taught freedmen, S.C. 1862–68	Port Royal, SC, 1868	Amistad
Harriet P. Hills	Williston, VT, 1832	Lamoille Cty. Grammar Sch.	Warsaw, IN 1853–54	NPEE: B,L VT VR	single		Waterbury, VT, 1868	VT VR
Julia M. Hitchcock	Bergen, NY, 1826	Mt. Holyoke Sem.	1853	NPEE: B Cen. 1850	Rev. James Walker, 3?		Hisperia, MI, 1875	Alum.: M.H.

Teacher	Home Town / Birth Year	Academy or Seminary	Places Taught for NPEB, Dates	Sources: Early	Marriage	Later Life	Death Place & Year	Sources: Future
Mary A. Hitchcock	Ft. Covington, NY, 1831	Malone Acad.	Beardston, Princeton, IL 1852–53	NPEB: B,L	William B. Montgomery, Cass Cty., IL, 1853			Cty. VR NPEB: L (Doty)
Jane A. Holbrook	Poland, NY, 1830 Lima, NY	Genessee Wes. Sem. Albany Normal	Mobile, AL 1850–52	NPEB: Admin., A,B Cen. 1850	single		died East "at home," 1852	Alum.: Alb. Norm.
Martha A. Hooker	Sacketts Harbor, NY, 1827	Utica Fem. Acad.	Geneseo, Wethersfield, IL 1852–54	NPEB: A,B,L				
Harriet P. Hoppin			East Bend, MO 1848–49	NPEB: L,R				
Amanda Hosford	VT, 1823		Stillwater, MN 1848–49	His.: MN Bishop, Floral Home: 103	Henry L. Moss, Stillwater, 1849 (50?), lawyer	widowed 1892	St. Paul, MN, 1910	His.: MN Cen. 1860
Delia L. Hosford	Charlotte, VT	Burlington Fem. Sem.	Ottawa, IL 1850	NPEB: R,L Arch: U.VT				Cty. VR
[Sena] A[nn] (?) Hoyt			Springfield, IL 1854	NPEB: L	Edward T. Walker, Sangamon Cry., IL, 1856 (?)			
Augusta E. Hubbell	N. Bergen, NY, 1834	Le Roy Sem.	Tipton, IA 1853	NPEB: B,L Cen. 1850		home in 1853		NPEB: L
Almira C. Hudson	Hudson, OH, 1826	Mt. Holyoke Sem.	Manlius, MI 1851–52 Kalamazoo, MI 1852 Crawfordsville, IN 1855	NPEB: B,L	single		Fennville, MI, 1906	Alum.: M.H.

Teacher	Home Town / Birth Year	Academy or Seminary	Places Taught for NPEB, Dates	Sources: Early	Marriage	Later Life	Death Place & Year	Sources: Future
H. M. Hurtin	Long Island, NY	Albany Normal	De Witt, IA 1853–55	NPEB: B,L	Stevens in IA			NPEB: 9th Report: 24
Mary Johnson	Sodus, NY, 1820		La Grange, TN 1850–52	NPEB: B		reapplied to NPEB 1855 from home		NPEB: L
Mary Johnson	Lowell, MA, 1817		(Ohio, 1842) Higginsport, OH 1850–53	NPEB: Admin. A,L				
Hannah Johnston	Northumberland, NY. 1824		1853	NPEB: B His.: Saratoga Cty.	Henry L. Ellis, Northumberland		Northumberland, 1860	His.: Saratoga Cty.
Rolinda A. Jones	Hubbardton. VT	Troy Conf. Acad. W. Poultney	Northport, IN 1852–53	NPEB: B,L				
Fanny L. Joslyn	Fayston, VT Waitsfield, VT	Burlington Fem. Sem.	Platteville, WI 1849–52	NPEB: Admin., A,L,R Town VR (Waitsfield) Arch: U.VT				
Nancy C. Kidder	Skowhegan, ME, 1821		St. Charles, IL 1850–51	NPEB: A,L (Arnold)	David L. Eastman, Kane Cty., IL, 1851, lawyer	widowed 1860, 4 children	Chicago, IL, 1882	NE His. Gen. (Kidder fam. his.)
Abigail Kies			Fort Wayne, IN 1847	Fletcher D: II: 387, 352–93				
Abby D. Killgore	Topsham, ME, 1825		Mooresville, IN 1850–52	NPEB: A,R ME VR	James S. Kelley, Mooresville, 1852 merchant	widowed 1862		Fletcher D: VII: 518, 570, 595

Teacher	Home Town Birth Year	Academy or Seminary	Places Taught for NPEB, Dates	Sources: Early	Marriage	Later Life	Death Place & Year	Sources: Future
Mary Jane Ladd	Meredith, NH 1815	Mt. Holyoke Sem.	Lewisville, IN 1850	NPEB: Admin., A,R Town VR	William T. Hatch, Henry Cry., IN, 1851		1861	Cty. VR Alum.: M.H.
Helen M. Landon	Burlington, VT	Burlington Fem. Sem.	Knightstown, IN 1850	NPEB: A,R Arch: U. VT	William H. Martin, Burlington, VT, 1855			VT VR
Hannah Langdill	Andover, MA		Clark Cry., IN 1851–52	NPEB: B	Austin Warren, Clark Cty., 1853			Cty. VR NPEB: L (Child)
E. L. Lawton	Dummerston, VT	Saxton River Sem.	Lebanon, Carlyle, Lawrenceville, IL 1852–54	NPEB: B,L				
Ellen P. Lee	Princeton, MA, 1832	Westminster Acad.	Hamilton Cry., Indianapolis, IN 1851–55	NPEB: B,L Town VR Cen. 1850 Fletcher D: V: 11, 344	Charles W. Livingston, Worcester, MA, 1856			MA VR
Elizabeth H. Lincoln	Portland, ME, 1817		Oregon City, Astoria, OR 1851–56	His.: OR	Judge Alonzo A. Skinner, Astoria, 1856		Eugene, 1895	His.: OR
Keziah Price Lister	Farmington, ME, 1816	Kents Hill Sem. Readfield, ME	Indianapolis, IN 1851–54	NPEB: A Fletcher D: IV: 285, et seq.	Calvin Fletcher, Indianapolis, 1855, lawyer/farmer	widowed 1866, returned East	Boston, 1899	His.: IN Fletcher D: V: 474–75
Susan A. Lord	Boston, MA area, 1825	Charlestown Sem.	Wisconsin 1850–51 Benicia, CA 1852–53 Bidwell, CA 1853–54	NPEB: A,R 6th Report: 7 His.: CA State Lib.: CA	Judge Thomas H. Wells, Butte Cty., CA	moved to NV 1864; to CA, 1890; widowed 1901	His.: NV Cen. 1870 (Carson City, NV)

Teacher	Home Town / Birth Year	Academy or Seminary	Places Taught for NPEB, Later	Sources: Early	Marriage	Later Life	Death Place & Year	Sources: Future
Mary E. Lyon	Charlotte, VT, 1828	Troy Conf. Acad., W. Poultney	Louisville, KY 1853–54	NPEB: B,L Cen. 1850				
Abba U. Mace	New Vineyard, ME, 1817	(Shakers, Sabbathday Lake, ME, 1836–50)	IN 1852	NPEB: A,B L (Ware) Shakers	Newell Carr, IN, 1854			Shakers[5]
Ann Mann	Charlestown, NY, 1823		Winnebago Cty., IL 1851	NPEB: B,L (P.Brooks)				
Sarah J. Matthews	Lee, NY		Peoria, IL 1852–53	NPEB: B,L	Alexander McCoy, Peoria		died before 1900, Peoria	Arch.: Bradley U. Alum.: M.H.
Laura Maynard	Potsdam, NY	Mt. Holyoke Sem.	Bellemonte, MO 1852 New Durham, IN 1852–54	NPEB: B,L, L (Barrett)	Franklin Fint, 1859		Denmark, IA, 1908	
Mary E. Mead	Essex, VT, 1820	Burlington Fem. Sem.	Clinton, IN 1851–52	NPEB: B,L Town VR Arch.: U. VT	John Vonn, Pike Cty., IN, 1858 (?)			Cty. VR
Elisa E. Meech	Chazy, NY E. Haddam, CT, 1824		1853	NPEB: A,B His.: E. Haddam				
Rebekah M. Merriam	Johnson, VT, 1833	Lamoille Cty. Grammar Sch.	1851	NPEB: B Cen. 1850				
Mary I. Merrill	Castleton, VT, 1825	Castleton Sem.	Petersburg, IN 1852	NPEB: B,L Cen. 1850				
Elizabeth Miller (also Millar)	S. Argyle, NY, 1830	Albany Norm.	Forest Grove, OR 1851–52	NPEB: A,B Cen. 1850 His.: OR	Joseph G. Wilson, OR, 1854, lawyer	postmistress, The Dalles, 1874–86; widowed 1873; 4 children	The Dalles, 1913	His.: OR Cen. 1880

5. Information supplied by Brother Theodore E. Johnson from the archives of the United Society of Shakers, Sabbathday Lake, Poland Spring, Maine.

Teacher	Home Town Birth Year	Academy or Seminary	Places Taught for NPEB, Dates	Sources: Early	Marriage	Later Life	Death Place & Year	Sources: Future
Amorette M. Mills	Colchester, VT	Burlington Fem. Sem.	German Township, South Bend, IN; Jefferson City, MO 1853–54	NPEB: B,L Arch: U. VT				
Sarah M. Mills	Tunkhannock, PA, 1818		1850	NPEB: Admin., A				
M. Augusta Moore	Bangor, ME, 1826		LaSalle, IL 1850	NPEB: Admin., A				
Lucretia M. Morrill	Boscowen, NH, 1827 Lowell, MA	Concord H.S. (Lowell Mills)	IL 1853	NPEB: B Cen. 1850	Donaldson, in IL			His.: NH (Boscawen Town History)
Mariam A. Moulton	NY, 1828 Cuyahoga, OH	Burlington Fem. Sem.	1851	NPEB: B Cen. 1850 Arch: U. VT				
Frances M. Nelson	Lewis, NY	Castleton Sem. Burlington Fem. Sem.	Frankfort, IN 1852–54	NPEB: B,L L (Tatterson) Arch: U. VT				
Mary Newell	N. Wilbraham, MA (?)		Cascade, Lyndon, Sheboygan Falls, WI 1849–51	NPEB: L				
Julie Newman	Egremont, MA	S. Egremont Acad.	Allensville, IN 1853	NPEB: B, L (Woodin)				
Abbie T. Newton	Colchester, CT	Mt. Holyoke Sem.	Elkhorn, WI, 1847	NPEB: 4th Report: 26	George W. Arms, Elkorn, WI, 1849			Alum.: M.H.
Lucia A. Nichols	Weathersfield, VT, 1828		Bertrand, MI 1850	NPEB: Admin., A Cen. 1850	William Danforth, Weathersfield, 1857			VT VR

Teacher	Home Town Birth Year	Academy or Seminary	Places Taught for NPEB, Dates	Sources: Early	Marriage	Later Life	Death Place & Year	Sources: Future
Lucy A. Ordway	Amesbury, MA, 1811	Mt. Holyoke Sem.	Greensburg, IN 1852; Liberty, MO (?)	NPEB: B,L Town VR	single	taught MA	Amesbury, MA, 1905	Alum.: M.H. MA VR
Emma C. Orvis	Bangor, NY, 1828	Troy Fem. Sem.	Montgomery Cty., IN 1850	NPEB: A,L,R				
Sarah M. Parker	Foxcroft, ME, 1824		IN 1853 (?)	NPEB: B, L (Barrett) Town VR		may have taught freedmen, Port Royal, SC, 1862–63		
Mary E. Parsons	Newbury, MA, 1814	Mt. Holyoke Sem.	Greensburg, IN; Oxford, OH; Crown Point, IN 1852–60	NPEB: A,B, L	single		Crown Point, IN, 1860	Alum.: M.H. Cen. 1860
Catharine R. Paul	Danville, VT	Burlington Fem. Sem.	La Porte, IN 1849	NPEB: L Arch: U. VT	Cadwallader, before 185?	lived Cincinnati, 1853		NPEB: L
Mary I. Paul	Danville, VT, 1834	Phillips Acad.	1852 or 1853	NPEB: B, L (Cadwallader)		home in 1855		NPEB: 9th Report: 24
Harriet E. Pease	Wells, NY, 1830		1849	Cen. 1850 NPEB: A,R				
Mary C. Pease			Franklin, IN 1847	Fletcher D: III: 387; IV: 41				
Elisa A. Peck	E. Haddam, CT		1847	NPEB: A		returned, reapplied 1851		
Catharine Peirce	Barnard, VT, 1825		Evansvil e, IL 1850	NPEB: Admin., A VT VR				

Teacher	Home Town / Birth Year	Academy or Seminary	Places Taught for NPEB, Dates	Sources: Early	Marriage	Later Life	Death Place & Year	Sources: Future
Arozina Perkins	Johnson, VT, 1826 Marshfield, MA New Haven, CT	Lamoille Cty. Grammar Sch.	Fort Des Moines, Fairfield, IA 1850–51	NPEB: Admin., A,B,L Diary (CHS) Cen. 1850	single		Marshfield, MA, 1854	MA VR His.: Marshfield
Lisette Perkins			Mooresville, IN 1852–53	NPEB: L				
Annie Perry			Kokomo, IN; New Madrid, MO 1853–54	Fletcher D: V: 336				
Lucy W. Pierce	Royalston, MA, 1835; Warwick, MA		TN 1854	NPEB: A,L (Tatterson)	Charles D. Lincoln, Raynham, MA, 1860, merchant		Raynham, 1906	MA VR
Jennette Pitkin	Marshfield, VT, 1831 Winchendon, MA	W. Newton Norm.	Boonville, MO 1852–53	NPEB: L Cen. 1850	Joseph W. Stone, Winchendon, MA		Winchendon, 1920	MA VR Alum.: Framingham NE His. Gen. (Pitkin fam. his.)
Charlotte C. Plimpton Olive M. Porter	Hopkinton, MA	Hopkinton Acad.	Westfield, PA 1850 Mt. Pleasant, MO 1854	NPEB: A, L,R NPEB: L				
Elvira M. Powers	Morristown, VT, 1823	Bakersfield Acad.	Hillsboro, IL 1850–51	NPEB: Admin., A	Rev. Thomas W. Hynes, Montgomery Cty., IL, 1851	4 children, 2 to maturity	Greenville, IL, 1859	Cty. VR His.: Montgomery Cty. PL: Greenville

Teacher	Home Town Birth Year	Academy or Seminary	Place Taught for NPEB, Dates	Sources: Early	Marriage	Later Life	Death Place & Year	Sources: Future
H. E. Pratt	Dalton, NH		Calhoun, MO 1852–53	NPEB: B,L				
Maria E. Preston	Danville, VT		Perkinsville, IN 1852–53	NPEB: B,L				
Mary Purinton	Truxton, NY, 1832	Fayetteville Acad.	Joliet, IL 1850	NPEB: Admin., B				
Maria Putnam	Colrain, MA Greensboro, VT, 1824	Burlington Fem. Sem.	Cedarville, IL 1850–52	NPEB: A,B, L (Birge) Arch: U. VT				
Sarah B. Quick	Braman's Corner, NY	Albany Norm.	Georgetown, Il 1852–??	NPEB: B,L	Elwood R. Aukrum, Georgetown, 1857	lived Danville, IL	after 1895	Alum.: Alb. Norm.
Marcella A. Ranny	Westport, NY	Burlington Fem. Sem.	Lake Mills, WI 1850	NPEB: L (Warner) Arch: U. VT				
Mary A. W. Richardson	Otisfield, ME, 1829	Gorham Fem. Sem.	Clay Ctr., MO 1853–54	NPEB: B,L Town VR				
Abbie A. Rogers	Northfield, NH, 1817		Guntersville, AL 1851–53	NPEB: A, B,– Town VR	Kingman Cross, Canterbury, NH, 1861	1 daughter		NH VR
Martha M. Rogers	Champlain, NY, 1821		Cassville, Waldo, Erie, MO 1850–53	NPEB: A,L, R Cen. 1850 (Barry Cty., MO)				
Lydia A. Rood	Stockholm, NY, 1822		IN 1853–56	NPEB: B, 8th Report: 30; 10th Report: 23				

Teacher	Home Town / Birth Year	Academy or Seminary	Places Taught for NPEB, Dates	Sources: Early	Marriage	Later Life	Death Place & Year	Sources: Future
Fidelia C. Root	Skaneateles, NY, 1826		1849	NPEB: A,R				
Mary Augusta Roper	Templeton, MA, 1833	Mt. Holyoke Sem. (?)	Mill Point, MI 1852–53	NPEB: B,L Town VR	Lyman J. Taft, Worcester, MA, 1854, restaurant owner		Worcester, 1909	MA VR City Dir.: Worcester
—— St. John	Westport, NY		St. Paul, MN	NPEB: *10b* Report: 23	Amidon in MN by 1856			His.: Essex Cty., NY
L. M. Sanborn	Hardwick, VT, 1831	Derby Acad.	1851	NPEB: B				
Almira B. Savage	Stowe, VT, 1826		Neosho, MO 1850–53	NPEB: A, L (M. E. Adams, De Puy) Cen. 1850				
Ann E. Sawyer	Franklin, NH, 1829	Mt. Holyoke Sem.	Pleasant Retreat, MO 1849–53	NPEB: A,L, R	John Chandler, Coldwater, MI, 1859	helped start MI State School for dependent children; 1 son, minister	Amboy, IL 1899	Alum.: M.H.
Sarah M. Scales	Henniker, NH	Mt. Holyoke Sem.	Alexandria, MO 1854	NPEB: L			Alexandria, 1855	Alum.: M.H.
C. Flavilla Schenck	Fulton, NY, 1827		MI 1849	NPEB: A,R	Gassh (?), MI, before 1852			NPEB: L (Winslow)
Mary A. Scofield			St. Paul, MN 1849	Bishop, *Floral Home*: 104				
Sarah E. Shedd	Pepperell, MA, 1816		Sugar Creek, WI 1849	NPEB: A,R	single		Sugar Creek before 1852	NPEB: L (Eddy)

Teacher	Home Town, Birth Year	Academy or Seminary	Place Taught for NPEB, Dates	Sources: Early	Marriage	Later Life	Death Place & Year	Source: Future
Sarah Smith	Lima, NY, 1821	Genesee Wesleyan Sem.	Oregon City, OR 1851–52	NPEB: A Cen. 1850	Rev. Alanson Beers, OR, 1852 John L. Kine. OR, 1855	widowed 1853 with 6 step-children; 2nd marriage 6 more step-children	Portland, OR 1872	His.: OR
Virginia Smith	Chateaugay, NY, 1831	Burlington Fem. Sem., Albany Normal	Sterling, IA 1853	NPEB: B,L Cen. 1850 Arc: U. VT	Arnoldie in IL, 1850			NPEB: 9th Report: 24
Ardelia A. Spencer	Gouverneur, NY, 1825	Mt. Holyoke Sem.	1849	NPEB: A,R	Rev. Howard Burnside, 1850; James McClung, 1854	widowed 1852 and 1872	Westfield, NY, 1878	Alum.: M.H.
Celia Sprague	Plymouth, VT, 1830	Black River Acad.: Ludlow	Huntington, IN 1852 Centreville, MI 1853	NPEB: B,L L (Hill) Cen. 1850 Town VR		taught Glenbulah, Greenbush, WI, 1858		His.: VT (Brigham File)
Abby Willard Stanton	St. Johnsbury, VT, 1820	Phillips Acad., Danville, VT Mt. Holyoke Sem.	Greenville, KY 1853–55	NPEB: B,L Cen. 1850	widowed before 1853		Concord, NH, 1856	Alum.: M.H
Augusta Stevens	Hardwick, VT, 1816	Burlington Fem. Sem.	Albany, IL 1850–51	NPEB: Admin., A,B,L (Crosby) VT VR				
Ursula Stevens	Hardwick, VT, 1804	Cazenovia Sem.	Albany, IL 1850–51	NPEB: Admin., A,B,L (Crosby) VT VR				

Teacher	Home Town Birth Year	Academy or Seminary	Places Taught for NPEB, Dates	Sources: Early	Marriage	Later Life	Death Place & Year	Sources: Future
Jane E. Stiles	NY, 1828 Marshall, MI		1852	NPEB: B Cen. 1850				
Ann Olivia Strong	Cleveland, OH, 1822 Hopkinton, NY		CA, 1851–57	NPEB: B, *6th Report*: 26; *11th Report*: 21				
Josephine M. Sweet	Montpelier, VT	Montpelier Acad.	Muscatine, IA 1853–54	NPEB: B				
Almira Swetland	Chicopee, MA		IN, 1853–54	NPEB: B, *8th Report*: 30				
M. Tatterson			Centre Square, IN 1854	NPEB: L				
Emilie M. Taylor	Hinsdale, NH, 1832		Boonville, MO 1850 Returned West 1853	NPEB: B,L	Rev. Moses H. Wells, Hinsdale, 1857			NH VR
Caroline Thayer			Iberia, OH 1850	NPEB: Admin.				
Louisa Thayer			Berlin, OH 1850	NPEB: Admin.				
Elisa D. Thomas	Cayuga, NY, 1820 Clinton, NY	Oneida Sem.	1850	NPEB: Admin., A,B				
Bertha E. Troeger	Nazareth, PA		Upper Sandusky, OH 1852	NPEB: B,L				
Harriet N. Tucker	Randolph, VT, 1820		(WI 1847–50) Jericho, IL 1850	NPEB: A,L,R				

Teacher	Home Town Birth Year	Academy or Seminary	Places Taught for NPEB, Date	Sources: Early	Marriage	Later Life	Death Place & Year	Sources: Future
H. A. Tuttle			Sarcoxie, MO 1852	NPEB: L				
Rebecca B. Veazie	Quincy, MA, 1814	Oberlin	(OH before 1852) Taylorsville, IN 1852; Covington, KY 1852–53; IA	NPEB: B,L Alum.: Ober.	single	taught for AMA: Jamaica 1860–63; Portsmouth, VA; New Orleans; Jacksonville, FL; 1864–1870	Jacksonville, 1870	Amistad
Fidelia M. Wait	Hatfield, MA, 1827	Mt. Holyoke Sem. (?)	Pleasant Retreat, MO 1851–53	NPEB: A,B, L (Sawyer) Cen. 1850	Smith, Pleasant Retreat, MO, 1853			NPEB: L (Rogers)
Mila L. Walker			Georgetown, MO 1854	NPEB: L				
Margaret B. Wands	Albany, NY		Durham's [Oswego], OR 1851–52	His.: OR	Gov. John P. Gaines, OR, 1852			His.: OR
Julia S. Ware	Orrington, ME, 1822	W. Newton Norm., MA	Lexington, MO 1852–53	NPEB: A,B, L Town VR	B.F. Bradford Oxford, NY	widowed 1858, returned to NY, 1 daughter	Oxford, 1897	Alum.: Framingham, MA
Fanny A. Warner	Sunderland, MA, 1827		Aztalan, WI 1850–51	NPEB: A,L R Cen. 1850	Alonzo M. Morrison, Ft. Atkinson, WI, 1851, trader	living in Koshkonog, WI, 1860, 1 son		MA VR His.: WI Cen. 1860
A. Mary Washburn	Burlington, VT, 1826	Burlington Fem. Sem.	Henrietta, OH 1850	NPEB: A,L,R Arch: U. VT				
Sarah B. Watson	Lincoln Cty., ME		Knightstown, IN 1852–53	NPEB: B,L				

Teacher	Home Town Birth Year	Academy or Seminary	Places Taught for NPEB, Dates	Sources: Early	Marriage	Later Life	Death Place & Year	Sources: Future
Maria S. Welch	Homer, NY, 1833	Cortland Acad.	GA (?) 1853	NPEB: B His.: Cortland Cty. Cen. 1850	Dr. Samuel Harris, Homer, 1868	widowed 1869, taught in Syracuse 10 years; wrote book on travels	Homer, 1905	His.: Cortland Cty.
Arvis Wellington	Boylston, MA	New Ipswich Acad., NH	1852	NPEB: B				
Harriet N. Wellman	Napoli, NY, 1830	Erie Cty. Acad., NY	Montrose, IA 1853–54	NPEB: B,L His.: Cattaraugus Cty. Cen. 1850				
Sarah Ellen Wheeler	New Haven, CT, 1833		La Grange, TN 1850	NPEB: Admin., A				
Martha Wheelock	Warren, MA	Mt. Holyoke Sem.	KY 1849	NPEB: R	Dr. H. M. Matthews	taught Paducah, Frankfort, Louisville, Shelbyville, KY; Bedford, IN	St. Louis, MO, 1892	Alum.: M.H.
Annie T. Wilbur	Newburyport, MA		MI 1849 Returned West 1852	NPEB: L				
Elizabeth J. Wilder	Keene, NH	Mt. Holyoke Sem.	Logansport, IN	NPEB: A	Gates, Logansport, IN, 1855		Logansport, 1856	Alum.: M.H.
Caroline Wilkinson	Brandon, VT, 1831		Bellevue, OH 1850–51 Poplar Corner, TN 1852–54	NPEB: A,L,R				

Teacher	Home Town / Birth Year	Academy or Seminary	Places Taught: for NPEB, Dates	Sources: Early	Marriage	Later Life	Death Place & Year	Sources: Future
Mary Wilkinson	Brandon, VT		Bellevue, OH 1850	NPEB: A,L,R	Emerson Covel, Bellevue, OH 1850	to New York city, 1853		NPEB: L (C. Wilkinson)
Frances L. Willard	Lunenburg, VT, 1798 Towanda, PA	Hanover Acad, NH	1849	NPEB: A,R,				
Harriet Willey	Newbury, VT	Newbury Fem Sem.	IN 1852-53	NPEB: B,L				
Mary A. Wilson	Temple, NH, 1824	New Ipswich Acad., NH	Mooresville, IN 1850	NPEB: Admin., A				
Mary G. Wilson	Bethel, VT, 1824		Charlottesville, IN 1848	NPEB:A Fletcher D: IV: 62 VT VR				
Flora Davis Winslow	Hallowell, ME, 1824 Portland, ME		Trenton, MI 1852-53	NFEB: B,L Town VR	widowed before 1852	son from first marriage		NPEB: B,L
Abby Wood	Leominster, MA 1825		Indianapolis, IN 1851-53	NPEB: B Town VR Fletcher D: IV: 336; V: 41				
Lydia L. Woodin	Hamden, CT, 1833	Church St. Sem., New Haven	Allensville, IN 1853	NPEB: B,L Cen. 1850				
Ruth C. Wright	Maryland, NY, 1819		Mt. Pulaski, IL 1853	NPEB: B,L Cen. 1850				
Elizabeth W. Young	Canastota, NY, 1830	Oneida Conf. Sem.	Crown Pt., IN 1850	NPEB: Admin., A				

SELECTED BIBLIOGRAPHY
≈≈≈≈≈≈≈≈≈≈≈ OF PUBLISHED WORKS ≈≈≈≈≈≈≈≈≈≈≈

Ahlstrom, Sydney E. *A Religious History of the American People.* New Haven: Yale University Press, 1972.

Allmendinger, David F., Jr. "Mount Holyoke Students Encounter the Need for Life-Planning, 1837–1850." *History of Education Quarterly* 19 (Spring 1979): 27–46.

———. *Paupers and Scholars: The Transformation of Student Life in Nineteenth-Century New England.* New York: St. Martin's Press, 1975.

Armitage, Sue. "Western Women: Beginning to Come into Focus." *Montana, The Magazine of Western History* 32 (Summer 1982): 2–9.

Barron, Hal S. "After the Great Transformation: The Social Processes of Settled Rural Life in the Nineteenth-Century North." Paper given at the Social Science History Association, Nashville, TN, October 1981.

Beecher, Catharine. *Educational Reminiscences and Suggestions.* New York: J. B. Ford & Co., 1874.

———. "An·Address to the Protestant Clergy of the United States," in *The Evils Suffered by American Women and American Children: The Causes and the Remedy.* New York: Harper & Bros., 1846, pp. 17–35.

Billington, Ray Allen, ed. *The American Frontier Thesis: Attack and Defense.* Washington, D.C.: American Historical Association, 1971.

———. *America's Frontier Heritage.* New York: Holt, Rinehart, & Winston, 1966.

Bird, Isabella. *A Lady's Life in the Rocky Mountains.* Norman: University of Oklahoma Press, 1960.

Bishop, Harriet E. [M'Conkey] *Dakota War Whoop; or, Indian Massacres and War in Minnesota.* St. Paul: D. D. Merrill, 1863.

———. *Floral Home; or, First Years of Minnesota.* New York: Sheldon, Blakeman & Co., 1857.

———. *Minnesota: Then and Now.* St. Paul: D. D. Merrill, 1869.

Bolin, Winifred D. Wandersee. "Harriet E. Bishop, Moralist and Reformer," in Barbara Stuhler and Gretchen Kreuter. *Women of Minnesota: Selected Biographical Essays.* St. Paul: Minnesota Historical Society Press, 1977, pp. 7–19.

Bowden, Angie Burt. *Early Schools of Washington Territory.* Seattle: Lowman & Hanford Co., 1935.

Bowers, William L. "Crawford Township, 1850–1870: A Population Study of a Pioneer Community." *Iowa Journal of History* 58 (January 1960): 1–30.

Brown, Dee. *The Gentle Tamers: Women of the Old Wild West.* Lincoln: University of Nebraska Press, 1958.

Bushman, Claudia, ed. *Mormon Sisters: Women in Early Utah.* Cambridge, MA: Emmeline Press, 1976.

Butchart, Ronald E. "Education and Culture in the Trans-Mississippi West: An Interpretation." *Journal of American Culture* 3 (Summer 1980): 351–73.

———. *Northern Schools, Southern Blacks, and Reconstruction: Freedmen's Education, 1862–1875.* Westport, CT: Greenwood Press, 1980.

Cleland, Robert Glass, ed. *Apron Full of Gold; The Letters of Mary Jane Megquier from San Francisco, 1849–1856.* San Marino, CA: Huntington Library, 1949.

Clifford, Geraldine Joncich. "Daughters into Teachers: Educational and Demographic Influences on the Transformation of Teaching into 'Women's Work.'" Paper given at the History of Education Society meetings, New York University, October 1982.

——— "Home and School in Nineteenth-Century America." *History of Education Quarterly* 18 (Spring 1978): 3–34.

Cott, Nancy F. *The Bonds of Womanhood: "Woman's Sphere" in New England, 1780–1835.* New Haven: Yale University Press, 1977.

———. "Young Women in the Second Great Awakening in New England." *Feminist Studies* 3 (1975): 15–29.

Cremin, Lawrence A. *American Education: The National Experience, 1783–1876.* New York: Harper & Row, 1980.

Cross, Whitney R. *The Burned-Over District: The Social and Intellectual History of Enthusiastic Religion in Western New York, 1800–1850.* Ithaca, NY: Cornell University Press, 1950.

Curti, Merle. *The Making of an American Community: A Case Study of Democracy in a Frontier County.* Stanford: Stanford University Press, 1959.

Daily, Christie. "A Woman's Concern: Millinery in Central Iowa, 1870–80." *Journal of the West* 21 (April 1982): 26–32.

Degler, Carl N. *At Odds: Women and the Family in America from the Revolution to the Present.* New York: Oxford University Press, 1980.

De Voto, Bernard. *The Year of Decision: 1846.* Boston: Houghton Mifflin, 1943.

Dublin, Thomas, ed. *Farm to Factory: Women's Letters, 1830–1860.* New York: Columbia University Press, 1981.

Dublin, Thomas. *Women at Work: The Transformation of Work and Community in Lowell, Massachusetts, 1826–1860.* New York: Columbia University Press, 1979.

Dyer, Thomas, ed. *To Raise Myself a Little: The Diaries and Letters of Jennie, a Georgia Teacher, 1851–1886: Amelia Akehurst Lines.* Athens: University of Georgia Press, 1981.

Eblen, Jack E. "An Analysis of Nineteenth-Century Frontier Populations." *Demography* 2 (1965): 399–413.

Eggleston, Edward. *The Circuit Rider: A Tale of the Heroic Age.* New York: J. B. Ford, 1874.

Elson, Ruth Miller. *Guardians of Tradition: American Schoolbooks of the Nineteenth Century.* Lincoln: University of Nebraska Press, 1964.

Engle, Flora A. P. "The Story of the Mercer Expeditions." *Washington Historical Quarterly* 6 (October 1915): 225–37.

Faragher, John Mack. *Women and Men on the Overland Trail.* New Haven: Yale University Press, 1979.

Farnham, Eliza W. *Life in Prairie Land.* New York: Harper & Bros., 1846.

Filler, Louis, ed. *An Ohio Schoolmistress: The Memoirs of Irene Hardy.* Kent, OH: Kent State University Press, 1980.

Fischer, Christiane. *Let Them Speak for Themselves: Women in the American West, 1849–1900.* New York: Dutton, 1978.

Fuller, Wayne E. *The Old Country School: The Story of Rural Education in the Middle West.* Chicago: University of Chicago Press, 1982.

Garland, Hamlin, "Lucretia Burns," in *Other Main-Travelled Roads.* New York: Harper & Bros., 1892, pp. 81–115.

Gherman, Dawn Lander. "From Parlour to Tepee: The White Squaw on the American Frontier." Unpublished Ph.D. dissertation, University of Massachusetts, 1975.

Goldman, Marion S. *Gold Diggers and Silver Miners: Prostitution and Social Life on the Comstock Lode.* Ann Arbor: University of Michigan Press, 1981.

Graber, Kay, ed. *Sister to the Sioux: Memoirs of Elaine Goodale Eastman, 1885–91.* Lincoln: University of Nebraska Press, 1978.

Gray, Dorothy. *Women of the West.* Millbrae, Ca: Les Femmes, 1976.

Green, Elizabeth Alden. *Mary Lyon and Mount Holyoke: Opening the Gates.* Hanover, NH: University Press of New England, 1979.

Guilford, Linda T. *The Use of a Life: Memorials of Mrs. Z. P. Grant.* New York: American Tract Society, 1886.

Harte, Bret. "The Idyl of Red Gulch," in *Luck of Roaring Camp and Other Sketches.* Boston: Houghton Mifflin, 1869, pp. 72–88.

Hine, Robert v. *Community on the American Frontier.* Norman: University of Oklahoma Press, 1980.

Hoffman, Nancy. *Woman's "True" Profession: Voices from the History of Teaching.* Old Westbury, NY: Feminist Press, and New York: McGraw-Hill, 1981.

Holliday, J. S. *The World Rushed In: The California Gold Rush Experience.* New York: Simon & Schuster, 1981.

Horner, Patricia V. "Mary Richardson Walker: The Shattered Dreams of a Missionary Woman." *Montana, Magazine of Western History* 32 (Summer 1982): 20–31.

Jeffrey, Julie Roy. *Frontier Women: The Trans-Mississippi West, 1840–1880.* New York: Hill & Wang, 1979.

Jensen, Joan M., and Miller, Darlis A. "The Gentle Tamers Revisited: New Approaches to the History of Women in the American West." *Pacific Historical Review* 49 (May 1980): 173–214.

Johnson, Paul E. *A Shopkeeper's Millennium: Society and Revivals in Rochester, New York, 1815–1837.* New York: Hill & Wang, 1978.

Jones, Jacqueline. *Soldiers of Light and Love: Northern Teachers and Georgia Blacks, 1865–1873.* Chapel Hill: University of North Carolina Press, 1980.

Kaestle, Carl F., and Vinovskis, Maris A. *Education and Social Change in Nineteenth-Century Massachusetts.* Cambridge, Eng.: Cambridge University Press, 1980.

Kaiser, Leo M., and Knuth, Priscilla, eds. "From Ithaca to the Clatsop Plains: Miss Ketchum's Journal of Travel." *Oregon Historical Quarterly* 42 (September 1961): 237–87; (December 1961): 337–402.

Kerber, Linda K. *Women of the Republic: Intellect and Ideology in Revolutionary America.* Chapel Hill: University of North Carolina Press, 1980.

Labaree, Leonard W. "Zilpah Grant and the Art of Teaching: 1829; as Recorded by Eliza Paul Capen." *New England Quarterly* 20 (September 1947): 347–64.

Larcom, Lucy. *A New England Girlhood, Outlined from Memory*. Boston: Houghton Mifflin, 1889.

Lerner, Gerda. "The Lady and the Mill Girl: Changes in the Status of Women in the Age of Jackson." *American Studies* 10 (Spring 1969): 5–15.

Lee, L. L., and Lewis, Merrill. *Women, Women Writers and the West*. Troy, NY: Whitson Publishing Co., 1979.

Leonardo, James S. "The Postal History of Des Moines, Iowa." *Postal History Journal* 21 (June 1977): 37–47 and 21 (October 1977): 27–37.

"Letters of a Pioneer Teacher [Arozina Perkins]." *Annals of Iowa* 35 (Spring 1961): 616–20.

Luchetti, Cathy, and Olwell, Carol. *Women of the West*. St. George, UT: Antelope Island Press, 1982.

McLoughlin, William C. *Revivals, Awakenings, and Reform*. Chicago: University of Chicago Press, 1978.

McMillan, Ethel. "Women Teachers in Oklahoma, 1820–1860." *Chronicles of Oklahoma* 27 (Spring 1949): 2–32.

Marr, Harriet Webster. *The Old New England Acadmies Founded Before 1826*. New York: Comet Press, 1959.

Mathews, Lois Kimball. *The Expansion of New England: The Spread of New England Settlement and Institutions to the Mississippi River, 1620–1865*. Boston: Houghton Mifflin, 1909.

Mayo, Rev. A. D. "Development of Common Schools in the Western States from 1830–1865," in *Report of the Commissioner of Education, 1898–99*. Washington, D.C., 1900, vol. 1, pp. 357–450.

Morain, Thomas, "Departure of Males from the Teaching Profession in Nineteenth-Century Iowa." *Civil War History* 26 (June 1980): 161–70.

Morton, Zylpha S. "Harriet Bishop, Frontier Teacher." *Minnesota History* 28 (June 1947): 132–41.

Mountain Charley or the Adventures of Mrs. E. J. Guerin, Who Was Thirteen Years in Male Attire. Norman: University of Oklahoma Press, 1968.

Myres, Sandra L. *Ho for California! Women's Overland Diaries from the Huntington Library*. San Marino, Ca: Huntington Library, 1980.

————. *Westering Women and the Frontier Experience, 1800–1915*. Albuquerque: University of New Mexico Press, 1982.

Nash, Roderick. *Wilderness and the American Mind*. New Haven: Yale University Press, 1973.

Nelson, Margaret K. "Rural Vermont Schoolteachers: Community Building; Community Restraints." Paper given at the Women's History Conference, Seneca Falls, NY, July 1982.

————. "Vermont Female Schoolteachers in the Nineteenth Century." *Vermont History* 49 (Winter 1981): 5–30.

Norton, Mary Beth. *Liberty's Daughters: The Revolutionary Experience of American Women, 1750–1800*. Boston: Little, Brown, 1980.

————. "The Paradox of 'Woman's Sphere,'" in Carol Ruth Berkin and Mary Beth Norton. *Women of America: A History*. Boston: Houghton Mifflin, 1979, pp. 139–49.

Novak, Barbara. *Nature and Culture: American Landscape Painting 1825–1875*. New York: Oxford University Press, 1980.

Patterson-Black, Sheryll and Gene. *Western Women in History and Literature*. Crawford, NB: Cottonwood Press, 1978.

Peterson, Susan. "Religious Communities of Women in the West: The Presentation Sister's Adaptation to the Northern Plains Frontier." *Journal of the West* 21 (April 1982): 65–70.

Reiter, Joan Swallow. *The Women (The Old West,* vol. 23). Alexandria, VA: Time-Life Books, 1978.

Reps, John W. *Cities of the American West: A History of Frontier Urban Planning.* Princeton: Princeton University Press, 1979.

Riggs, Stephen Return. *Mary and I: Forty Years with the Sioux.* Chicago, 1880.

Riley, Glenda. "European Views of White Women in the American West" and "Suggestions for Additional Reading." *Journal of the West* 21 (April 1982): 71–88.

————. *Frontierswomen: The Iowa Experience.* Ames: Iowa State University Press, 1981.

Royce, Sarah. *A Frontier Lady: Recollections of the Gold Rush and Early California.* New Haven: Yale University Press, 1932.

Ryan, Mary P. *Cradle of the Middle Class: The Family in Oneida County, New York, 1790–1865.* Cambridge, Eng.: Cambridge University Press, 1981.

Sandoz, Mari. "The Kinkaider Comes and Goes," in *Sandhill Sundays and Other Recollections.* Lincoln: Univesity of Nebraska Press, 1970, pp. 23–50.

————. *Miss Morissa, Doctor of the Gold Trail.* New York: Hastings House, 1955.

Sanford, Millie. *Mollie, the Journal of Mollie Dorsey Sanford in Nebraska and Colorado Territories, 1857–1866.* Lincoln: University of Nebraska Press, 1959.

Schlissel, Lillian. *Women's Diaries of the Westward Journey.* New York: Schocken Books, 1982.

Scott, Anne Firor. "The Ever Widening Circle: The Diffusion of Feminist Values from the Troy Female Seminary, 1822–1872." *History of Education Quarterly* 19 (Spring 1979): 3–26.

————. "What, Then, Is the American: This New Woman?" *Journal of American History* 65 (December 1978): 679–703.

Sklar, Kathryn Kish. *Catharine Beecher, a Study in American Domesticity.* New Haven: Yale University Press, 1973.

————. "The Founding of Mount Holyoke College," in Berkin and Norton, *Women of America,* pp. 177–201.

Smith, Henry Nash. *Virgin Land: The American West as Symbol and Myth.* Cambridge: Harvard University Press, 1950.

Snell, Joseph W., ed. "Roughing it on Her Kansas Claim: The Diary of Abbie Bright, 1870–71." *Kansas Historical Quarterly* 37 (Autumn 1971): 233–63 and 37 (Winter 1971): 394–428.

Stratton, Joanna L. *Pioneer Women: Voices from the Kansas Frontier.* New York: Simon & Schuster, 1981.

Thomas, Louise Porter. *Seminary Militant.* South Hadley: Mount Holyoke College, 1937.

Thornbrough, Gayle, Riker, Dorothy L., and Paula Corpuz, eds. *The Diary of Calvin Fletcher, 1817–1862.* Indianapolis: Indiana Historical Society, 1972–80, 7 vols.

Throne, Mildred. "A Population Study of an Iowa County in 1850." *Iowa Journal of History* 57 (October 1959): 305–30.

Topping, Gary. "Religion in the West." *Journal of American Culture* 3 (Summer 1980): 330–50.

Unruh, John D., Jr. *The Plains Across: The Overland Emigrants and the Trans-Mississippi West, 1840–60.* Urbana: University of Illinois Press, 1979.

Welter, Barbara. "She Hath Done What She Could: Protestant Women's Missionary Careers in Nineteenth-Century America." *American Quarterly* 30 (Winter 1978): 624–38.

Western Writers of America. *The Women Who Made the West.* New York: Doubleday & Co., 1980.

Wilson, Elizabeth M. "From New York to Oregon, via the Isthus of Panama in 1851." *Oregon Historical Society Proceedings* (1900): 99–112.

Wishy, Bernard. *The Child and the Republic: The Dawn of Modern American Child Nurture.* Philadelphia: University of Pennsylvania Pess, 1968.

Wister, Owen. *The Virginian: A Horseman of the Plains.* New York: Macmillan, 1902.

Woody, Thomas. *A History of Women's Education in the United States.* New York: Science Press, 1929, 2 vols.